HAPPY
FOR NO
GOOD
REASON

Dedication

For my parents,
Herbert and Selma Kruckman and
my teacher, Swami Muktananda,
and the great beings of Mother India.
Gurus of body, heart and soul,
I love and honor you all.

HAPPY
FOR NO
GOOD
REASON

Swami Shankarananda

Foreword by Garry McDonald

SHAKTIPAT
PRESS

Published by Shaktipat Press

27 Tower Road, Mt Eliza, Vic. 3930
Telephone: (03) 9775 2568 Fax: (03) 9775 2591
www.shivayoga.org Email: askus@shivayoga.org

4th Printing

The National Library of Australia
Cataloguing-in-Publication entry:

Shankarananda, Swami.
Happy for no good reason.

ISBN 0-9750995-1-5
1. Meditation 2. Self (Philosophy) I. Title
294.543

Design: Alistair Hay (Monogram Graphic Design Pty Ltd)
Printed in Australia by BPA Print Group

Acknowledgements

I WISH TO EXPRESS my deep appreciation to Ma Devi Saraswati, not only for contributing her Preface and her wisdom, but also for her loving support and belief in this project and for her editing skills. I am also grateful to Garry McDonald for his delightful Foreword. I owe special thanks to Dr Isobel Crombie, Sarah Hudson and Nancy Jackson for their work with the manuscript at various stages and to Kaymolly Morrelle for her editorial work during the final sprint to publication. I am grateful Alistair Hay for his excellent design work. Thank you also to Roger Anderson and Glenn Sharp for their meditative music and for producing the accompanying CD.

I want to acknowledge the many students of my Learn to Meditate and Intermediate Meditation Courses, and also those who went on to participate in the Shiva Process work. These teachings were forged in the fire of our relationship.

I am very grateful also to my students, the ashramites and householders, who serve these courses with such love and unselfishness. The light of the Self burns bright within them. If they get tired of hearing these teachings over and over again, they never let me know it.

Finally, I must acknowledge the yogis and great beings of all the traditions who have blazed the trail that I follow.

Contents

About the title

RECENTLY ONE OF my students told me that one morning he had awakened feeling remarkably happy. He wondered at his joy. He inventoried his life and the events of the previous day. He did not recall anything unusual or particularly positive. During his contemplation the thought came to him: *I'm happy for no good reason!*

He relished this thought and then remembered that he had been meditating for several weeks. "Aha!" he realized, "I am happy because I have been meditating!"

If making money, finding a lover, winning an award, or reaching a goal is a good reason to be happy, then meditation certainly seems like "no good reason". Ironically, of course, happiness through meditation is the best reason of all, since it directs us to the source of happiness itself—the inner Self.

Happiness that has "no good reason", no cause in the outer world, is the most stable happiness. It cannot be destroyed when the outer world cause is removed.

It is my wish that everyone learn the secret of happiness for the best reason of all—the inner reason—the inner Self.

Swami Shankarananda
May 2000

PREFACE

MA DEVI SARASWATI

ONCE IN A while a special voice speaks old truths in a compelling new way. Such voices belonged to J. Krishnamurti and Sri Ramana Maharshi. Another such voice is, I feel, Swami Shankarananda. While Swamiji is a traditionalist, he is also an innovator who has developed and expressed unique spiritual ideas in his distinctive style. Here is a short list of some of his characteristic ideas:

- We live simultaneously in two worlds.
- Thought and feeling are intimately related.
- Feeling should be taken inside and resolved into the Self rather than dumped.
- "Tearing thoughts" and "inflating thoughts" are wrong movements in "self-talk".
- Self-talk is purified and uplifted by **Accurate** and **Beneficial Statements**.
- Asking empowering questions is Self-inquiry.
- One should learn to recognize and follow the upward shift of energy in daily life as well as in meditation.

Swamiji's yearning for inner wisdom led him to India where he studied for 12 years under Baba Muktananda, an enlightened meditation master. This is the traditional length of time a seeker spends with his or her spiritual mentor when seeking self-realization. He was one of the first Westerners to be given the title "Swami" under his teacher and to establish an ashram in the West. He immersed himself in the philosophy and practice of yoga and emerged as a guru in his own right.

Swamiji describes the state of enlightenment as one of "becoming present". He says that no matter how painful or happy the past, or how painful or happy we think the future may be, it is the present moment, the *now,* that holds the key to everything. The method for attuning to the 'now' is Self-inquiry, turning inward and asking the right questions. This simple practice will eventually lead to the goal of all yogas, Self-realization.

Swamiji is a master of the great spiritual tradition of *Shakti,* the powerful and compassionate energy dormant within every person. In the book he explains that spiritual energy is the substance of meditation. It is the mysterious force that enlivens and gives bliss to life. It electrifies everything we do. When we nurture the energy of meditation our inner world blossoms like a radiant garden.

The book is divided into two parts. **Part I, Meditation on the Self**, is based on the successful "Learn To Meditate" course where Swamiji imparts the fundamental techniques and understandings of the practice of meditation. Here he directs us to commit to a meditation practice and discusses the various ways to do that, with personal anecdotes, stories and instruction based on his many years of practice. **Part II, Meditation in the world**, teaches us how to integrate the teachings into daily life. We learn to use the meditative energy in the world. He is deeply committed to the idea of *yoga in the world*. He says the real test of meditation and yoga is when we can overcome difficulties in our "real" life - at work, with our dear ones or when life becomes difficult.

At the end of the book there is an appendix with a written version of the Chakra Meditation, a glossary of Sanskrit terms and a selection from the *Bhagavad Gita*, translated by Swamiji, relevant to meditation and the teachings in this book.

Part I, Meditation on the Self, concentrates on the basics of meditation—the "inner" world, the inner Self, the goal of meditation and the obstacles to recognizing the inner Self. Meditation is the single most important spiritual practice. Without it we remain at the mercy of habits and tendencies that cause suffering. Swamiji gives various classical meditation techniques and contemplations to deal with that which prevents us from seeing the inner Self, the "villain" of the saga - the mind.

Everyone has an inner Self, a place deep within which is the true resting place of the mind. Swamiji reassures us that meditation is as natural as sleep and that the ability to enter deep states of peace is as easy as falling asleep, once you know how. He calls it "sleep sitting up" and believes that everyone can learn to meditate. His years of teaching have shown him that not everyone will resonate with every technique given, and so he offers an "arsenal" of meditation techniques and yogic practices. You can experiment with each one to discover the techniques that give you the peace of the inner Self. It is important to go with what works and to not struggle with what does not.

Near the end of the book Swamiji tells an amusing story about his mother, who had come to India to visit him while he was living there with his teacher. One morning she approached him concerned that she was falling asleep during meditation. He reassured her that she was not sleeping, but meditating. At first she was filled with disbelief but she soon realized it was true. She quickly learned the difference between meditative sleep and normal sleep. She and her husband, Herbert, became avid meditators.

My first meditation experience happened in 1974 when I was working at the University of Michigan Counselling Centre. A friend and I were invited to meet Baba Muktananda at a meeting for health professionals. I had never met a swami or a guru and was intrigued by the idea of the "mystic" East. I walked into the room where he was sitting, sat down on the floor cross-legged, looked up at Baba, our eyes met and he nodded. The last thing I remember is my head falling forward onto my chest. I was suddenly awakened to a poking on my shoulder. Twenty-five minutes had passed. My friend was standing over me, telling me it was time to go. I reluctantly stood, keenly aware that I had touched a place deep within myself. As we drove away, I turned to him and said: "I don't know what it is, but that man definitely has something."

A few months later, pulled by a number of synchronicities and the meeting with Baba, I returned to where I had met Baba, which was now a meditation centre run by Swamiji. At an Intensive a few months later I again had that deep experience of meditation. I learned that meditation like that only happens around great beings, spiritual masters, who are established in the inner Self.

Meditation is at the heart of these teachings and practice. However, it is also important to "think deeply" and "love abundantly". In **Part II, Meditation in the world**, Swamiji teaches us how to do that. He gives a brilliant path that uses meditative awareness to become more "awake" and happy in daily life. His method is groundbreaking because it successfully manages negative emotion like anger, fear, sorrow and depression.

Usually when we are caught in negative emotion we want to "blame" or "dump" the feeling. The impulse to express negative emotion to others or to act irresponsibly is something we all do. Swamiji is adamant that the way to navigate negativity successfully is to not push the feeling outside, but to turn within and investigate it by means of Self-inquiry. By looking at what is hidden within the negative emotion we can see what we are doing, have an understanding and return to peace.

Swamiji points out a truth so obvious it is easy to overlook - the subtle inner voice that chatters negativity in the mind. There is no doubt that this voice is the single most disempowering and destructive phenomenon in life. This is truly a breakthrough insight. He calls this negative voice "tearing thoughts".

Tearing thoughts are subtle thoughts, arrows that pierce the heart. He says they live and breed in our minds as our worst enemy and they prevent us from merging with the highest that is in us. He also says that once we see them, they no longer have power over us and we can and should disarm them. Swamiji's ideas present the possibility of overcoming what we may view as the deepest possible ignorance, the unconscious tendencies that plague us and create the painful and stressful situations of our lives.

This book represents Swamiji's deepest spiritual values. Love plays a major role in his navigation of the inner world. With determination he stubbornly refuses to accept anything less. He knows, from his own struggle with the mind, that the temptation to become negative and critical of others, to blame others, to become caught in self-pity, to whine and complain about life and its hard knocks is difficult to break. He implores us to break it. And break it we must. He knows that these habitual tendencies disempower us.

Swamiji often uses humour to help dispel brooding temperaments into a lighter way of viewing life. His lectures and courses are made joyful by his lightness of being and his unique gift to uplift the heart and mind even in the most difficult times.

An introvert by nature, I used to fall into melancholy and restlessness, which could turn into irritability, impatience and then anger. I have always had trouble controlling and seeing this inner movement. It bothered me and I disliked being at the mercy of it. I was keenly aware that it led to frustration and created difficult situations. When I would be in "mood" or react like this, Swamiji took to calling me "bad" Devi. One day when I went to talk to him about an ashram matter, I became upset. The conversation became difficult and the impulse to get angry grew strong in me. He suddenly turned to me and with a twinkle in his eye asked: "Is this good Devi or bad Devi?" His question forced my attention inward and a picture of a sullen pouting two-year old girl who wanted her own way popped into my mind. The picture was so clear that I had to laugh and get off it. I became aware that this tendency often came up when I had an intuition about something and could not articulate it.

Thinking about it I later I realized that impatience, anger and fear arise in me when I have not thought deeply enough about what I want to say. There was a valid conversation I could have if I slowed down and considered in the moment what was important to me. I saw that if my conversations are coloured by anger or fear then I would be disempowered and eternally frustrated. I also saw that when I speak from negative emotion, a feeling of separation arises in me. Swamiji's question moved my energy from the outer to the inner and I was instantly rewarded.

I have had many moments like this when he has used his insight and humour to help me see when I was indulging negative emotional states. He has taught me that no matter what happens, or no matter what I want or expect, it is always better to move toward peace and love in my inner world and to move away from despair and anger. His persistence has shown me a higher value – that is to try to remember the Self at all times and under all conditions.

Swamiji points over and over to the innate transforming power of our own consciousness. He encourages us to turn the light of awareness, which we share generously with others, within and reflect on the inner Self. This simple yet crucial "doing" frees us from the fickle and unreliable mind.

Swamiji is a brilliant spiritual teacher, a lover of God, a knower of the truth in the highest sense. He is a man of great compassion, humour, intelligence and love. "Happy For No Good Reason" reflects his serious and thoughtful outlook on spirituality and the dilemmas in life we all face.

15 February 2000

Ma Devi Saraswati is an accomplished practitioner of Shiva Yoga. She teaches meditation and yoga and assists Swamiji in the running of the Shiva Ashram.

Foreword

ME AND MY SWAMI

GARRY McDONALD

I FIRST MET Swami Shankarananda in 1981 but it was a good 12 months before I tried to pronounce his name. I had just completed a lengthy cabaret tour of "Can't Stop the Gunston", a groundbreaking show about man's need to pay his outstanding tax bill. I had decided to say farewell to Norman, the mainstay of my career for six years. I was excited about the future, relaxed and relatively free of debt.

During the last days of the tour I'd picked up a copy of *The Bulletin* magazine. The cover story was on stress and it had a picture of a businessman sitting on his desk meditating. Now I'd always been quite keen to learn to meditate since the Beatles took it up because ... well, because the Beatles took it up. Then I met up with a Melbourne friend of mine whom I hadn't seen in ages. He said that he was in Sydney to give a talk on meditation and that I should come along.

So I went off to this program called "Meditation and Creativity". It was held in the Sydney Masonic Hall and upon entering I thought I had mistakenly gone to an Actors Equity union meeting. It was full of actors. I felt very comfortable. Just like a night at the Logies except tonight we were all going to win. David made his speech and then introduced a Swami Shankarananda.

"Swami" I thought to myself. David didn't mention anything about a swami! Then out comes this European guy with a shaved head - before it was popular - he's wearing orange robes and he's got a red dot on his forehead. "Oh my God," I thought. "This is terrible, what has David got himself into. What's he trying to get me into?"

But it got worse, much worse. This swami opened his mouth and he was an *American!* Now remember this is 1981, well and truly before Australia signed the World Trade Organization treaty and we got used to the yanks dumping all their surplus swamis on our fair shores.

He spoke. I didn't listen to a word of it. I was irritated and couldn't get past my initial reaction. Then he said: "We'll chant the mantra for five minutes and meditate by silently repeating it for 10 minutes," Well this is what I came for, so I decided to try it. I immediately had a response. I felt very pleasant and started seeing coloured lights. This was good! Afterwards I asked David what to do next. He suggested I sign up for this two-day intensive that Swamiji was coming back to Sydney for in 10 days. I thought for a minute. "He dresses like an Indian, talks like an American and has a skinhead haircut. It can't get any worse."

I was certain that I didn't want any of that Hindu stuff. I decided to buy a book on meditation, although it was nearly impossible to buy such a thing in a mainstream bookstore in those days. I went into a Christian bookstore and was nearly thrown out. "We don't sell books like *that* here!"

There was no way around it, I had to go to the Theosophical Society bookshop, but I made it very clear that I wanted a sensible book on meditation. Preferably written by a doctor. I found the perfect one, a "Learn to Meditate" primer. As I was paying for it my eye caught an *Om Namah Shivaya* chant tape. This was the mantra we used at the introductory program. I grabbed that as well. I practised every day and I thought I was progressing pretty well.

So when the day of the intensive came around I was pretty excited. I walked into the hall and they had done it to me again! What had been a normal lecture hall 10 days ago was now Little India. The chairs were gone and everyone was sitting on the floor. The men and women were segregated. There were big pictures everywhere of an Indian man I didn't recognise. The air was sweet with incense and Indian chants were playing softly on the sound system. I started to wish I'd had my typhoid shots.

Various speakers got up and talked about the inner Self, *Kundalini* energy, the spiritual awakening and something about Swamiji blessing us in the traditional manner with peacock feathers. I couldn't take any of it in and I was feeling slightly uncomfortable. Then I noticed that I was sitting next to George Ogilvie the well-known theatre director. Now I'd never met George but his reputation as a director was excellent. I began to feel reassured by his involvement. In fact, I was thinking, "Maybe this is a chance to make an impression, I'll play it cool now but after the spiritual awakening I'll let him know that I'm available for work."

Then Swami Shankarananda spoke and introduced the hour-long meditation but he changed the technique. Great! I'd been practising Om Namah Shivaya for 10 days, I was practically Olympic standard and now I'm back to square one. What is it with these people!

Anyway I closed my eyes and began to meditate. Then a few minutes in I heard moaning coming from the women down the front. And it was getting louder and louder until this moaning and wailing was filling the whole hall. It was as though they were all auditioning for Meg Ryan's role in *When Harry Met Sally*! I could have sworn I heard someone yell out: "I'll have whatever she's having!" It was extraordinary, bizarre. "What a mob of hysterical tossers," I thought.

Then I heard this swishing sound coming towards me and wondered if these guys were into flagellation as well. But my Scottish ancestry came to the fore, the $80 course fee was non-refundable, so there was no way I was going to open my eyes and leave. I told myself to ignore it and stick to my technique.

A few minutes later the swishing got closer and a strong, beautiful smell wafted over me. My heart suddenly started racing. It was pounding. I felt like it was going to jump out of my chest. "This is crazy," I thought. "I don't believe in any of this stuff. Why is this happening to me?" Then I was whacked on the head with the peacock feathers and Swamiji's hand brushed my forehead twice and pinched the bridge of my nose.

In the next moment an extraordinary rush of energy went up my spine and exploded into white light in my head. I started to sob, great big heaving sobs. I wasn't sad but I was sobbing. Oddly enough a Norman Gunston line popped into my head from Norman's *Dreamtime* stories. "Kookaburras laugh because they know it's all a big joke." Well I found this hysterical. I started laughing and laughing and laughing. Everyone else disappeared and there was only me in the hall. I felt like my being had expanded to fill the room, there was nothing but me. It was the most beautiful, beautiful experience. The next thing I was aware of was music softly playing and the lights being raised. The hour of meditation was over.

At lunchtime a friend came up to me and said: "It looks like you got it." Obviously the time was right to make myself known to George Ogilvie. As we were leaving I shook my head in disbelief and pointed back into the hall: "Pretty bloody noisy in there today, wasn't it?"

"You should know," he shot back. "You were the noisiest!"

The second day could not happen soon enough. Before the program commenced I made a quick bathroom stop. I got a huge shock. I rushed into the hall and sat down beside a silently meditating George.

"George," I whispered, "are there any physical side effects of *Kundalini?*"

"Like what Garry?" he asked.

"Like colon cancer. I just went to the loo and there seems to be a lot of *blood* around, you know, around my stool."

He shook his head. "No," he said. "I've never heard of colon cancer striking 12 hours after Kundalini."

"Yeah," I said. "Maybe you're right, maybe it's just something simple like a haemorrhaging ulcer!"

During the first meditation I suddenly remembered that I had had three bowls of beetroot soup for dinner last night. My self-diagnosis had been a little extreme! I started laughing all over again. Poor George.

After the intensive I was ecstatic for months. Occasionally a great wave of bliss would rise up out of nowhere and engulf me. It was like being in love but there was no object of my love that was causing this. My new career took off. I did some of my best work in years and was well reviewed and nominated for various awards. Everything was perfect.

Then in 1982 Swami Shankarananda left Australia and I lost contact with him and the yoga. I was very fond of Swamiji, but I never thought of him as my guru. Gurus weren't European; they were Indian and enigmatic. He was witty, articulate and loved the blues. Anyway, only weak people had gurus. I'd learned all I needed in that one weekend. In moments of stress or emotional crisis all I had to do was close my eyes, repeat the mantra for 20 minutes and it would all go away. This was a metaphysical equivalent of valium.

In the early nineties I started to struggle with anxiety and panic attacks and eventually they got the upper hand. I was in Melbourne in 1994 about to open in my first play since my very public breakdown when I received a letter at the theatre from Swamiji. He had returned to Australia for good and said he would love to see me. I was thrilled. I thought I would never see him again.

It has taken three years of visiting the ashram, taking intensives, doing the occasional retreat and, most importantly, observing Swamiji, before I accepted him as my teacher, the one I trusted to teach me what he had learned. There was no doubt about the effect that he had on me but I still had to convince myself that he was a meditation master, a Self-realized yogi. I watched him deal with difficult people, emotional people, his elderly parents who came to Australia to live with him and I saw the changes in myself. I started to have purpose and meaning in my life and my mind began to turn outwards. I started to see the divinity in others. And, I started to experience a contentment that I never thought I would find. This contentment has nothing to do with public recognition or material success but everything to do with self-acceptance.

It is a wonderful journey, sometimes confronting, sometimes blissfully intoxicating but never disappointing. I have learned that people need meaning and purpose in their lives. I no longer see myself as separate from others. The deeper my experience of the Self the more I realize how we are all connected. I find that so comforting. Life is no better or worse than it was before. However, my attitude is and for this I am eternally grateful.

Mind you, I've known Swamiji for nearly 20 years and he still hasn't managed to teach me how to pronounce his name with any degree of confidence.

Sydney, January 2000

Garry McDonald is a much-revered comedian, actor and director known throughout Australia for his personal sincerity and heartfelt relationship with the Australian public.

Introduction:
MY SECOND EDUCATION

Aim for heaven and you will get earth thrown in.
Aim at earth and you will get neither.
C.S. Lewis

WE ARE THE MOST educated and affluent people in human history, the most literate, the most technologically proficient. We can replace one person's heart with another's, we can fly people to other planets, and we can send tiny cameras into people's organs to inspect them from within. We are able, or will be able, to do almost anything in the physical world. However, we find this world stressful and demanding. We have trouble motivating our teenagers and keeping them away from negative influences. We find it difficult to control anger, fear or depression. We are confused by the world within ourselves.

Our situation becomes intelligible if we recognize that we actually live in two different worlds simultaneously. One is the outer world of people and objects and the other is the inner world of thoughts and feelings. Each has its own laws and each has its own form of education. We have explored the outer world in detail, however we have neglected the inner world.

In my early life I was an academic, deeply involved in Western education. I call this form of conventional education *First Education* or the "knowledge" tradition. The focus of First Education is the outer world, on science and technology, facts, events and history. This knowledge education embellishes us but does not transform us. We can acquire more and more information and still have the emotional sulks and tantrums of a child.

Over the past 30 years I have been involved with what I call *Second Education*, or the "wisdom" tradition. Second Education says that true happiness lies not in the outer world but *within* each of us. Not only that, it can be realized. The process of awakening to Second Education is called inner work. In all my years involved with institutions of higher learning, both as a student and a teacher, no one had ever spoken about conquering depression, overcoming fear and anger and attaining happiness and self-mastery. I learned so much about history and the stuff of the external world, but almost nothing about myself.

By contrast Second Education works on "being". It does not give much information in the usual sense, but it empowers us. It turns a weak person into a strong one, an unhappy person into a happy one, a confused person into a person of clarity and wisdom. Only through work on our being can such alchemy take place. Meditation is the bedrock of such change.

MY SECOND EDUCATION

I grew up in Brooklyn, New York, surrounded by loving family and friends. My father was a well-known artist and my mother a high school teacher. Every few years I have occasion to visit New York. When I do I usually meet some of my high school friends for lunch. One of them is a CPA. Another is a wealthy entrepreneur. Another is a professional bookie. Another is a doctor, and another owns a grocery store. In those days piano lessons were *de rigueur*. Arthur, the CPA, and I took lessons from Mrs. Bloom. I found them discouraging and soon quit because Mrs. Bloom would tell me: "Barry plays so beautiful!" I knew Barry - he went to school with me and lived in Arthur's building - Barry Manilow.

I was a good student and I am listed in my high school yearbook as "most likely to succeed". It makes me smile to remember that, and it is difficult to evaluate it without being overcome by delicious ironies. It is certain, however, that I am the only one in my neighbourhood who became a *swami*.

During the late '60s I was living on the Lower East Side of New York, studying for my PhD in English literature. On weekends I enjoyed walking over to the Fillmore East to listen to the great bands of the time—the Grateful Dead, Jefferson Airplane, Janis Joplin, Ten Years After and so many others. One day some friends and I dropped in on another friend while on the way to a party. We were sitting chatting when there was a knock on the door. Being closest to it I went to answer it. I had then what you could call "a New York moment". I opened the door to a gun in my face. I instantly became present. I looked down the gun barrel and could clearly see the bullets in the chambers. Years later, while being shown a gun collection, I identified it as a .38.

I felt no fear but two powerful thoughts came into my mind. The first was: "This is it, I'm going to die, *what a waste of all that education.*" The second thought was: "*What's it all about* if it can end so abruptly?"

The gunman told us to lie down. He searched for and then checked our identification. He told us he was looking for someone who had "burned me for two hundred dollars in a drug deal". When he discovered that none of us was the person he cordially said: "I've got to apologize to you guys", and left. That was a lot of money in those days, so I didn't point out that he was overreacting.

Looking back I recognize that that encounter awakened the spiritual seeker in me, the quest for Second Education. I began to search for explanations, for personal growth and wisdom. My search was intellectual and personal. Intellectually I began to read widely, outside my field. I investigated Western philosophy, anthropology and psychology. At this point I knew nothing about Eastern thought and had something of an aversion to it. A friend called me a "quintessentially rational man" and, although he underestimated my emotional nature, I thought of myself as firmly standing in the Western rational tradition. I was particularly interested in the evolution of culture and how technology impacted awareness. Not surprisingly, Marshall McLuhan was one of my heroes.

These stories are perhaps entertaining, but I tell them for another reason also. While I was in high school and college, if I could have glimpsed the future course of my life I would not have believed it. Maybe I could have become a physicist or an academic—possibly a writer, a poet—all right, but a swami? A meditation teacher was not in the realm of the possible. But I think that large historical and evolutionary forces, of which I had no awareness, were at play. They make my story not so much the quirky individual history of a fellow who was "too smart for his own good" (as some of my old friends surely believe), but a story that illustrates my belief that wisdom education is entering our culture.

In my 25 years of teaching meditation my audience has changed from groups of fringe, bohemian, artistic people to mum and dad, sister and uncle. Everyone is meditating now or intends to learn one day. Medical science has established the value of meditation for health as well as stress reduction. I get referrals from many medical doctors and psychologists. What was a trickle in 1970 is a flood today. Further, inner transformation has become big business. My story is a single instance of a cultural and spiritual phenomenon that includes many lives. The signs of a "new age" are everywhere. Recently I saw meditation instructions written on the back of a box of *Kellog's Special K*. It said: "Meditation is a deeply relaxing state that helps relieve stress and promotes self-esteem. It can help slow down your breathing and calm your mind."

My own search led me towards humanistic psychology—the work of Fritz Perls, Rollo May and Carl Rogers. I joined a group in Chicago, near the university where I was teaching Shakespeare and Humanities, and began to investigate the swirling mysterious world of emotion and personal motivation. The process of my awakening was exciting but frustrating. None of my friends or associates had any idea of what I was talking about when I made comments like: "Everything we do is tied to ego. It is time for a new truth. It is possible to live beyond ego. Such a life would be a constant ecstasy". In fact, I had little idea what was happening to me. I felt like a solitary explorer in an uncharted land. I did not know then that my world was about to change forever.

On February 20, 1970 I was invited to a small dinner party held by the head of my group in his luxurious apartment in a high rise on Lake Michigan's gold coast. The guest of honor was an emerging superstar of the consciousness movement, a former Harvard psychologist named Richard Alpert, now known as Ram Dass.

We were asked to shed our clothing and wear Japanese kimonos. I was seated on the floor at a low table next to Ram Dass. He was dressed in white, had a long beard and was serene and friendly. I spoke easily to him. Within five minutes of talking with him I realized that far from being a voyager where no man had previously gone, I was just qualifying for kindergarten in the inner path of yoga.

I told Ram Dass that I had been speculating about states of consciousness and that I thought a highly evolved person would have his awareness totally in the present. I asked him: "How would such a person cross a street? Would he not get run over? How could he function?"

"A being who is present," replied Ram Dass, "plans for the future in the present."

His answer, as banal as it looks today, had a remarkable effect on me. I was overwhelmed by a certainty that he was in touch with *higher wisdom*. I knew that I would go to India and I also knew that forever hence I would divide my life into two parts: before that question and after that question. Something had shifted within me. I had discovered *the path*.

He told me that thousands—millions—had walked that path and had left profound records and detailed maps. Most exciting, Ram Dass told me that there were beings *alive today*, who had walked the path to the end and who had attained Self-realization. And, he *knew and had studied* with some of them.

By November of 1970 I was in India. India welcomed me by magically creating situations that enabled me to meet a number of great beings. I met Ananda Mayi Ma, the bliss-filled mother, India's greatest woman saint. She was nearing the end of her life but exuded an otherworldly sweetness that was palpable.

I met and studied with Hari Dass Baba, a teacher of hatha yoga, who had been silent for 20 years. I lived with him for several months and he taught me physical postures, breath exercises and yogic esoterica like swallowing a 24-foot long bandage-like cloth and then pulling it up to help digestion.

I studied with Sri Goenka, the leading guru of Vipassana, Buddhist meditation. In a humble apartment in Bombay I met Sri Nisargadatta Maharaj, the great *jnani* (exponent of the path of wisdom). He was a man of love as well as wisdom.

I spent time with the mysterious saint Neemkaroli Baba. Wrapped in a blanket he seemed like a child, even though he must have been in his 70s. He radiated love and some of the things he said to me still have impact.

And, I met Swami Muktananda, the most remarkable of all. Equal to the rest in love and wisdom, he also radiated spiritual power, *Shakti*, to a most extraordinary degree. Seekers regularly had spontaneous meditation experiences in his presence and sometimes became grabbed by the inner power—the Kundalini. His ashram near Bombay was a model of disciplined regularity—a laboratory of inner growth.

In the months between meeting Ram Dass and going to India I read avidly in spiritual literature. One book that fascinated me was P.D. Ouspensky's *In Search of the Miraculous*, a history of his days with the great teacher G.I. Gurdjieff. Ouspensky had been searching in the East for "mystery schools", as he put it. These were hidden monasteries in which the esoteric mystical knowledge, the wisdom education of mankind, was still a living tradition handed down orally from teacher to student. Muktananda's ashram was an overwhelming experience. It was the first true "school" I had encountered. I stayed there for three years.

The surface of life in the ashram was extremely regular. Every day was exactly the same—wake up bell at 3:30 a.m. and a packed succession of meditation, chanting, ashram work, an after lunch rest and study period and more chanting and meditation until lights out at 9:00 p.m. But underneath the surface everyone was on the boil.

I faced every demon in my past, opened every door in my psyche. I had a constant flow of illuminations and new understandings about myself and about life. I saw a thread ran through my life: I had always been looking for happiness, for truth and meaning. I would pin my hopes on something—a career or a person—only to be disappointed. That disappointment would spur me on.

I had had occasional intimations of higher Consciousness—earliest watching my father paint. He could be as complex and petty as the next person in ordinary circumstances. But poised, brush in hand before a canvas, he became transfigured. Then he would be childlike with an excitement and joy that spread to anyone who was watching.

Later I had experiences listening to music that must have approached Pop's state. Several times the music spoke to me in abstract terms, giving me exquisite wisdom too perfect for ordinary language. Meditation showed me that these fleeting experiences were moments of access to the deepest part of me, the inner Self.

The Self is eternally present within each of us, yet we lack the means of access. Occasionally something works—my father's painting, great music—and an opening occurs. We think "what great music" but the truth is that the greatness of the experience is always within us; *it is us*.

In my years at Muktananda's ashram my inner being woke up. I had spiritual experiences—energy rushing through me, the vision of lights and high beings, out of the body experiences and glimpses of states of perfect peace and freedom. Most significantly, the experience of the Self became more and more my daily and normal experience. I felt anchored in a part of myself that I had previously scarcely known. I accompanied my teacher on his second world tour in 1974 and later that year he sent me away to teach and develop an ashram in Ann Arbor, Michigan. From an educator in the knowledge tradition I became an educator in the wisdom tradition. A long, winding road led me back to Australia in 1991 and the founding of the Shiva School of Meditation.

It is not that knowledge education should be replaced by wisdom education. In fact, the two complement each other. The lack of the latter constitutes a shocking gap in our culture, and we pay the price for that. How good it would be if young people learned meditation and Self-inquiry!

I vividly remember one Year 12 Psychology class I spoke to a while ago. I led them through the same Chakra Meditation you will be doing in this book. There were about 20 in the class and 16 or 17 of them felt a block in the throat chakra. This was an extremely interesting and revealing result. A block in the area of communication epitomizes teenage angst. Teenagers often feel misunderstood by parents and teachers and anxious about their image and personality with peers.

I worked with several of them on specific issues. One girl's block was related to her mother. She found "angry words" in her throat and because they were angry she could not speak them. Investigation separated the true content of what she wanted to say to her mother from the anger and the block left her throat. She knew what she wanted to say to her mother and how to say it with love.

Such work is as rewarding to the meditation teacher as it is to the student.

Greater Self-knowledge and better communication would be of enormous benefit to children. It is my conviction that meditation—in non-sectarian form—should be taught from the earliest years of our schooling. Wisdom must be joined to knowledge.

Nonetheless for us, although we may have missed the meditation boat in our earliest training, it is not too late to begin. Meditation allows each of us to explore our own Consciousness and discover the joy that is inherent within us. It is an inner journey, and a marvellous quest. The investigation of the inner Self is a process of endless unfolding. It gives wisdom and peace and it also enhances the quality of our ordinary life. Following the techniques given in this book and doing the practice, you will become a skilled meditator.

ABOUT THIS BOOK

In the years that I lived with Muktananda I would hear him lecture almost every night. He always taught essentially the same thing, though he found creative ways to say it. The substance of his message was: meditate on the Self, God dwells within you as you. He also told his audience to see God in each other, to welcome others with love and respect. Though he repeated his message I always felt uplifted by it.

In this book, also, the argument is simple. I talk about the mind and I talk about the Self. I give three main techniques of meditation and subsidiary contemplations. About the mind I say that it can be positive and reflect the light, or negative and reflect darkness. A positive mind can lead us beyond the mind to the inner Self, which is the goal of meditation. We have to make effort to quieten the mind and educate it to move in positive grooves. I go back and forth over this ground, looking at it in many ways from many perspectives.

I will explore the practice and philosophy of meditation and the traditional meditation techniques of mantra (the repetition of a phrase) and witness-consciousness (watching the thoughts). Other topics include the emotions and "tearing thoughts". You will also learn a technique of Self-inquiry. It is a method of meditation that directs the mind to the power and wisdom of the inner Self. In the latter part of the book I emphasize active meditation, or meditation in life, a 24 hours-a-day awareness.

I think you will be able to tell that I love meditation. I also have great faith in the inherent wisdom of the inner Self. If we learn to hear it, the Self provides us with *wisdom-in-the-moment* to meet situations as they arise. Rather than a consistent theory, I would like meditators to have a quiver full of possible responses to meet each moment freshly. Hence the "arsenal approach" of this book suggests many meditative possibilities

This book is first and foremost a meditation and Self-inquiry manual *cum* workbook. But, it is also a textbook of Second Education. The reader will not fail to notice a very large number of stories. I have culled these from Yoga, Zen, Tibetan Buddhism, Sufism, and other sources including Western ones. Some I have come across in my reading, but mostly I have heard them directly from spiritual teachers, especially, my own.

Teaching stories and parables are the lingua franca of spiritual teaching. Many dramatize a teaching given by a guru to a disciple. The wisdom tradition is based on the guru-disciple archetype. I have also included a number of vignettes from my own relationship with my teacher.

Most people do not have the opportunity actually to sit "at the feet" of a spiritual teacher. In general our culture is suspicious of gurus, perhaps with good reason. Nonetheless, we continue to be fascinated and touched by the mentor archetype: the man (or woman) of wisdom and experience who imparts the truth to the young aspirant seeking relief from ignorance and suffering. Think of Jesus, the Buddha, Don Juan, Socrates, Obe Wan Kinobe, Black Elk, the Dalai Lama and numberless other sages, seers, Boddhisattvas and realized beings.

I have always been moved by this archetype in all its forms, even the Hollywood version where an old gunslinger teaches an impetuous youth the wisdom of the violent frontier and how to shoot a gun. The presence of the mentor archetype tells us that we are encountering Second Education. Sometimes in First Education an encounter with a great teacher engages us emotionally in an unusual way. In such cases First Education is moving towards Second Education. The ideal student is open, earnest, eager to learn and respectful. His heart swells with admiration and love for his teacher. He is willing to follow and not argue with the teaching. On his side the teacher is moved by the student's love. Compassion and spontaneous wisdom flow from him, as much to his surprise and delight as the student's. Openness and love are the context of transmission in Second Education.

USING THIS BOOK WITH THE CD

The compact disc that accompanies this book is called the *Chakra Meditation*. It has four tracks to help you establish your meditation practice. The first two tracks taken together form the heart of your practice. When I refer to the Chakra Meditation I mean these two tracks. They help you move your mind from the outer world to the inner world. I will explain the other tracks later.

In the book I will suggest a number of ways to make the best use of the techniques on the CD. Of course, you will also learn to meditate "on your own"— that is without the CD. However, most important is your commitment to practise. Try to use the CD every day. Every spiritual effort reaps large rewards. Give meditation at least 20 minutes a day and I guarantee that your life will become calmer and more peaceful.

Read the whole book, then go back and do each chapter one at a time. Do the practices accompanying some of the chapters. Let them work in you. Contemplate the teachings. Think about them. Explore their effect on you. If you feel uncomfortable with a teaching, put it aside. Use the teachings that uplift and expand your awareness. When you feel ready, move on to the next.

Once a day meditate with the first two tracks on the CD. You can begin immediately. Later you can experiment with the other practices as they are described. For more detailed instructions refer to chapter two.

USING THE BOOK WITHOUT THE CD

Because many things happen in the course of the life of a book, it may be that the book has been separated from the CD. Do not panic! Every time the text tells you to meditate with the CD follow the meditation outlined in the appendix on Page 217.

Great beings of all traditions have walked the inner path. Let us set out in their company, with the Buddha, with Jesus, with Sri Ramakrishna, with Bhagawan Nityananda and with my teacher, Swami Muktananda. Their blessings are with us.

KEY IDEAS OF THE INTRODUCTION

- We live in two worlds simultaneously: the outer world of people and objects and the inner world of thoughts and feelings.
- First Education is the knowledge tradition. It focuses on facts and information.
- Second Education is the wisdom tradition. It works on being and empowers us.
- The wisdom tradition is based on the mentor archetype.
- The essential practice in this book is the Chakra Meditation (see Chapter two: Your First Meditation).
- Two other important meditative techniques taught are mantra and witness-consciousness (the breath meditation).
- There are contemplations that help expand your understanding of meditation.

Part 1

ATMA VYAPTI
MEDITATION ON THE SELF

Chapter one:
THE INNER SELF

suddhatattva sandhanadva apashushaktihi

Contemplation of the inner Self frees the individual
from his suffering and feeling of limitation.

Shiva Sutras I:16

ONCE A SEEKER went to a great master. Bowing reverentially in the traditional manner he said: "O master, I seek enlightenment, please initiate and teach me so that I may attain That!"

The master replied in a kindly manner: "Certainly my son, *tat twam asi*, you are That, the divine Self lives within you. Meditate on that Self, know that Self, merge in that Self, realize that Self!"

The seeker was disappointed. "O master, I know all that already. Why, that very teaching was featured in this month's *Yoga Journal*. Please give me the secret teachings, I want the real stuff!"

The master said: "That is all I know. That is my entire teaching, I have no secrets. There is nothing that I have not given you. However, if you are not satisfied, you can go down the road to the next swami's ashram and see if he has something more suitable for you."

The seeker approached the other guru and said: "O master, I seek enlightenment, please give me the initiation and your most secret teaching so that I may attain That!"

The guru said: "I do not give my teachings so easily. You must earn them. You must do *sadhana*, spiritual practice. If you are sincere then you can stay here and work for 12 years. Only in this way will you earn my initiation."

The seeker was delighted: "That's just what I wanted. That is real spiritual life, real sadhana. I'll begin at once."

The guru assigned him the job of shovelling buffalo dung in the back paddock.

The years went by. Each day as he shovelled the dung the seeker dreamt of his future enlightenment. He ticked the passing days and months off his calendar. Finally 12 years were up; the great day arrived. He approached the guru with hands folded palm to palm.

"O my guru, I have served you faithfully for 12 years. I request your teachings and initiation as you have promised. Please bestow your grace on me."

The guru said: "My son, you have served me well. You truly deserve my teaching. Here it is: "*Tat twam asi*. You are That, the divine Self lives within you. Meditate on that Self, know that Self, merge in that Self, realize that Self!"

The seeker became enraged. "What! Is that all? The guru up the road gave me that the first time I met him and I didn't have to shovel buffalo dung for him for 12 years!"

"Well," said the guru. "The truth hasn't changed in 12 years."

What is this inner Self? It is our deepest nature, at the very core or source of the mind. It is the place of love, wisdom and contentment, the place we have touched in our most profound experiences in life. It contains the restorative peace of deep sleep and the vivid joy of our best experiences in the waking state.

The inner Self is the essence of a person: it is also called the *soul*. When a person dies, his Self leaves the body and moves on. The body is left lifeless and inert. If you see a dead person you become aware that it is no longer the person you knew. The body is a vehicle for our true essence, the inner Self.

In another version of the 12 years story the seeker became enlightened as soon as he heard the teaching of the second guru, even though it was word for word the same as that of the first guru. After shovelling dung for so long, the seeker had prepared the ground inside him and was now ready to absorb the teaching. This version also has merit. The Self (I also refer to it as the inner Self or the awakened Self) is paradoxical. It is very close at hand, closer than the closest. My teacher once told me: "Everyone knows his own Self." It is also very elusive.

Over the years mystics have debated whether there is a Self or not and some claim that the core experience is not the Self but the void or emptiness. When I look here and now to the core of my experience I discover my awareness. Awareness contains both understanding and feeling in their most basic forms: understanding that precedes specific thoughts, feeling that precedes specific emotions. There is also a sense of "I" that does not identify with my body or my life story, but with awareness itself. If you want to call this a void you can, but it is a feeling, conscious, Self-aware void.

About a year after I began to meditate I had a significant experience. I was meditating one day in India when I began to feel myself levitating. I floated to the top of the room and hovered near the ceiling. I thought: "I am doing the Indian rope trick, I will be in *Ripley's Believe it or Not*." I had no doubt that my whole body was floating in the air until I opened my eyes and looked down. Then I saw that my body was still sitting in meditation. So it wasn't that my body was levitating, *I had left my body*. Whatever *I* was, was on the ceiling. I understood in that moment, *by direct experience beyond any doubt*, what is meant when the teachings say that you are not the body, you are the Self.

In India the quest for the experience of the peace of the Self is given the generic term yoga. The term yoga is derived from the Sanskrit root *yuj* to "join" or "harness". The English word "yoke" comes from the same root. The yoke was an important instrument in Vedic society since it controlled the horses which pulled the plough or the cart. In the Vedic mind there was a correspondence between joining the horse to the plough and joining the mind to the Self. Thus, yoga means "union", the uniting of different aspects of a person in order to uplift him. Yoga encompasses techniques such as breathing exercises, chanting, service, and especially contemplation and meditation that bring about this union.

In the West the term yoga is most often associated with the physical postures of *hatha yoga*. The term yoga has a much wider application. When I use the term I particularly refer to meditative practices which increase self-knowledge and connect us to the inner Self.

A definition of yoga I like is: "*Yoga is intelligent effort*". Yoga does imply effort. One school of thought claims that since the Self is always present no effort need be made to attain it. This is an attractive thought, but in practice it is nonsense and even harmful. The Self can be experienced spontaneously by grace, or by accident, but to stabilize in the Self, a consistent, intelligent and passionate effort must be made for a long time to realize it completely. Few become anchored in the Self when they first hear the teaching. Most of us have to go through a long practice of meditation and contemplation and make inner progress little by little, bit by bit.

No amount of effort that goes in the wrong direction will attain the goal. We may run with courage, stamina and speed, but if we are going in the opposite direction we will not reach the finish line. There must be true insight and understanding. Meditation helps us understand ourselves and shows us in what direction our effort can be profitably harnessed.

THE ART OF MEDITATION

In the field of meditation the main authority is the ancient sage Patanjali. Patanjali lived at least 1500 years ago and wrote the *Yoga Sutras*, a concise treatise of 196 aphorisms on the art of meditation, as relevant today as it was then. Patanjali's second aphorism (after introducing his topic in the first) is probably the most famous statement about meditation ever made:

yogas citta-vritti-nirodhaha

Yoga (i.e. meditation) is the effort to still
the thought and feeling waves of the mind.

Yoga Sutras of Patanjali I.2

Usually this aphorism is translated "Yoga is to still the thought waves of the mind". This translation, while technically accurate, has created the illusion that there is no meditation unless the mind becomes completely still. The effect of this notion has been to make generations of meditators insecure and dissatisfied with their meditation. Of course in deep meditation the mind becomes completely still, but it is not correct to say anything less than that is not meditation. In valuable states of meditation, thoughts continue to play in the mind. Thoughts in themselves do not stand in the way of meditation. Negative thoughts and negative feelings are, however, another matter and must be pacified.

The statement "yoga is the *effort* to still the mind" is more in the spirit of Patanjali's teachings. A practical teacher, he would have called any and all movement to still the mind meditation.

The idea of quietening or stilling the mind gives meditation a unique place, since in most of our other activities in life we want the mind to be active. The one exception is in sleep, and, in fact, meditation and sleep have a strong relationship. In both activities the mind is turned inside and becomes still. In both activities the still mind approaches the inner Self and draws nourishment and refreshment from it. The difference is that in sleep the Self is approached *unconsciously*, while in meditation it is approached *consciously*.

In his next aphorism Patanjali introduces the idea of the inner Self:

tada drashtuh svarupe 'vasthanam

Then the Seer is established in his own essential
and fundamental nature.

Yoga Sutras of Patanjali I.3

The Seer is the inner Self or witness. When the mind is still, the Self shines forth. One of the commentators compares this situation to the moon's reflection in a still pool of water. When the water is still, the reflection is perfect.

Patanjali then tells us what happens when the mind is not still:

vrtti-sarupyam itaratra

In other states, the Self is obscured by the thoughts
and emotions that play in the mind.

Yoga Sutras of Patanjali I.4

The Self is obscured by an agitated mind—be it anger, fear or despair. Continuing the analogy, if a wind stirs up the pool, the reflection of the moon is refracted and colored by the agitation of the water. In practical terms this means that when we are gripped by agitation we are "no longer ourselves". Anger, paranoia and intense desire can be forms of temporary insanity in which we do things we later regret. Under their influence the force of the Self is obscured.

Meditation is a method of quietening the mind and experiencing our deepest nature, the Self. The value of experiencing the Self is incalculable. It is an awakening, an upwelling of energy, joy and wisdom. There are a number of ways that this awakening takes place. It can even happen spontaneously for no apparent reason. .

Over the years I have heard many accounts of the inner awakening. One man was lying in his bed when he felt a bolt of energy enter him. Another was driving along a freeway and had to pull over because he became absorbed in Cosmic Consciousness. At the age of 16, the great sage Ramana Maharshi underwent an intense fear-of-death experience and in one half hour was completely transformed. Similar experiences are more common than you might expect.

The awakening can also happen in the presence of a self-realized being, as it did for me in the presence of my teacher, and as it did for him in the presence of his teacher. In my case I felt energy rushing through me. I had a series of experiences of higher Consciousness similar to the out-of-body experience I have already described. The awakening can also take place through meditation techniques like the ones in this book, which have been passed down in a strong tradition of great souls from teacher to student .

KEY IDEAS OF CHAPTER ONE:
THE INNER SELF

- The inner Self is our deepest nature, the core, and the source of our mind.
- The quest for the experience of the Self is given the name yoga.
- Yoga is intelligent effort.
- The essence of meditation is to still the thought waves of the mind.
- When the mind is still, the Self shines forth.
- The awakening is an up-welling of energy, joy and wisdom.

Chapter two:

YOUR FIRST MEDITATION

magnaha svachittena pravishet
Meditation is achieved by diving into the
deeper levels of the mind.
Shiva Sutras III.21

TAKING ADVANTAGE OF modern technology you can immediately begin to meditate. The value you receive from these teachings will depend, most of all, upon your commitment to a daily practice of meditation. I suggest you sit down and listen to the Chakra Meditation, the first two tracks, after reading this short chapter. If you do not have the Chakra Meditation CD to play, please do the meditation described on page 217 in the Appendix.

The first part, the *Self-inquiry* section, is just under eight minutes long. I use this technique in all my meditation courses. It helps you become aware of inner tension. In this meditation you investigate the thoughts and feelings in four of the seven chakras: the navel, the heart, the throat and the brow. I ask questions like: "Is the feeling pleasant or unpleasant, tense or relaxed?" This gives you an awareness of the tensions and blocks you may be carrying and also puts you in touch with expanded and uplifting feelings.

The second part is the *Healing Meditation*. Here relaxation and wellbeing are emphasized. You return to the four chakras with a view towards acceptance, love and peace. Follow my narration using its statements and images to release the tension. Experiment with each idea and image. At the end you can find the best feeling and focus on it for the rest of the meditation.

The third track is a musical interlude with the *tamboura*. The tamboura is a four-stringed Indian instrument that creates a meditative mood.

ESTABLISHING YOUR PRACTICE: WHERE AND WHEN

The traditional time for meditation is early morning. Your mind is calm, the phone is not ringing and the children are asleep. Another good time to meditate is at night before you go to bed or early evening just after you have come home from work. Experiment and see what works for you.

A proper meditation posture helps the energy of meditation flow throughout the body. Zen meditation quite rightly describes two ways not to meditate. The first is called *Kontin,* the posture is too "mushy," too loose—the chin falls, the back bends. The second, *sanran*, is the opposite. The meditator manifests too much rigidity and tension in the body. One is too easy going and surrendered, the other too tight and self-willed.

You can sit in a comfortable easy chair or on a cushion on the floor. Your posture should be relaxed and comfortable but also alert. It is best to sit with your back straight and hold your head erect but without tension. It is all right if your head falls forward or backward after you have been meditating for a while.

Wear comfortable clothes. You may want to keep a blanket or a favorite sweater handy in case your temperature drops. You may feel cool one moment and warm the next.

Hatha Yoga has become very popular in the West and is practised to prepare the body to sit for meditation. The postures increase flexibility, strengthen the spine and release tension. Hatha Yoga works on every aspect of the body, including the organs. It is physical culture for the 21st Century. Good health and suppleness are by-products. I suggest you find a good teacher in your area and learn the postures. It will help you meditate effectively.

Where possible set aside a room or a niche for meditation. When you meditate in the same place every day, the meditation energy builds. You can create an energy-filled space by placing pictures of great beings or symbols of higher Consciousness around the area—whatever objects or music you find conducive for entering meditation. You might want to burn some essential oils or incense. This creates a positive atmosphere.

I knew a woman whose husband was violently opposed to meditation. If her meditation paraphernalia was visible it caused turmoil in the house. She cleaned out her closet and created a meditation "cave". She put her meditation pillow in there and had a tape of the mantra playing constantly. She would tell her family: "I am going to my cave to meditate." She was, in every sense of the word, a closet meditator.

Meditation is the single most important discovery I have ever made. Without doubt it has transformed my experience of life. It gives me great joy to welcome you to the practice.

YOUR FIRST MEDITATION

Now is a good time to sit down and become familiar with the Chakra Meditation. Close your eyes, turn within and follow the instructions on the CD or do the written meditation in the appendix. Meditate to the first two tracks. Even if you have the CD it is useful to read through the written form in the appendix one time.

KEY IDEAS OF CHAPTER TWO:
YOUR FIRST MEDITATION

- The traditional time for meditation is early morning.
- Proper posture helps the energy flow.
- Sit comfortably. Keep your back straight but relaxed. Do not become rigid.
- Hatha Yoga helps prepare the body to sit for meditation.
- You can create an energy-filled meditation space.
- Meditating in the same place every day builds the energy.
- Use your CD or your Chakra Meditation every day for at least half an hour.

Chapter three:
WE LIVE IN TWO WORLDS

drishyam shariram

My awareness is a second body in which
everything I experience is contained.

Shiva Sutras I.14

When I open my eyes to the outer world,
I feel myself as a drop in the sea;
but when I close my eyes and look within,
I see the whole universe as a bubble
raised in the ocean of my heart.

Inayat Khan, Divine Symphony

WE CAN DEFINE three major areas of life: career (includes money and objects), relationships (includes partner, parents, children, friends and colleagues), and body (health, fitness and body image). Our usual strategy in life is simple: *we go after what we want and we try to avoid what we do not want.* Unfortunately life includes *not getting what we want and getting what we do not want.* This creates stress. Disappointing outcomes are mitigated by experiences of joy when life goes well or relief when we avoid unpleasant situations.

When life does not go the way we would like we acutely feel the indifference of a vast universe that is unresponsive to us, to our needs, to that which we value and to that which is important to us. We struggle to provide for our families, for love, for creative expression and to become what we intuit we can be. Struggle is inherent in the nature of life and creates tension within us. Meditation comes as a welcome ally and can dissolve that tension if we let it work on us.

The first meditation course I did upon arriving in India was Vipassana, a Buddhist technique. My teacher Goenka, who is now well known, had been a successful businessman for many years before being plagued by migraine headaches. The pain was so unbearable that he could not work. He went to many doctors but nothing alleviated the pain. Finally he met someone who told him he should try meditation. He did as a last resort, and his headaches went away. They had been caused by stress. He was so enthusiastic that he studied meditation profoundly and became a teacher. He is quite elderly now but continues to teach in India.

Over the past 30 years, medical science has begun to make serious studies of meditation. Measurable benefits, such as lowering blood pressure, reducing heart rate and strengthening the immune system, have been documented.

I have been able to use meditation to control heart palpitations (paroxysmal auricular tachycardia), which have troubled me since the age of nine. Meditation has been recognized as a supreme form of stress reduction, and a great aid to controlling negative emotions and moods.

There is a fourth area of life insufficiently understood in our culture. It includes our emotional and intellectual lives as well as the world of imagination that we associate with the artist. The core of the fourth area of life is spirituality, the Self, the realm of meditation.

I LIVE IN TWO WORLDS

Corresponding to the two forms of education there are two worlds. In one world there are gross objects like cars, horses, pencils and other people—the outer world. In the other world there are subtle objects like hope, fear and memory—the inner world. You cannot find *hope* at the supermarket, you cannot buy a thought at the chemist. The inner world and the outer world are the two environments in which we live. We live in them *simultaneously.*

Once Sheik Nasruddin was involved in a murder at a bar. The bartender immediately called the police, who were baffled when they saw that the head was missing from the body. "Who are your regulars," the police asked the bartender.

"Mulla Nasruddin," replied the bartender.

The police immediately called Nasruddin in. "We understand that you come here regularly. Can you identify the body for us?"

"Bring me a mirror," exclaimed Nasruddin.

The police brought him a mirror. Nasruddin examined himself at length in the mirror. "Well," he said: "it's not me!"

The punch line affirms that you do not have to look outside to recognize the Self. You know, without looking in a mirror, that the corpse cannot be *you*. We know the inner world via *knowing*—introspection.

The inner world is our closest, most intimate environment. The essential ingredients of our inner world are thought and feeling. The outer world changes if, for example, we travel to New York, Paris or Cairns. But wherever we go, we take our inner world with us.

It is impossible to arrange our outer world so we continually feel fully satisfied. There are bound to be areas of stress and disappointment. Gossip magazines are a billion-dollar business, at least part of which is to demonstrate that people who "have everything" are still not necessarily happy. For this reason, some people despair of ever controlling their outer life and seek to numb themselves through substance abuse. Drugs and alcohol are inner world strategies—they deal directly with the condition of the inner world—but have disastrous side effects.

There is, however, a strategy that is entirely positive: it helps the inner world and has excellent side effects—meditation.

TRUE EMPOWERMENT

Many years ago a western academic was travelling in the East. A friend took him to the ashram of a noted sage. The professor asked the sage: "What is the purpose of meditation and yoga?"

The sage answered: "People are aware of the outer world of people, actions and objects, but they are generally unaware of the laws of the inner world of thoughts and feelings. The purpose of meditation is to become familiar with the inner world. Beyond that, the goal of meditation is to reach the source of life, Consciousness."

The inner and outer worlds each have their own laws. Through science and technology we have understood physical principles and made our physical life easier. If I throw a ball against a wall one thousand times I expect the ball to bounce back one thousand times. Not once—even in a billion tries—will the ball pass *through* the wall. In the West the inner world has been left to a few artists, philosophers and psychiatrists, whom we respect and revere but scarcely understand. In the East investigators have studied the inner world for centuries. A good meditator is an inner scientist. His own Self is his laboratory and he experiments with thoughts and feelings and meditative techniques to gain inner mastery. Clarity, objectivity and hard-headedness are qualities of the inner world science.

The East has thousands of strategies for understanding the transcendent Self but it lacks outer world technology. East and west, inner and outer—a cultural exchange is happening. With the integration of the inner and outer worlds the collective unconscious of humanity is healing. Our time promises exciting developments.

The inner world is governed by subtle principles and *is just as lawful as the outer world*. If you are depressed, there are reasons for it. If you are happy, there are reasons for it. If you understand the reasons for the condition of your inner world, you are well on the way to being able to return to, or stay in, a state of joy and peace. It is good sense to investigate these inner laws.

The outer world is a shared experience. The same automobile exists in your outer world and in mine. But in your inner world only one person exists—*you*. No matter how much you and your beloved love each other, he/she can never enter your inner world, nor you theirs. Another may be very attuned to your thoughts, moods and emotions, but he can never know them with certainty *from inside*. It is in your enlightened self-interest to learn as much as you can about your inner world to gain the power of inner transformation.

What is the relationship between the outer world and the inner world? The conventional understanding is that the inner world is decisively affected by events in the outer world. When our life goes well we are happy. When our life goes badly we are unhappy. So we try to control events, which we can do only to a limited degree. Hence, we are significantly disempowered, and our moods go up and down when events prove to be beyond our control. In addition, there is inevitable loss due to disease, old age and death.

Certainly, outer events affect us. But by working on our inner world we can develop such strength and independence that we can always return to peace or happiness, no matter what happens. We may be happy when we get what we want, *but we can also be happy when we don't get what we want*. I call this condition of inner independence *true empowerment*. Meditation is an important means to this goal.

While in India I studied a number of philosophical systems, including Vedanta. Vedanta says that the world is a dream. As in a dream, everything is experienced through our thoughts and emotions, the inner environment. You can probably think of someone who has a negative mental attitude. No matter what positive things happen to him, even if he wins the lottery, he says: "But it was only so much, not more!"

We firmly believe that we see the world *as it is*, but in reality the world is filtered through the sunglasses of the mind. Those glasses may be rose-colored or jaundiced. The ancient scripture *Yoga Vashishta* states: *"ya drishti, sa shrishti"*, which means, the world is as you see it, or: "as the vision, so the world". We have been strongly affected by conditioning from infancy, by our parents and the culture. Often when a person thinks he is objective he is actually seeing his own concepts, judgments and prejudices. In fact, a *psychic* filter prevents us from seeing clearly.

Meditation cleans our psychic filter. When we meditate we rid ourselves of the unnecessary impressions we gather from daily life. Through meditation we can experience our true nature, which is full of bliss and wisdom. We have within us the power to uplift ourselves. This power is our own awareness. We should investigate our own consciousness, and ask the following empowering questions:

1. What is my true Self?
2. What blocks hold me back?
3. How can I move from contraction to freedom?

Our inner world is constantly changing. In meditation we discover exactly how this is true. We become aware of the enormous range of thoughts and feelings we hold within. By Self-inquiry and meditation we understand it is not the world outside but our inner world, our own consciousness, which confuses us. And that it is not so much events as our reaction to them that creates our problems.

We can cultivate the strength that leads us to the freedom to choose how we react. If someone criticizes you, there is a range of responses you can have. You might feel crushed and go to bed for a week, or you might shrug it off as nothing. You might consider the other person and graciously put it down to a cranky mood or a "bad hair day" and forgive the person. You might dismiss it by asking yourself: "Why should I listen to her?" When someone whose opinion you value judges or criticizes you, you probably feel quite hurt. However, if a two-year-old criticizes you, you are not affected. Our reaction is everything. The good news is that we can change our reactions. We do not have to react with anger or fear.

I HAVE A CARROT IN MY EAR

If you have ever tried to shift out of a bad mood you know that it is not easy. That is why some people resort to substance abuse. Meditation gives us a much better means to change our inner world for the better. To make this change two prerequisites are necessary. The good news is that we can change our reactions. We do not have to react with anger or fear. We can cultivate the strength that leads us to the freedom to choose how we react.

1. You have to see the problem.
2. You have to know what to do.

In our Chakra Meditation the first part, Self-inquiry, helps us to see the problem. The second part, the Healing Meditation, is a positive *doing*.

In every field: science, business, art or sport, the first step is to examine the situation. The golfer surveys the green hoping to predict the way his chipshot or his putt will roll. The businessman watches the fluctuations of the market. The scientist observes the patterns of nature. Meteorologists watch the movement of warm and cold fronts. The artist reflects on his subject. The meditator sculpts the landscape of his inner world.

Sometimes when we investigate a particular situation, the truth is hidden. Even though more and more evidence pointed to the fact that the earth revolves around the sun, the medieval churchmen refused to accept it. Their preconceptions and dogmatism kept them from the truth. In the inner world, fear and desire or the ego can keep us from seeing what is so, or hearing the truth. I call this *having a carrot in one's ear.*

When I was in high school I heard an enigmatic joke. Two men are walking along the street. One of them says to the other: "You know, you have a carrot in your ear."

The second man replies: " I can't hear you. I have a carrot in my ear."

This odd little joke has kept coming up in my mind all these years. It strikes me as funny, because the man knows he has a carrot in his ear. Did he put it there for quiet, or is he fatalistic about it and feels he cannot get rid of it? It is easy to see the carrots in others' ears, hard to see our own. In some areas of our life we are 'stuck', not listening, not seeing clearly and not hearing. We have had our carrots for so long they seem natural and right. They are comfortable and removal seems dangerous, even life threatening. The ego circles the wagons around it, and prepares to defend an insignificant bit of terrain until death.

The path of Vedanta describes a three-fold process of inner growth. The first is *hearing*: the student listens to the teaching in an open, non-argumentative way. He lets the words of the teacher or the text he is reading enter him and work on him without resistance.

The second is *thinking*: the student tries to understand what he has heard by using his mind in a positive way. He tries to make the teaching relevant to his understanding. He brings up doubts with a view to clearing them.

Thirdly there is *assimilation*: the student merges with the teaching. He lets it take him deep within himself, where he discovers the teaching already exists as his own Self. He makes it his own.

To *hear* properly, we must pay attention and remove all carrots. The first step is to observe the inner world as vigilantly and objectively as possible. When I began my own process of self-observation, I was stunned to see that the way

I *actually* was, was far different from the way I *thought* I was. When I saw selfishness, ego and other negative qualities I began to judge myself harshly. Later my attitude towards self-observation changed. I came to enjoy breaking my own illusions and seeing myself as I am. Every time I did that, I felt more empowered.

Each day we have innumerable encounters with the world. We meet other people. Events take place. We have a reaction to every event and encounter. Sometimes our reactions are open, loving and marked by delight. Other times we react with anger, fear or grief.

In some cases our reaction is too subtle for us to notice. Freud would call it "unconscious". Nonetheless, it is quite real. Even when our mind is not aware of it, impressions are recorded within and some of them show up as tension or contraction. By meditation these subtle contractions can be discovered and their causes worked out and released.

Our speech and actions broadcasts our conscious ideas and feelings. They also broadcast *unconscious* ideas and feelings that form subtle contractions. These contractions motivate us to act in various ways. Psychologists call these subtle contractions the "shadow". From the point of view of meditation and Self-inquiry the shadow is *unconsciously held contractions created by past reactions to events and people.* These reactions show up in the subtle energy centres in the body. As we carefully observe our reactions and contractions, we begin to remove the carrots from our ears.

KEY IDEAS OF CHAPTER THREE:
WE LIVE IN TWO WORLDS

- We live simultaneously in two worlds, the inner world and the outer world.
- The inner world, not the outer world, is crucial to our empowerment.
- The inner world is just as lawful as the outer world.
- It is possible to be happy even if we do not get what we want.
- The search for happiness is the search for the inner Self.
- Meditation is true empowerment.
- Meditation is the care and feeding of the inner world.
- By self-observation we can discover the carrot in our ear.
  By meditation we can remove the carrot.

Chapter four:
KUNDALINI-
THE INNER POWER

Contemplate Kundalini, who is supreme Consciousness,
who plays from the muladhara to the sahasrara,
who shines like a flash of lightning,
who is as fine as a fibre of a lotus stalk,

Who has the brilliant radiance of countless suns and
is a shaft of light as cool as hundreds of nectarean moonbeams.

Swami Muktananda

ALL MEDITATIVE PATHS define energy centres within the body, and the findings of all of the systems are remarkably similar. The system of yoga defines seven chakras, each one governing particular areas of life.

Chakra	Sanskrit Name	Position	Area of Life
First	Muladhara (Base chakra)	Anus (precisely: mid-way between the anus and genitals)	Basic security. (home and money, survival and instinct)
Second	Svadhistana	Genitals (precisely: at or just above the genitals)	Sexuality and reproduction.
Third	Manipura	Navel	Action and will; career drive.
Fourth	Anahata	Heart (centre of the chest)	Love, feeling, emotion. (relationship and family)
Fifth	Vishudha	Throat	Communication and expression.
Sixth	Ajna	Brow (3rd Eye)	Inspiration into life issues; wisdom and intuition. (philosophy)
Seventh	Sahasrar	Crown of head (thousand-petal lotus)	Transcendent Self; transpersonal reality. (spirituality)

I have found that one of the most effective ways to unblock tension is to begin by examining four of the energy centers. This investigation provides a vast amount of information and puts one in a position to become empowered. Self-inquiry confirms again and again that the areas of life listed relate to the chakras indicated. You can verify this in your own practice. Although no heart surgeon has ever found a heart chakra, you probably will agree that when you say: "I love you" to your beloved you feel the love in your heart area, not in your earlobe or elbow.

If you read widely in the field of yoga, you will find elaborate descriptions of the chakras. They will include colors, sacred syllables, images and so on, for each one. Most of these are traditional descriptions that were arrived at clairvoyantly by early meditators. Some of these details are debatable, so I have kept it simple.

Yoga and Chinese medicine both affirm that there is a "subtle body" and that it has its own energy system. This takes a form similar to nerve channels except they are not physically visible. Chinese medicine calls them meridians, and an acupuncturist places needles at certain key points in the energy system to open blocks. Yoga calls them *nadis* and some texts say there are 72,000 nadis, others 720,000. Whatever the number, when the energy (or prana) flows nicely in these channels, there is health, wellbeing and happiness.

Among the nadis, three are particularly significant. They are the *ida, pingala* and *sushumna*. The sushumna is the central canal in the centre of the body along which the chakras are arranged. The energy that moves along the sushumna is called Kundalini—divine spiritual energy. When this energy is awakened, a person begins to evolve spiritually. Most of humanity at the present state of human history is not very evolved in an inner sense—their *Kundalini Shakti* is unawakened. Gurdjieff said: "Man is a machine"; the Hindu sages say: "Man is asleep". Listening to the evening news verifies this judgement.

Hence it follows that many disciplines, including Zen, yoga and Vedanta, talk about an awakening. In my tradition it is called *Shaktipat*, the descent of grace.

My teacher was famous for the awakening people received from him. He would hold meditation intensives (weekend workshops) and at the start of meditation he would walk among the meditators (often more than a thousand people) and bless each person with a wand of peacock feathers and touch them between the eyes at the third eye. The Kundalini energy became thick in the air and people would manifest it in dramatic ways. Some shook with energy, some had physical movements, some spoke in tongues. It sometimes seemed like a primeval swamp full of strange creatures.

In my early years in India, there was an Indian man who visited the ashram every weekend. When there was a program of chanting, the Shakti would hit him. He would begin while sitting, by shaking all over, and his body would gyrate in a wave-like manner. Suddenly his head was thrown back and he was flat on his back. He would move backwards (head first) on his back at great speed through the chanters. Because of his unique motion we called him "the snake". Many understood this was a manifestation of Kundalini, but some new people were terrified.

I was hall monitor at the time, and my colleagues and I made a plan. The next weekend we were on the alert. As he started to gyrate we sprang into action. When he hit the ground four of us were on him. We each grabbed a limb and lifted him neatly up and out into the courtyard where he continued to slither harmlessly. Strangely enough we had caught some of his energy and were quite ecstatic as a result.

Years later I was leading my own intensive in Sydney, Australia. I gave the touch and though I was aware that there was a lot of Kundalini activity going on, I settled down for a nice meditation. After a while a hall monitor tapped me on the shoulder. He was worried and wanted me to make sure everything was all right. He took me to the back of the hall where a row of meditators was creating an extraordinary commotion.

Earlier in the week I had met a gentle, middle-aged doctor. He was polite and soft-spoken. Now there he was in the centre of the row, roaring like a lion. Each roar would send a shock wave of energy through his neighbors and they would react in various ways. I saw that none of them wanted to run away, but on the contrary, they all showed signs of enjoying the experience mightily. I could feel the floor shaking under them and I could feel waves of bliss coming from them. I stood there basking for a while, and then reassured the hall monitor and returned to my own meditation.

Shaktipat is not confined to my tradition, of course, but is found in all the paths. The experience recorded in the gospels of the manifestation of the holy spirit on the Pentecost after Jesus' death is such an event, as is this one from the Jewish Hassidic tradition. The Bal Shem Tov was an inspired being, the founder of Hassidism. Martin Buber recounts a story from the Bal Shem Tov's successor, the Maggid of Mezritch. One holiday the Bal Shem was praying in front of the altar with great fervour and in a very loud voice. The Maggid of Mezritch was ill that day and stayed in the small room to pray there alone. At one point the Bal Shem came into the room to put on his robe. The Maggid looked at him and could see that he was not in this world; the Bal Shem's face was shining and he was transported. As the Bal Shem put on his robe, it wrinkled at the shoulders and the Maggid put his hand on it to smooth out the folds. As soon as he touched it, he himself began to tremble. The Bal Shem went on into the big hall but the Maggid remained standing there, trembling half in ecstasy and half in terror.

Of course many people who receive the awakening manifest nothing externally but go deep within. My teacher wrote about seeing a series of inner lights: red, white, black and blue in that order. Each light represents a deeper layer of contact with the Self. Especially significant is the blue light. Even today many of my students report seeing this light in their meditations. Every meditator will awaken in some way. It may not be this dramatic, but it will be real. People feel energy running through them, others waves of love or deep peace. Two of the most useful forms of awakening are the awakening of true understanding and the awakening of the ability to act strongly in life.

Early in the book I wrote about two kinds of education, conventional education (the First Education) and wisdom education (the Second Education). The awakening belongs to the Second Education, but there is overlap. Andrew Delbanco, a professor of humanities at my old university, Columbia, finds the roots of literary studies in religion. He quotes Emerson, who, in the 19th Century said:

> The whole secret of the teacher's force lies in the conviction that men are convertible. And they are. They want awakening. Every great teacher seeks to get the soul out of bed, out of her deep habitual sleep.

Delbanco calls this "education as illumination and deliverance". I see it as an area in First Education where there is an intimation of awakening to Second Education. Unfortunately—or inevitably—literary studies have gone in a direction far from Second Education.

In 1976 Muktananda called me in and told me to awaken people by touch the way he did. He gave me his wand of peacock feathers, instructed me how to do it and recited some mantras for me to learn. As he sang the mantras I felt them enter my brain as the worst headache I had ever experienced. The headache lasted all that day and I spent a sleepless night in agony. Early the next morning I went to his house and told him of my headache. He said: "Take an aspirin."

Later in the day he was more sympathetic and told me to put clarified butter (ghee) in my nose and lie briefly in the sun. Eventually the headache went away and the realization came that my wiring had been somehow changed for the work ahead of me. I still use those feathers at meditation intensives.

KEY IDEAS OF CHAPTER FOUR:
KUNDALINI - THE INNER POWER

- The subtle body is an energy system.
- Blocked energy is the result of our reactions.
- Unblocked energy is love and joy.
- The great Kundalini power slumbers within us, waiting to awaken.
- A master of meditation can awaken the Kundalini of a seeker by means of the process of Shaktipat.

Chapter five:

WAKING, DREAM, DEEP SLEEP & MEDITATION -THE FOUR STATES OF CONSCIOUSNESS

jagrat svapna sushupta bhede turyabhoga sambhavaha

*Beyond and pervading the waking, dream and deep sleep states
is the blissful fourth state—"Turiya" (meditation).*

Shiva Sutras I.7

THE INNER SELF exists within everyone, not only people of genius, like Shakespeare or Mozart. There is a blazing sun that lives within you as your own awareness. Meditation will help you get in touch with it.

The commitment to meditation is more important than specific techniques. By meditating every day you will become more and more sensitive to the tensions in your body. Gradually, you will understand how they have arisen and you will learn the skilful means to release them.

Your consciousness is a sensitive and intelligent medium that records every nuance of your life. This is true even when you are not particularly aware of your reactions to people and events. Sometimes you may find it difficult to get in touch with one or more of the chakras. It is common for one or another of your chakras to hold little feeling. The important one to work with is the one where tension, stress and bad feeling cluster.

Think of the Self as the source of the mind and emotion. It is the place within where the highest and noblest thought and feeling reside. When you are in touch with the inner Self, awareness expands. Joy and illumination are revealed.

As you meditate you build a true identity. That identity gets stronger and stronger as you continue to meditate. Then you recognize the voice of wisdom, love and truth. That inner voice is the voice of the inner Self.

The inner Self has energy associated with it. When your meditation touches the inner Self you can palpably feel that energy. Sometimes your meditation comes with a feeling of grace, you move into a beautiful rhythm. You effortlessly glide into deep states of peace. At other times it does not come so easily and you may need to make an effort. These are the two wings of the bird of spiritual practice: grace and self-effort. We cannot control grace, since that is a gift from the Divine. We can—at least to some degree—control effort. It is important for us to do our practice of meditation. God is generous and therefore grace is inevitable. But we should create the proper conditions for it.

THREE STATES OF CONSCIOUSNESS

Day after day we habitually pass through three states of consciousness, one after the other. They are the waking, dream and deep sleep states.

- The waking state is a state of awareness in which the senses and the mind are active.

In the waking state, we absorb information through our senses and we analyze it with our mind. We think, we act and we converse. We live our outer life. After a number of hours we become tired and we crave a change of state.

Think about this for a moment. Imagine that you have been having the best day of your life. Your oil well struck oil. Your novel was given the Nobel Prize for literature. You have won the lottery. The man (woman) of your dreams has just called you up to tell you that he (she) secretly loves you. That would be a good day, but even with your luck running that hot, at some point you wouldn't be able to stay awake for another moment.

The question is: what is it about sleep that is so refreshing and so desirable that oil wells, honors, money and love cannot replace it?

In sleep we move to the interior of our being. We leave the outer world and dwell, for a time, exclusively in the inner world. We move closer to the inner Self. Just as when we move closer to the sun we get hot, so when we move closer to the blazing sun of the Self, we become refreshed, inspired and reinvigorated.

- Dreaming is a state of awareness in which the mind is active and the senses are not.

Dreaming is entirely subjective. We create a world that is convincing in its apparent reality. We see other people, tigers, bears and castles. Good and bad things happen to us. Most of the time we are completely taken in, but a dream is an illusion. In fact, as we discover when we awaken, *there is no other person in that world but us.* The whole drama is played out in our own awareness.

Psychologists have observed that dreamers produce rapid eye movements (REM). They designed an experiment in which volunteers would sleep in the laboratory. Whenever there was REM activity, they would be awakened. Soon the subjects were having severe depression and nervous disorders. In this way they found that dreaming performs a necessary function. We can say that as we dream, the energy of life is harmonized by the energy of sleep, as awareness moves deeper towards the Self.

To dream is not the state for which we hunger. If we dream the whole night we wake up feeling agitated and grumpy. The state we seek is deep sleep. When we have had the required deep sleep we say: "I slept like a log, I slept like a dead person!" We feel renewed and refreshed.

- Deep sleep can be defined as a state in which the senses and the mind are turned off. Awareness is absorbed within.

Everyone loves and values deep sleep. Although it appears as if nothing is going on, we are actually having a profound experience. In deep sleep awareness is close to the inner Self.

Consider for a moment the good and bad aspects of waking and deep sleep. Variety, beauty, excitement, colors and sounds mark the waking state. It is a brilliant world. The problem is that it can be stressful. We often experience fear, anger, worry and depression.

On the other hand, deep sleep has none of these stressful features. It is sheer peace, perfectly secure and strangely blissful. But, it lacks the brilliance and variety of the waking state.

One wonders, is it possible to combine the good features of both these states? It surely is, but I am reminded of a story—probably of doubtful authenticity—about the famous early 20th Century dancer Isadora Duncan. In those days there was a fascination with eugenics, the idea that a higher type of human being could be created by selective reproduction. Isadora, who was well-known for her beauty, had the desire to have a child with the smartest man in the world. Upon deciding on the playwright George Bernard Shaw, she wrote to him requesting his assistance in her project.

"Dear Mr. Shaw, would it not be wonderful if we had a child? The child would be blessed with my beauty and your brains."

He replied: "Madam, your proposal is the most intriguing one I have had in quite some time. One matter worries me, however. What if the child were to have *my* beauty and *your* brains?"

Likewise, our meditation should not have the agitation of waking and the inertness of sleep. It should have the brilliant awareness of waking and the deep peace of sleep.

THE FOURTH STATE

The four states of consciousness can be summarized in the following diagram.

Every person experiences the first three states of consciousness. Even animals experience them. Sometimes I have to wake up my dog, Bhakti, when she is having a nightmare. She whimpers and has Rapid Paw Movements. There is a state beyond or within these ordinary states. In Sanskrit it is called *turiya*, which means: "the Fourth State". Only a person who makes a conscious effort to experience this state of awareness can achieve it.

Meditation is the means to enter the Fourth State. In the Fourth State we go close to the Self as in sleep, but we remain aware. It is not hard to see that attaining such a state of awareness is extremely valuable.

You may already have had a taste of *turiya* while using the Chakra Meditation. You may have felt a floating sensation. You may have entered an inner space that was something like sleep but clearly different from sleep. You may have felt an energy or peace. These are all experiences of the Self and the Fourth State of Consciousness.

A meditation master of the last generation was invited to lecture behind the Iron Curtain. When preparing for his trip, it was mentioned that the people in that particular culture knew little about meditation and tended to be hostile to it. He laughed and said: "Don't worry, tell them I teach a method of sleep sitting up!"

I suggest that you stop reading now and try the following for 10 minutes or so.

Contemplation 1: "I am asleep sitting up".

This contemplation gives a good hint at what a still mind feels like and also illustrates the connection between sleep and meditation. You will probably stay awake, but your mind will become quiet, if you stay with it long enough.

1.   Sit in a relaxed manner.

2.   Close your eyes.

3.   Let go, as if you were going to sleep.

4.   Pretend you are asleep sitting up.

CONTINUING YOUR PRACTICE

Continue using the Chakra Meditation as you have been doing. This will make you more and more sensitive to your inner world. You will eventually discover the underlying causes of the tensions you hold in your body. I also hope that you are learning how these tensions can be released. Using the Chakra Meditation will build your concentration and your ability to be comfortable and effective in your inner world.

We go to astrologers, therapists and psychics to find out about ourselves. Meditation is truly the most direct way to learn about yourself. As a Zen master once told his student: "You want to know about yourself? Look! Look! Look!"

Sometimes when we begin to meditate, the inner world is stirred up. It is like a lake that becomes muddy when there is a disturbance. After a while the mind quietens down and the lake becomes clear again. In the same way, continue your daily practice. Your inner world will sort itself out.

MEDITATION TIME-OUTS

Use meditation when you feel stress or tension in the course of the day. If you are at work, close the door of your office, or find a quiet spot somewhere and do the Chakra Meditation. Focus on the uplifting feeling and centre yourself. This has a powerful and calming effect. Three-minute breaks a few times a day will help your day run more smoothly. It is quality time with the inner Self.

Remember; a great untapped power is within you. You are full of wisdom, joy and light. This is your true Self. Never put yourself down or give way to despair. By walking the path of meditation you are affirming the greatness that is within you.

KEY IDEAS OF CHAPTER FIVE:
THE FOUR STATES OF CONSCIOUSNESS

- By meditating every day you will become more and more sensitive to the tensions in your body.
- As you meditate, you build a true identity.
- The inner Self has an energy associated with it.
- The three states of consciousness are waking, dream and deep sleep.
- There is a fourth state beyond them: it is the state of meditation.
- The Self can be realized through effort, meditation and understanding.
- A Zen master said: "Do you want to know about yourself? Look!"
- Within you is an untapped power, full of wisdom, joy and light.

Chapter six:

WHAT IS THE CONDITION
OF MY INNER WORLD?

svasvarupa vismarana

Ignorance is simply forgetfulness of one's inner Self.

Sri Shankaracharya

THE FIRST PURPOSE of meditation is to become familiar with the inner world. Beyond that, the goal is to reach the source of life, the inner Self, the Awakened Self. Many of us have a sense of this inner source, or at least of a great potential within that we have rarely tapped.

Sometimes we doubt ourselves. I vividly remember a woman who came up to me after a meditation class and said: "When you spoke I imagined that you looked at me and thought, 'You are the first person I have seen who does not have an inner Self.' Do I have an inner Self?"

I reassured her that the inner Self is at the core of every human being. But afterwards I thought about her doubt. Why did she have a problem with the concept of the Self? Sometimes when you give names to subtle things in the spiritual realm you do create a difficulty. She thought of the inner Self as mysterious and far away, outside her usual experience. On the contrary, it is close at hand. It has been with us through all the changes and vicissitudes of our lives. It is our most intimate self, the place we refer to when we say "me".

The Awakened Self is the deepest, clearest region of the inner world. There is peace, energy and wisdom in that region. As we move from states of suffering towards states of joy we are "approaching the Self". Or, you could simply say we are improving or uplifting our inner world.

- Meditation is a movement towards expansion or better feeling in the inner world, entirely by inner means.

Taking this view, we do not have to wonder: do I have a Self, do I have the "right stuff"? How long it will take to attain it? Instead, we focus directly on present experience with a view towards uplifting the mind.

The Awakened Self is that area, space or condition of our inner world, which is characterized by light, joy, wisdom, energy and peace. It is positive and contented. Even if we rarely experience such harmonious states, we know that the *potential* to feel good or better exists within us.

UPLIFTING THE INNER WORLD

A good meditation could be defined as:

- One in which you felt better or more peaceful when you finished than when you began.

I tell my students that they have achieved a spiritual triumph when they resist the temptation to avoid meditation or to quit early when they are in an agitated state. It increases the triumph when they manage, in the course of the session, to shift to a state of peace or joy.

My emphasis in my own meditation is always on the present. I sit down and ask myself: "How do I feel now?" I observe areas of tension or unpleasantness. I spend time trying to work out what has caused that tension. Then I give all my effort to achieving an upward shift, using techniques I will explain later.

Contemplation 2: What is the condition of my inner world?

For the moment let us discard the notion of the Self and just see what is inside right now.

1. Close your eyes and bring your attention inside to your inner world.
2. Notice your breathing. Notice any inner sensations or subtle movements.
3. Bring in the thought: "This is my inner world".
4. Let yourself become familiar with it as you would a new city or country.
5. Question: "What is the present condition of my inner world?"
6. "Is it happy, sad, angry, fearful, contracted or expanded?"
7. "Do I feel weak, agitated, confused or pained?"
8. "If I compare the present condition of my inner world to remembered positive states, where does it rate on a scale of one to 10?"
9. "If I am presently at four, how can I get to five or eight?"
10. Think of a pleasant memory, a peaceful scene, or an uplifting thought that *improves the feeling in your inner world.*

In repairing the inner world use your common sense: "If it ain't broke, don't fix it". Patanjali, the ancient theorist on meditation, listed many techniques, but his final comment was: "Or, meditate as desired". It means that we can use whatever works.

Tradition supports this practical approach. The Buddha elegantly said that the essence of meditation is to get rid of bad states when they occur, and perpetuate good states when they occur. This makes good states more likely in the future. The *Vijnanabhairava*, a classical compendium of meditation techniques says: "Meditate on whatever gives deep joy without agitation."

Meditation has a marvellous side effect in that it develops and increases intuition. Intuition is that "sixth sense" we all have, but do not always heed. After something goes wrong we often think: "I *knew* I shouldn't have done that." Listen to your intuition! Cultivate it. Use your intuition in your meditation. You will develop a "feel" for your inner world and an instinct for what will help you in life as well as in your meditation.

KEY IDEAS OF CHAPTER SIX:
WHAT IS THE CONDITION OF MY INNER WORLD?

- The first purpose of meditation is to become familiar with the inner world.
- Meditation is a movement towards expansion by inner means.
- A good meditation is one where you feel better when you have finished.
- The awakened Self is the deepest, clearest region of the inner world.
- Meditate on whatever gives joy without agitation.
- Listen to your intuition. Cultivate your intuition.

Chapter seven:
MANTRA -
THE POWER OF THE WORD

vidyasharirasatta mantrarahasyam
*The luminous energy of pure Awareness
is the secret of mantra.*
Shiva Sutras II.3

*The essence of a mantra lies not in its syllables,
but in the spiritual power it delivers.*
Swami Shankarananda

SO FAR YOU have been working with the Chakra Meditation. In this chapter I will introduce the second meditation technique—one very dear to my heart—mantra.

My first encounter with the practice of mantra came many years ago when I read J.D. Salinger's short novel, *Franny and Zooey*. In the book the character Franny is reading a charming narrative called *The Way of a Pilgrim*, written by an anonymous 19th Century Russian peasant. The pilgrim is on a quest to understand the teaching in the Gospels when they say: "Pray ceaselessly". He wanders from holy man to holy man, searching for an explanation.

After a long time he meets a hermit who explains that repetition of the Jesus Prayer, *Lord Jesus Christ have mercy on me*, is the practice referred to in the Gospels. The hermit initiates the pilgrim into *mantra* practice.

The pilgrim pursues his prayer with single-minded enthusiasm, logging many thousands of repetitions a day. As his practice intensifies, he experiences deep ecstasies and visions.

The ancient sages had a full arsenal of meditative means at their disposal. Perhaps the most pervasive of the techniques they used is mantra. A mantra is a word or phrase that you repeat silently to prepare the mind for meditation. '*Man*' is from '*manas*' which means mind. The syllable '*tra*' means "to protect" or "quieten".

Mantra repetition is the method most often used to enter meditation. When we first learn to meditate we confront a mind that may be unwilling to cooperate. The mantra pushes unwanted thoughts away. It soothes negative emotion. When the mind settles down, the inner Self shines forth.

Om Namah Shivaya is the mantra of Shiva Yoga. When repeated, it calms the mind and brings peace to the senses. It destroys ignorance and expands awareness. It is charged with the energy of the inner Self. It is alive with spiritual power. By repeating it or by listening to it you can awaken Kundalini Shakti, the dormant meditative energy. Once awakened, Shakti illumines the inner world. It connects the individual to universal awareness. It deepens and enlivens meditation practice.

In my early days in the ashram in India I went through a period of intense fear. I felt so hopeless and disempowered that I could not bring myself to speak to my teacher. One day, as I was doing my work in the ashram garden, he came up to me. He stood an inch from my face, nose to nose.

He whispered to me: *"Om Namah Shivaya, Om Namah Shivaya, Om Namah Shivaya."*

He forcefully said: "Repeat this twenty-four hours a day. Meditate intensely for four hours a day!"

I began at once. Less than a day later I was again experiencing joy bubbling in my heart. I felt triumphant and empowered; I had shifted my mood without recourse to unhealthy diversions.

When you go through a particularly difficult period of depression, it is hard to make rational decisions. The mind dwells on negativity. You can uplift your mind by intense mantra repetition.

Mantras are given in all the traditions of meditation including the Hindu yoga tradition, the Buddhist tradition as well as the Pilgrim's Eastern Christian tradition. That tradition continues today in monasteries like Mt. Athos in Greece and other places. Monks have been meditating in caves for 30 or 40 years, repeating this prayer and attaining inner ecstasy.

There are many effective techniques of meditation. However, it is possible to get overly caught up in various techniques, to the detriment of the goal. The first step is to concentrate the mind on one thought. The mantra is a single thought. With practice, the mind can become concentrated and move beyond thought to deep meditation.

Dr. Herbert Benson of the Harvard Medical School thought that you could repeat any word or phrase as a mantra. His idea was to say the word "one" repeatedly. He called it the "relaxation response". Actually, "one" is rather a good mantra, but ordinary words will not have the same effect as a mantra. Some words are simply more powerful than other ones. Even an effective mantra should be received from the proper source.

Ramana Maharshi used to tell an amusing story of mantra initiation. Once there was a king whose Prime Minister used to practise mantra repetition. The king, aware of its positive effect, asked him for initiation. The Prime Minister told the king that he could not do it. Later the king called the Prime Minister before him and asked him why he refused his request for initiation. The Prime Minister called a palace guard and ordered him to take hold of the king. The guard just stood there. The Prime Minister again repeated the order. The guard did not respond. Angry at the minister's impudence, the king ordered the guard to seize him. The guard immediately took hold of him.

"Do you see?" laughed the Prime Minister "you and I gave the same order to the same guard. My order to seize you had no effect, whereas your order to seize me had the authority and power of the throne behind it. It is the same with mantra."

The sage Goraknath said: "The word is the lock and the word is the key. An awakened word received from an awakened master, is the only way to awaken the dormant word in the heart of the sleeping disciple. Upon introducing the word, the gross articulate word merges into the eternal word"(*Gorakabani 21*).

The mantra I am giving you is a mantra that has been passed down through generations of meditators. It is *alive* because it comes from a true line of meditation masters. I have used this mantra for more than 25 years and it is one of the most effective tools of meditation that I have come across. It calms and strengthens the mind.

Om Namah Shivaya is a Sanskrit mantra. Sanskrit is an ancient language similar to Latin, Hebrew or ancient Greek. No one actually speaks Sanskrit any more but it is still used for mantra repetition and chanting. *Om Namah Shivaya* is a different sort of statement from "Pass the butter, please", or "I would like a copy of *The Herald*, please". It has no outer world meaning, only inner world reference. *Om Namah Shivaya* points us to the inner Self. It directs our attention within. It means: "I turn to my own deepest truth", "I turn to my own inner Self".

Om refers to the Absolute, the highest principle in the universe. Patanjali, the great authority on yoga says: "His (i.e. God's) designator is *Om*." For religious or spiritual people, *Om* is synonymous with God. Others say that *Om* is all the sounds of the universe condensed into one sound.

An alternate and more phonetically correct spelling of *Om* is *Aum*. The *Mandukya Upanishad* says that the "A" in *Aum* refers to the waking state of consciousness. The "U" refers to the state of dreams. The "M" refers to the state of deep sleep. Taken all together, *Aum* refers to the fourth or transcendental state of Consciousness.

Shivaya refers to universal Consciousness. This divine Consciousness is full of energy, bliss and wisdom. It contains all the objects in the universe and lives within them as their inner Self.

Namah means: "I honor" or "I orient myself towards".

Om Namah Shivaya means that we have turned our awareness away from outer objects and focused it on the divine space of the inner Self. We invoke and remember that Self.

Please accept **Om Namah Shivaya** as your mantra.

It has been a faithful friend to me all these years and it would not be an exaggeration to say that, even in the most agitated times of my life, it has always connected me with the inner Self.

You pronounce the mantra **OM na—MA shee—VY—ah.**

The mind is "many-pointed", like the spikes of a porcupine's coat. It jumps and moves in many directions. Your job is to focus the mind, to make it one-pointed and to eliminate obtrusive thoughts. When you repeat the mantra watch your reactions. There will be a never-ending flow of thoughts and feelings. Watch them and keep repeating the mantra. Meditation is the time when you can allow your thoughts to come and go. Sit as if you are watching a movie while lightly concentrating on repeating the mantra.

Repeat the mantra until your mind becomes quiet. Eventually, after a little practice, the thoughts and feelings will slowly subside and a deeper experience will begin to emerge. If you find that you are drifting into a sleep-like state, let that happen. This is the state of meditation.

Be kind to yourself; remember that it is the nature of the mind to think endlessly. It is fickle and unsteady. Every meditator encounters this. When the mind wanders away from the mantra, lovingly and calmly bring it back to the mantra.

It is possible to say the mantra with little attention. Then it is as though the mantra is going on in one part of the mind, while the mind is thinking other thoughts in another part. It is better to have a fuller concentration on the mantra, though even the case I have just described is helpful.

"MANTRA AND THE GOOD GUYS"

You might become impatient when you are not able to silence your mind totally. Actually, it is not necessary. As you repeat the mantra you will notice other thoughts arise spontaneously. Some of these you will recognize as distractions, working against the flow of your meditation. I call them "the bad guys". They should be dismissed.

Other thoughts are in harmony with your meditation. I call these subsidiary thoughts "the good guys". These might be: "Relax, focus on the mantra. Surrender. Stay open."

Think of them as the retinue, or entourage, that accompanies the mantra. They are not part of the problem; they are part of the solution. They are perfectly acceptable and can be encouraged. The rule of thumb is that those thoughts that are friendly to the mantra and its goal are fine, while thoughts that move in another direction should be eliminated.

Healthy mental discipline or "mind culture" includes encouraging good thoughts and discouraging bad thoughts. You can turn away from unwanted thoughts or let them go. This approach refuses to give them energy by giving them attention. You can forcefully banish them or throw them out. Use whatever metaphor suits you.

The next time you meditate, become aware of the effect of the good guys and the bad guys that accompany your mantra repetition. When you stay with the mantra and the good guys for a while, your mind will spontaneously glide into a deeper state similar to gliding into sleep.

HELPFUL HINTS

Mantra repetition is an art that you will learn by doing. Here are several techniques I have found useful.

Visualizing the mantra

One method to increase the level of concentration is to visualize the letters of the mantra in your mind's eye. Some people find this extremely effective.

Hearing the mantra

Try to listen to the sound of the mantra with the inner ear. Try to hear every word in every repetition in your inner space. The greater the degree of concentration you attain, the more effective your mantra repetition will be and the greater the rewards. When you focus intensely on the mantra you effectively drive out other thoughts. You will start to feel energy and bliss moving throughout your body. However, be patient. It takes a strong effort and a lot of energy to achieve this degree of concentration, and you might not be able to do it every time.

Mantra and the breath

Another technique is to combine the mantra with the breath. When the mind is agitated from stress and tension, the breath is also agitated. Mantra repetition relaxes the mind and helps return the breath to its natural rhythm.

Silently repeat Om Namah Shivaya once to yourself on the in-breath and once on the out-breath. Let the mantra follow your natural breathing rhythm. Once you get the knack of this technique, you will find it powerful.

Open to the mantra

Next time you sit down to practise mantra meditation, carefully notice in which chakra the mantra repeats itself. Most people find that the mantra tends to gravitate towards the navel, the heart, or the 3rd eye. After you have found where it shows up in you, *consciously try to open that chakra and let the mantra in.*

This simple practice is the most enlivening technique of mantra repetition I have ever found.

Mantra in each chakra

One last technique is to repeat the mantra in each chakra successively. For example, five minutes in the navel, five minutes in the heart and so on. This is a very effective way to balance the inner energy.

JAPA

The mantra is a powerful inner friend. When unwanted thoughts and negative emotions rush in, the mantra is a superb antidote. I once heard a story that cleverly illustrates the power of mantra.

A farmer had a big farm. He was always worried about planting, harvesting, and getting all his work done. One day a famous magician visited the area. When the farmer met him the magician said: "You have a lot of cares and concerns, I have just what you need."

"What is that?" said the farmer.

"It is a demon who can do the work of thousands of men in no time at all."

The farmer was skeptical: "That would be nice…"

"There is one catch, though," said the magician. "If he runs out of work he will eat you up."

"No chance of that," said the farmer. "I'll take him!"

The farmer set him to plowing the fields the next morning. He watched in amazement as the demon moved up and down the field at lightning speed. The farmer started to worry. Soon the demon had done the planting, painted the barn and renovated the house.

The farmer began to feel scared. Fortunately, he sometimes visited a wise clairvoyant for past-life therapy. In desperation he visited her. She said: "I can solve your problem. Here is what to do: when the demon finishes his work tell him that his next job is to erect a tall pole in the barnyard. When he finishes that, tell him that his next job is to go up and down the pole, until you call him for his next job."

"Aha!" said the farmer. And they lived happily ever after.

Of course, this story is really an analogy. Have you worked out who is the demon and what is the pole? Who is the farmer? Of course, you are the farmer, and the demon is your mind. The demon pole is the mantra.

Like the demon, the mind is good when it is working. We do all of our work by means of the mind. The human mind is such a powerful instrument; look at what it has created. But, sadly, when the mind has nothing valuable to do, like the demon, it eats us up. The mind is always hungry. When it is not gainfully employed it will turn against us and think useless and painful thoughts. The thing to do then is to send it up and down the pole of the mantra. The mind will be kept out of trouble.

Japa is the practice of silent mantra repetition either during meditation or outside of meditation. The mantra is a wonderful means of cultivating and strengthening the mind. There are many times in a day when your mind may tend to go towards negativity or worry. It is at such times that japa can be practised.

Your external life and your meditation feed each other. It should be obvious that if your life is set up in such a way that you are constantly full of fear or hysteria it will be rather difficult for you to calm the mind in meditation. When you meditate effectively things in the outer world tend to go much more smoothly. Conversely, when your outer life is calm and harmonious, your meditation will be much better.

Yogic texts recommend a lifestyle that maximizes peace of mind. You can use this insight to evaluate actions in your external life. Ask yourself: "Will this create greater peace or greater stress?" Remember that meditation wants you to keep moving towards peace.

USING THE OM NAMAH SHIVAYA JAPA ON CD

The *Om Namah Shivaya Japa* track (4) on your CD makes mantra repetition effortless and it will help you establish your practice. It will teach you the proper pronunciation and help you remember it. Some of my students like it so much that they use it every day.

Sit down; turn on your CD player and listen to the fourth track. Press the repeat button if you wish. You may find that you enter a deep state of meditation. Let yourself enter that space.

Here is an important reminder: volume makes a considerable difference. Some meditators like to listen to the mantra at a barely audible level, others like to play it louder.

I recommend that you experiment with mantra repetition for at least a week. Meditate with the mantra track (22 minutes) at least once a day. If you like, meditate with the Self-inquiry track first.

KEY IDEAS OF CHAPTER SEVEN:
MANTRA-THE POWER OF THE WORD

- The most pervasive technique for meditation is mantra.
- Mantra prepares the mind for meditation.
- The mantra keeps a hungry mind out of trouble.
- The mantra will calm a restless mind.
- The mantra is an access to the higher self.
- Om Namah Shivaya has been handed down from powerful masters for thousands of years.
- Om Namah Shivaya is full of spiritual energy and can awaken one who practises it.
- Eliminate thoughts that work against your mantra repetition and meditation, but encourage thoughts that support them.
- Japa is the practice of mantra repetition outside of meditation.

Chapter eight:
I CAN ALWAYS HAVE THE MEDITATION I AM HAVING

prayatnaha sadhakaha

Right effort is the means.

Shiva Sutras II.2

THE MIND CONTINUALLY and normally fluctuates between three conditions. The best condition is one of harmony when the mind is clear and insightful. In the middle condition the mind is active and emotional. In the worst condition the mind is dull and stupid. Thus, it is natural for the mind to be in different conditions when we meditate. This will certainly affect our meditation, but discipline tells us it is important to meditate no matter what the condition of the mind. When you feel more energy and more mental strength let your concentration be deeper. The main thing here is not to beat yourself up if your meditation seems less focused than you would want it to be.

Early in my practice I achieved a *samadhi* state effortlessly on a few occasions. A samadhi state is a deep absorption into the Self. In this state there is a feeling of great peace and great oneness and meditation becomes effortless and natural. I craved to attain that state every time I sat down. To my chagrin I discovered that it rarely came. Indeed, often my mind droned on in a mundane and boring way. I became desperate to find that state again.

One day in the midst of this torment, understanding dawned on me like a great light: *I cannot always have the meditation that I want but I can always have the meditation I am having!*

What relief accompanied this insight! I could relax and accept whatever was happening. The mind is a great trickster, ever ready to tempt you into comparing *what is* with what was or what might be. Not content with peace, the negative mind seems to crave dissatisfaction.

A surrendered attitude nurtures meditation because it is more in harmony with the mood of meditation: an accepting frame of mind rather than a striving, craving one.

When we first start to meditate the mind is more like a glass of Coca Cola than a quiet lake. When a Coke is poured, it becomes bubbly. After a while it quietens down and becomes flat. It is good for a coke to be full of bubbles, but the mind needs to be quieter. As we meditate we allow the bubbles of the mind to settle. However, sometimes it feels as though this will never happen. Imagine if you were to meditate until all anger, jealousy and fear were dissolved. What would it be like to endure everything that arises in the mind until you break through to a state of peace?

One of the most difficult obstacles to overcome is impatience, the impulse or voice that tells you to jump up and do something else. Another challenge is boredom. Our culture is chronically afraid of boredom. A little while ago someone sent me a Los Angeles magazine. What struck me was the sheer number of movies, shows, concerts, cabarets and other events that were listed. I lived there for a long time and know the cultural assault that is inherent in Los Angeles, but still I was surprised. It is certainly an extreme example, but the same phenomenon is true everywhere else as well.

We are the most entertained people of all time. We are desperate for diversions to take us away from ourselves. Meditation is an affront to the fear of boredom: sitting, turning within and thinking of nothing! It is a radical approach. However, intuition tells us that it is precisely the cultural medicine we need. Instead of endlessly running from our demons, we turn and face them.

The most common obstacle that new meditators report to me is the idea "I cannot meditate". Allied to this idea are the following:

- I cannot quieten my mind.
- My mind is scattered.
- My mind is restless.
- This state of mind is not meditation.
- When will meditation (or samadhi) happen?
- I will never be able to meditate properly.

These thoughts are all based on dissatisfaction. The thinking process, which may be unconscious, goes something like this. *This* state is not meditation (or at least not good meditation). I can *imagine* another state, which I cannot attain, that would be better.

In fact, these thoughts—along with the underlying feeling of anger and agitation at "Self"—are great enemies to meditation.

> **Contemplation 3: Having the meditation you are having.**
>
> Here are some thoughts I have used to conquer the disease of "meditation dissatisfaction". Use them as a contemplation to work with your mind. Begin by closing your eyes and turning within. Notice the condition of your inner world.
>
> Say to yourself:
>
> 1. This is the meditation I am having.
> 2. This is the perfect meditation.
> 3. This awareness is Shiva.
> 4. This is Consciousness.
> 5. This too is a state of meditation.
> 6. Meditation is whatever arises in my own Consciousness.

Just as you cannot force sleep, you cannot force meditation. Meditation, like sleep, will descend on you in its own time. The best way to prepare for it is by being calm, relaxed and open. Put one or more of these thoughts into your meditator's arsenal. They will save you a lot of needless pain and deepen your meditation.

In line with "having the meditation you are having" is another approach I call "being with the emotion you are having". Ordinarily people handle negative emotions either by (1) denial or (2) trying to shift them. In the former we suppress or we are not conscious of the negative emotion that nonetheless affects our dealings with others. People often, for example, hold a degree of anger without knowing it—though others often do.

In the other approach a meditator will try to move from negative states to positive states. Later in this book I will describe many ways of doing this. However, the best efforts sometimes fail and the emotion proves difficult to shift. It is then that you can try "being with the emotion you are having". In this approach you simply sit with the emotion, not trying to get away from it, not denying it. You can study it deeply and experience it fully. If nothing else happens you at least have a greater understanding and awareness of the emotion. But it is very likely that as you go deeper into the emotion and arrive at its centre you will experience a shift and discover the peace that exists at its core. In any event, even though you may not be able to change something, you always have the option of being with what is.

KEY IDEAS OF CHAPTER EIGHT:
I CAN ALWAYS HAVE THE MEDITATION I AM HAVING

- The mind fluctuates between three conditions: harmonious, active or lethargic.
- A samadhi state is deep absorption in the Self.
- I cannot always have the meditation I want, but I can always have the one I am having.
- A common obstacle is the thought: "I cannot meditate".
- You cannot force meditation.
- When you can't shift a negative emotion you always have the option of being with it, studying it and experiencing it fully.

Chapter nine:
EIGHT STEPS TO MEDITATION

yoganganushthanad ashuddhi-kshaye
jnana-diptir a viveka-khyateh

From the practice of the steps of yoga comes increased
purity and illumination, leading to the awareness of the Self.

Yoga Sutras of Patanjali II.28

AROUND THE 2nd CENTURY the sage Patanjali sketched an eight-fold path called *Ashtanga* (eight-limbed) *Yoga*. These steps or stages culminate in deep meditation. They are—*yama, niyama, asana, pranayama, pratyahara, dharana, dhyana* and *samadhi*.

STAGE 1 AND 2: YAMA AND NIYAMA - INTELLIGENT LIVING

Yama and niyama are concerned with how to live life. Guides for intelligent living, which include yogic disciplines, they involve ethical consideration like truth telling and non-violence and personal practices like cleanliness.

If you rob banks and murder people on a daily basis and then sit down to meditate at night, it would not be a surprise if your mind were agitated. On the other hand, if you spend your day in acts of peace and kindness, you are likely to have a stable mind. One of the charming things about Patanjali is that he is no moralist: he is entirely practical. These ethical and personal values and behaviors are designed fundamentally to keep your mind in a peaceful condition. They simply work better and make good sense.

STAGE 3: ASANA - LEARNING TO SIT FOR MEDITATION

Patanjali's third limb is asana. In the West we are increasingly familiar with *hatha yoga*, the collection of stretches and postures taught everywhere for flexibility and good health. Patanjali's emphasis is specific. For him, the main purpose of asana is to train the body to sit securely and comfortably for meditation. As a culture we are not used to sitting cross-legged on the floor. But, as one sage pointed out, the real "posture" is the posture of the mind. The mind should be made to rest in the Self, or in inner calm. To do this, it is quite all right to sit in a comfortable chair. We need not resemble a statue to be good meditators. Our posture should be relaxed and our back comfortably straight. However, we should try to remain alert.

STAGE 4: PRANAYAMA - BREATHING EXERCISES

Pranayama is Patanjali's fourth stage. This is the science of breath control and another traditional meditation technique. Centuries ago someone noticed that the breathing was directly related to the mind. Agitated breathing accompanies agitated mental states. Calm breathing accompanies calm mental states. That sage must have wondered: "Since the mind is so difficult to control directly, can it be controlled indirectly by controlling the breath?" And so it has proved: breath control is a popular method of quietening the mind. There are dozens of different forms of breathing exercises. I give a description of a very effective breath meditation - the *hamsa* meditation - in Part 1, Chapter 18.

STAGE 5: PRATYAHARA - FOCUS ON THE INNER

Patanjali's first four steps are preparation for meditation. The fifth step, pratyahara, is the transitional step when we move from the outer world to the inner world. In pratyahara we detach our senses and our attention from the outside and turn within, just as we do when we go to sleep at night.

STAGE 6: DHARANA - CONCENTRATION

The last three limbs deal with meditation directly. The normal mental condition is scattered. Thoughts follow each other almost randomly. In dharana the mind becomes concentrated. Patanjali, drawing his metaphor from the quills of a porcupine, calls this mental condition "many pointed". As the mind becomes focused in meditation, it moves towards *ekagrata,* one-pointedness. Here the meditator can keep his focus on whatever he is contemplating without serious breaks or distractions.

STAGE 7: DHYANA

As concentration continues to deepen it moves to Patanjali's seventh stage, dhyana, or "meditation". Now focus is perfect. The mind holds the object of contemplation without wandering. Patanjali says that there is an unbroken flow of thought similar to the unbroken way that oil is poured from one vessel to another. Certainly, powerful focus like this is valuable in our outer life, as well as in meditation.

STAGE 8: SAMADHI

The final step in Patanjali's *Ashtanga yoga* is called samadhi, the deepest state of meditation. This word might be familiar to you from "samadhi tanks", which were in vogue in the '70s. These were sensory-deprivation tanks, designed for deep relaxation and inner exploration. The subject floated in water, in darkness; the goal was to take away outer world consciousness. Patanjali's samadhi is a trance-like state of perfect absorption. This is deeper than the previous stage. In dhyana you are still aware that you are meditating, and are still making effort to stay with the practice. In samadhi there is no effort at all. You are not aware of yourself as a separate person; you are totally and effortlessly merged with the object of meditation. Here we can speak of grace: in samadhi it is as if a higher power has taken us up and wrapped the mind in absorption. If this seems too religious, remind yourself of sleep. There also we get the "grace" of a higher power (the sandman?) and get lifted beyond ourselves.

SAMYAMA

The last three parts of Patanjali's yoga—concentration, meditation, and deep absorption (dharana, dhyana and samadhi)—represent the final steps of drawing the mind inward towards stillness. Patanjali gives the name *samyama* to the three taken together. He tells us that samyama is developed slowly, in steps, and once it is mastered, the meditator experiences the "light of higher Consciousness".

Patanjali's discussion of samyama develops into a discussion of psychic powers (*siddhis*). These powers of mind are achieved by performing samyama, intense focus, on specific objects. Here are a few typical examples of siddhis from the *Yoga Sutras of Patanjali*:

1. By direct perception of the image occupying the mind, knowledge of the mind of others (III.19.)
2. By performing samyama on friendliness, (or other qualities) comes the development of that quality. (III.24.)
3. By performing samyama on the strengths of animals, the strength of an elephant. (III.25.)
4. Knowledge of everything by intuition. (III.34)
5. By performing samyama on the heart, awareness of the nature of the mind. (III.35)

The essence of what Patanjali tells us in his discussion of samyama is that by focusing our mind on any object, we gradually acquire the knowledge and power of that object. The mind holds the object in awareness, and little by little, eliminates extraneous thoughts. The mind of the meditator moves closer and closer to the object, until it merges with the object. In that oneness the object yields its mystery. Like other yogis before and after him, Patanjali warns against getting caught up in powers of mind. They are a spiritual trap and increase, rather than diminish, the ego. The best object of meditation is, paradoxically, the Self. It is paradoxical because the Self can never be an object. Still, when the Self is lightly held by the mind, the highest Consciousness is attained.

Taking Patanjali's advice let us now try samyama. Using number 2 from the above list, you can experiment as follows:

Contemplation 4: Samyama
Part 1: Samyama on a desirable human quality

- Focus on a quality you would like to acquire or increase. Some possibilities are peace, contentment, strength, detachment, insight or energy.
- Hold the word and idea of the quality in your mind. Do not strain. Merely hold it. Contact it.
- Repeat the word, for example peace, love or wisdom, like you would a mantra. However, do not think about it.
- Throw away the thoughts that interfere with the image or quality of the attribute.
- Open to it. Experience the essence of it. Let the knowledge and feeling of it come to you.

Part 2: Samyama on the qualities of an object

Number 3 from the above list, Yoga Sutra III.25, says to use the mind to focus on an animal or object embodying the quality you seek. Some possibilities: strength, ease or unselfconsciousness.

- Choose an object or an animal that you love, or resonate with, or one that embodies the qualities you desire.
- Hold the image in your mind.
- Imagine yourself drawing the qualities of the object to you.
- Push away extraneous thoughts that interfere.
- Open to the experience and feeling of the object.

Part 3: Samyama on the image of a Great Being

A variation of the previous contemplation is to focus on a great soul, or a form of God, with the idea of drawing his/her desirable qualities to you. This was a favorite meditation of mine for many years. I would focus on my teacher and try to absorb his strength of mind and spiritual state.

- Hold the image of the Great Being or deity in your mind, and inwardly open to him/her.
- Imagine that his/her power and wisdom is flowing into you through your heart, third eye, or the top of the head.

The foregoing contemplations can be done for any length of time. Your intuition will tell you. One good method is to use one of them for five minutes or so at the beginning of your meditation to energize yourself.

KEY IDEAS OF CHAPTER NINE:
EIGHT STEPS TO MEDITATION

- Patanjali sketched an eight-fold path called Ashtanga Yoga.
- The goal of Patanjali's yoga is for the mind to rest in the inner Self.
- Patanjali's yoga moves from the outer world to the inner world.
- Calm breathing accompanies a calm mind.
- By turning the attention inside, focus becomes perfect.
- The deepest state of meditation is called samadhi.
- By samadhi one experiences "the light of higher Consciousness".
- By focusing the mind on an object (samyama), we gradually acquire the power and knowledge of that object.

Chapter ten:

BREAK THROUGH - INTENSIFYING YOUR PRACTICE

tatra shitau yatno'bhyasah

*The effort for becoming firmly
established in the experience of the Self is abhyasa.*

Yoga Sutras of Patanjali I.13

CLASSICALLY THERE ARE two schools of thought regarding the spiritual journey. *Yoga*, the school of intense practice, teaches that the path is long and arduous and only after many years of mantra repetition and meditation can the goal of Self-realization be achieved. Yoga embodies a strong work ethic, solid virtues, and small, incremental steps.

The other school of thought, *jnana* or wisdom, argues that since the Self is the eternal witness or background of all of our experience and since nothing that is permanent can be newly discovered, the Self is always present and does not have to be attained. No amount of practice can bring about Self-realization. It can be discovered, here and now. *Jnanis*, practitioners of the wisdom path, jet to the top and try to stay there.

The two views create a kind of white-collar / blue-collar debate in the inner world. There is merit in both views. It is important to have the understanding that under all conditions, in all circumstances, and at the core of all emotions, even negative ones, *the Self is always present*. At least in principle, it can always be contacted. On the other hand, it is realistic to acknowledge that a long process of spiritual work is necessary for all but the rare, extraordinary, spiritual genius. Even the Buddha and Jesus had difficult and arduous spiritual journeys. Effort is necessary.

Legend has it that after pursuing many paths and forms of asceticism Siddhartha Gautama sat down under a bodhi tree to meditate his way to the attainment of the Absolute. His years of effort and frustration had been distilled into a unique moment of resolution:

*Though my skin, my nerves and my bones
should waste away and my life-blood run dry,
I will not leave this seat until I have attained supreme enlightenment.*

This moment has come to be called "Buddha's Resolve" in the iconic renderings of his life. I have always found it impressive and stirring. Of course no one was there with a video recorder and later myths have elaborated the story of the Buddha. But, there is no mistaking the power of his determination and strength of purpose whether this is a literal or symbolic account.

Gautama then entered a profound meditation lasting perhaps a single night, perhaps several days. He penetrated to the core of every phenomenon, every obstacle his mind threw up. He sat down as a spiritual seeker and when he finally arose he was the Buddha, the Enlightened One. Hard work and determination pay off in the inner journey just as they do in the outer one.

Patanjali, the dean of all yogis, emphasizes the need for practice or *abhyasa*. The effort to pacify the mind must be "continued for a long time, without interruption and with devotion". Further he enumerates a list of obstacles that threaten our practice: disease, languor, doubt, carelessness, laziness, and desire for sense pleasures, delusion and instability. These either undermine our resolve or tempt the mind into less productive by-paths. Our determination to reach the truth of the Self clashes with our ignorance and bad habits and our weaknesses and produces a battle.

Shaivism says that spiritual work is sometimes gradual and serene. But at other times it calls for stronger means. One text describes *hatha paka*, a "violent digestion" in which we swallow up and destroy ignorance through a "dogged persistence".

SPIRITUAL MATERIALISM

Followers of the path of wisdom sometimes deprecate the type of spirituality that acknowledges effort and slow acquisition of spiritual power. They call it "spiritual materialism". But sometimes a naïve immersion in spiritual materialism is bracing. One such naïve (but strong) attitude is to take the notion that every mantra we repeat puts a *devi* dollar, a divine dollar, in our spiritual bank account. In India this idea is accepted without apology.

There is a practice called *purascharana*, which involves the repetition of a mantra for a fixed number of times over many days. For example, a seeker might make a decision to repeat the mantra Om Namah Shivaya 100,000 times. He may do sessions for six hours a day over many days.

These intense sessions of mantra are, in fact, quite beneficial. I once did a purascharana of one million repetitions over nine months. Quaintly, Swami Shivananda of Rishikesh, perhaps the godfather of spiritual materialism, gives a table, which says, in part:

Mantra	Speed per minute	Number of Mantras per hour	Time for one Purascharana (six hours daily, or 100,000 repetitions)
Om			
	Low: 140	Low: 8,400	Low: 11 hrs. 54 mins.
	Med: 250	Med: 15,000	Med: 6 hrs. 40mins.
	High: 400	High: 24,000	High: 4 hrs. 10 mins.
Om Namah Shivaya			
	Low: 80	Low: 4,800	Low: 17 days 2hrs. 10mins.
	Med: 120	Med: 7,200	Med: 11 days 3hrs. 30mins.
	High: 140	High: 9,000	High: 9 days 1.35 mins.

I give these numbers for your amusement but I heartily endorse periods of intense mantra practice.

When you go through a particularly difficult period of depression or anxiety, it is hard to make rational decisions. The mind dwells on negativity. At such times, sit down and tough it out with intense mantra repetition. I promise you, you will be uplifted soon enough.

As befits such a dyed-in-the-wool spiritual materialist as Swami Shivananda, the rates of mantra repetition in his chart are high, presumably with the understanding that the faster you repeat a mantra the more "divine dollars" you acquire in a shorter time. Donald Trump would certainly understand this. However, it is not good to let your spiritual greed get out of control. You should find a speed of repetition that is truly nurturing. When I am not combining the mantra with my breathing rhythm, I find that my normal rate of Om Namah Shivaya is about fifty repetitions per minute. That would not get me into Swami Shivananda's chart. It is however, the pace I prefer.

If spiritual materialism warms your heart you could consider acquiring a *mala* or mantra rosary. These beads are generally made of wood or the seeds of *rudraksha* or *tulsi* trees. These days they are also made of crystal and other precious and semi-precious stones. The number varies but generally there are 108 beads. It is worn around the neck when not used for mantra repetition. A mantra practitioner using a mala will count one bead for each mantra repeated so he will know how many mantras he has repeated. Enthusiastic contemporary meditators have been known to acquire a tally counter from their local stationers and click it once for every mantra, thereby keeping an accurate score. A true spiritual materialist enjoys keeping these statistics.

Another technique yogis love is the *breakthrough*. When the mind gets stuck in grooves causing suffering, it is possible to meditate until understanding dawns. This is what the Buddha did when he sat down under the bodhi tree and resolved not to move until he became enlightened. Resolution and endurance are the keys here.

Contemplation 5: Breaking through - Buddha's Resolve

1. Close your eyes and turn within.
2. Begin with a statement like: "I resolve not to move until understanding dawns. I let everything go. Let me understand. Let me be free of this."
3. Make your resolution.
4. Watch the images, thoughts and feelings come without getting trapped in what they mean.
5. Contemplate until you feel an upward shift, a lightening.

KEY IDEAS OF CHAPTER TEN:
BREAK THROUGH - INTENSIFYING YOUR PRACTICE

- There are two approaches to attaining Self-realization: by slow and arduous practice or by remembering that the Self is always present.
- Hard work and determination pay off in the inner journey.
- According to Patanjali, practice or *abhyasa* is concentrated effort over time with the goal to pacify the mind.
- Our determination to reach the Self clashes with our ignorance and bad habits.
- Followers of the path of wisdom sometimes deprecatingly call intense effort "spiritual materialism".
- Repeating the mantra earns spiritual dollars.
- Repetition of the mantra for a fixed number of times is beneficial.
- A mala can be used to count the mantra repetitions.
- You can fight negativity with mantra.
- Yogis love to break through into understanding.

Chapter eleven:

MIND CULTURE AND SELF-EMPOWERMENT

*The mind is one. Tendencies are of two kinds, auspicious and
inauspicious. When the mind is under the sway of auspicious
tendencies it is said to be a good mind. When it is under the sway of
inauspicious tendencies, it is said to be a bad mind.*

Ramana Maharshi

**Chanchalatvam manodharmo
vahner dharmo yatho shnata**

*Just as heat is the nature of fire,
so fickleness is the nature of the mind.*

Vyasdev

ONCE TWO ZEN monks were walking down the road. It was a breezy day.
One of them said to the other: "Look, the flag is flapping in the breeze."

The second monk replied: "No, that is foolish. The breeze is flapping the
flag!"

And so they spent an exciting quarter hour: "The flag is flapping!"

"The breeze is flapping!"

"The flag is flapping."

"The breeze is flapping the flag."

The debate became more and more heated, and they were about to affirm
their insights with fist and knee when the Zen master appeared on the road.
They ran to him. "Roshi, please settle our dispute. I say the flag is flapping in
the breeze, he says the breeze is flapping the flag. Which one of us is right?"

The master looked at them with a penetrating eye. "You are both wrong,"
he said. "Your *minds* are flapping!"

Most of the time our minds are flapping. Frank Zappa, the '60s music icon,
once asked the question in a song, "What is the ugliest part of your body?"

He answered humorously but accurately: "Some say your nose, some say
your toes, I think it's your mind."

Our minds are not always ugly or negative, but when the mind does go
south nothing is worse. The mind is our closest environment. Just as there is
an outer weather, there is an inner weather. The climate within our head may

be sunny and warm, or it may be damp and soggy, overheated or cold and forbidding. We may feel stress or be calm and peaceful. The sage Shivananda said:

> A sublime thought elevates the mind and expands the heart. A base thought agitates the mind and renders the feelings morbid and dark. Every thought and emotion vibrates in every cell of the body. Selfish, mean, worried thoughts create vibrations of disease, despair and death. Happy, noble thoughts create vibrations of life, joy and renewal.

Contemplation 6: Inner Weather

1. Sit down, close your eyes and turn within.
2. Let your awareness become familiar with your inner world.
3. Ask yourself the following questions:
4. Is my mind quiet or agitated?
5. Is my mood cloudy or sunny?
6. What is my inner weather?
7. Take note of the condition of your inner world. Do this for 3 minutes.

As I have already said, our inner world is composed of thought and feeling. Our inner weather is how it *feels* inside and this is closely allied to what we are thinking.

Before I practised yoga I worked hard with my mind. In high school I learned long vocabulary lists so that I could do well on my university entrance exams. I became an academic and I worked hard at French, Spanish and Latin. And, for a solid year before my Ph.D. exams, I studied every aspect of English and American literary history. During my tournament chess days I memorized openings avidly. Yet none of these activities are what I would call "mind culture."

In proper mind culture you do not fill the mind with new information. Instead, you investigate the mind, observe the mind and work *with* the mind to make it stronger. A weak mind dwells on anger, despair and fear. It harbors resentment and sees slights where none exist. It cannot uplift itself. A strong mind is a positive mind, one that swiftly handles negativity.

UNDERSTANDINGS BASIC TO MIND CULTURE

- Monitoring self-talk is self-observation.

Socrates said, "Know thyself." This is still the first principle of meditation and the inner life. It is important to observe what kind of thoughts and feelings arise both in meditation and in different life situations. As you get to know yourself in this new and more intimate way, you will gain more power in the inner world. Later you will be able to transform your states of fear and anxiety into peace and happiness. Self-observation and self-knowledge are an indispensable preliminary step to gaining that power.

THOUGHT AND FEELING ARE INEXTRICABLY CONNECTED

Often self-talk is subconscious—you are not aware of it. You can become aware of it by noticing feeling and understanding that a parallel self-talk must be present. If you search for it you are bound to find it. This is important because it is easier to work with thought than with feeling. If I ask you to change your mood you would have a hard time, but if I ask you to change your thoughts you could do that somewhat easily.

Once a spiritual seeker asked his teacher to sum up his teaching so that he could carry it away with him in a convenient form. The teacher pondered for a moment and then said, "My teaching is this: cease to be a problem to yourself!"

Thought and feeling are locked in an eternal dance; they are two sides of the same coin. If we feel depressed or unhappy it means that our thinking, our *self-talk*, must be negative. Conversely, when we are happy it means that our underlying self-talk is positive.

- Negative self-talk gives rise to negative moods and positive self-talk gives rise to happy moods.

Here indeed is meditation and spirituality in a nutshell. By bad habits of mind we go off the rails. It is important to be vigilant and become aware of the patterns of our thought process.

- Negative feeling indicates the presence of negative thoughts even when we are not aware of them.

Often we will be in a bad mood and not know why. Since thought and feeling are inextricably linked, you can be certain that when you feel bad, or if you are in a bad mood, you are in the grip of negative self-talk.

- There is always a reason for your bad moods.

Bad moods arise in time. They are always stimulated by some event, outer or inner, a reaction or a memory.

- Meditation is the process of making the unconscious conscious.

The unconscious becomes conscious by paying attention to it. If a room is dark, you turn on the lights. Immediately everything is revealed. There is no mystery to it. In the same way, awareness is a great light. When you turn the light of awareness toward the inner world, it illumines all of the objects of the inner world.

Freud's great discovery of the "unconscious" in the 19th Century was not new to the masters of meditation. They knew that we keep certain things from ourselves simply because it is too disturbing to look at them, or we haven't bothered to look at them. There is nothing to fear in the inner world. There is no monster lurking in the depths. Rather, there is love, peace and joy at the deepest core. The more we look, the more empowered we become, and the more understanding we have of our motives, our thoughts and our feelings.

As you meditate, the unconscious reveals itself; the light of awareness illumines your dark room.

- Thought, like the breath, but unlike the heart beat, is both voluntary and involuntary.

The involuntary nervous system is beyond conscious control. It is controlled by the intelligence of the body, not by personal will. You can decide to lift your arm, but digestion performs its function automatically. The heartbeat is independent of your volition. There are yogis in India who can slow the heart down to an amazing degree. Even ordinary people can change their heart rate to some extent if they work at it. Nonetheless, the heartbeat is clearly different from the breathing rhythm, which we can control to a much larger degree. You can slow your breath, you can speed it up, and you can hold it. But notice that although you have a large degree of control over your breath, you do not come near to 100 percent control. You cannot hold your breath forever, and breathing goes on involuntarily when you do not pay attention to it, as in sleep.

The mind is more like the breath than the heart. It produces thoughts involuntarily and voluntarily. That is, you can use the mind consciously to explore a train of thought. You can introduce thoughts for contemplation. But when you try to still the mind in meditation you discover (if you had not noticed already) that it produces thoughts all on its own. In fact the mind constantly produces thoughts: some of them are memories and fantasies, some of them give a negative or positive commentary on our lives as we live them. This background hum always goes on. It could be called a waking dream since its conscious or unconscious recitation determines the way we view and experience our lives.

Since we know that the mind can be negative or positive, and that this profoundly affects us, it makes a lot of sense to make some effort to achieve a positive mind.

KEY IDEAS OF CHAPTER ELEVEN:
MIND CULTURE AND SELF-EMPOWERMENT

- The mind is our closest environment.
- Mind culture is to work with the mind.
- Monitoring self-talk is self-observation
- Thought and feeling are inextricably linked.
- There is always a reason for bad moods.
- Meditation makes the unconscious conscious.
- Thought is both voluntary and involuntary.

Chapter twelve:
THE PRESENT MOMENT

The past is history, the future is a mystery,
only the present is real.

Anonymous

When you draw in a deep breath,
be aware that you are drawing in a deep breath.
When you draw in a shallow breath,
be aware that you are drawing in a shallow breath.
When you draw in a medium-sized breath,
be aware that you are drawing in a medium-sized breath.
This is the way to enlightenment.

Gautama Buddha

THE ZEN MASTER Hui Hai was asked by one of his students: "Do you make efforts in the practice of the Way, master?"

"Yes," the master replied.

"How so?" asked the disciple.

"When hungry," said the master, "I eat; when tired, I sleep.

"But does not everyone make those same efforts, master?"

"When they eat their minds are elsewhere. When they go to sleep their minds are elsewhere. When I eat I just eat and when I sleep I just sleep."

To be present means that our minds are here with our bodies. While the body can never be anything but present, the mind loves to wander in memory or fantasy. A little thought will convince you that the past and the present only exist in the mind. What time is it now? It is the present. No matter when I ask you that question your answer will always be "the present". The point of power is the present moment; the point of meditation is *the present moment.*

That Zen story reminds me of another Zen-like anecdote told about one of my college professors. In those days Columbia was an all-men's undergraduate school, and the occasional female who crossed the road from Barnard was seen as an intruder in our male paradise.

During one lecture a woman sat in the front row knitting while the professor, a distinguished scholar, discussed the concept of the "sublime" in 19th Century culture. Finally, he could stand it no longer and said: "Miss, do you know that knitting is a form of masturbation?"

"Professor," she coolly replied, "when I knit I knit, and when I masturbate, I masturbate!"

PLANNING VERSUS WORRYING

Even though we are always here and now, our mind is likely to be "there and then". When the mind is relishing memories, sadness or anger, energy gets stuck in the past. Or, it can be obsessed about the future, worrying about outcomes. This does not always involve negative emotions; some people who daydream carry positive fantasies about the future or pleasant memories of the past. Nonetheless, it is a still a way of not being present. Meditation is the royal road to becoming present.

Planning and worrying are entirely different activities. Planning is calm and can be completed. Worrying is endless.

- Worry is future-oriented mental activity fuelled by fear.

When you worry, you may have the illusion that you are planning. However, what you are probably saying to yourself is more like, "I am scared that...or, I am apprehensive that...or, I am frightened that...."

There is energy and pleasure when the mind is present. When you watch a movie that you are enjoying, you are entirely focused. If the movie is boring, your mind wanders and you notice your physical discomfort. Thoughts from your life intrude. When I played baseball as a boy and the game was close and interesting, my mind was focused on the game. I loved it. In my years in India and Australia I learned about the game of cricket. In cricket the fielding side can be in the field for hours, if not days. It becomes more difficult to focus as each ball is bowled.

Athletes often talk about problems in concentration as central to their success or failure. Concentration is natural at critical moments, but in those moments tension can have a negative effect. Sports psychologists have found that the best mind-set for an athlete is to focus on the task at hand and not on the outcome. Sometimes athletes call this "being in the zone", it is a spontaneous experience of clarity, joy and energy that sometimes happens. It is a Zen moment, and the athlete will perform at his or her highest level.

Seeking results is a future-oriented activity. Being present is meditation in action. This involves living your life without worrying about the results; the praise or blame that may, or may not come. You do what you have to do, as perfectly as you can, in the moment. In this sense, being present is the most effective way to do and act.

While the mind goes to the past and future, the body and the senses - and the emotions - can only be present. Some meditation practices make use of this fact to cultivate present-ness. Part I of the following contemplation uses sound, one of the best methods. The year before I left for India, 1969, I used the sound contemplation a lot. I would try to pay attention to all the sounds around me. I was struck by how much I usually did not hear because my mind was elsewhere engaged. One day after teaching I was crossing to my car in the university parking lot when I heard a can being blown across the asphalt. I really *heard* that tin can - it penetrated my awareness with a mysterious vividness. It is hard to convey but I heard that tin can so completely that it seemed to invoke divinity.

Contemplation 7: Being present

Part I Hearing the sounds

1. Take a few moments to contemplate the present moment.
2. Close your eyes and listen to the sounds around you.
3. Hear them as though they were a piece of music.
4. Listen in to the totality of all the sounds without identifying them or giving them meaning.
5. Hear them as pure sound.

You will notice many sounds that you were not aware of when you were not doing the exercise.

Part II

6. Be present to the bodily sensations of sitting.
7. Be present to the temperature of the room.
8. Be present to your breath going in and out.
9. Be present to thoughts playing in your mind.
10. Be present to your mood or feelings in this moment.

You might notice how rich the experience of the present is. I experience an unmistakable current of energy when I focus on the present. The past and the future which are mental constructs have relatively little energy, while the present which is rooted in actual experience is vibrant and alive. But it does take some effort to be and stay present. What does it feel like for you to be present?

Being present is closely allied to interest. When your mind is present you get a lot more from life. If you are interested in something you will stay present to it. If you are bored your mind will wander. In the ecstasy of new romance your mind is focused on your beloved 24 hours a day. I hope it is not too cynical to say that when new romance gives way to "going steady" and later to marriage, the mind is less focused on the beloved. Life becomes more normal.

Interest is connected with passion, with emotion, with pleasure. All of these attributes are within you! They are qualities of your inner Self. Why then do we often have trouble controlling our minds and staying present during meditation? The answer can only be that we are at war with ourselves: we have not found the place of peace, energy and joy that certainly exists within.

"Interest" is derived from *inter-esse*, "to be within it". We become one with something when the object inspires us and engages us. Skilful meditation makes use of our natural interest to focus the mind and access the inner Self.

KEY IDEAS OF CHAPTER TWELVE:
THE PRESENT MOMENT

- The point of power is always the present moment.
- Worry is future oriented mental activity fuelled by fear.
- There is energy and pleasure when the mind is present.
- Being present is always allied to interest.
- Good meditation is the ability to access the inner Self.

Chapter thirteen:
THE CYCLE OF THE MIND

atma chittam

*As individuals we are our minds. The mind is nothing
but a limited form of pure Consciousness.*

Shiva Sutras III.1

*Sow a thought, reap an action;
Sow an action, reap a habit;
Sow a habit, reap a character;
Sow a character, reap a destiny.*

Anonymous

THE MIND IS a fertile thought-producing factory. There is an endless creation of thoughts. Some thoughts pass lightly through our minds while others have more weight. Weight is based on two factors: feeling and interest.

Let us imagine that it is getting near dinnertime. The mind is thinking, "What will I have? Duck a l'orange? Veggie stew or pizza?" An inner signal is transmitted. "Pizza it is!" The *thought* of pizza has become the *desire* for pizza (see diagram below). When thought has intention it becomes a desire. Said another way; a desire is a thought that has acquired a feeling power through repetition.

When the desire for pizza becomes strong enough we spring into *action*. We jump into the car and go down to the pizza place. Sometimes the desire has to build to such an extent that it overrides other contrary thoughts like, "Pizza is fattening," "Pizza has too much cheese," and the like. Now, we are at the restaurant, surveying the menu. "Hmmm....pizza with egg, with pineapple, with sausage, with pepperoni...." We make our choice and after a wait, perhaps filled with pizza fantasy, the pizza is finally served. Now comes the pay-off. We bite into the pizza and taste it. We have arrived at *experience* and we now have the ecstasy of pizza. The mind that has been careening forward in desire saying "pizza, pizza, " stops. In that moment desire is fulfilled.

In the moment of satisfaction of a desire or a physical need, joy is released. When the desire of the mind is satisfied, consciousness turns within and the mind becomes silent. No wonder we are so committed to trying to satisfy our desires

At such a time we have at least a partial experience of the bliss of the Self.

Looked at in this way, we can say that satisfaction only *apparently* comes from the pizza (or any object of desire). It actually comes from the Self. When the mind stops at the moment of fulfilment, it turns within and we experience our natural state of inner satisfaction.

Unfortunately, our relief from the craving mind is only momentary. It starts up again: "Is this pizza as good as the one at Filo's?" (comparison); "I remember the summer of '87, I had a pizza one night and *she* was with me (nostalgia, memory)"; "Now, I need a coke (another desire)."

When a thought arises in the mind it sets off a subtle chain reaction that begins in the inner world and eventually manifests in the outer world. Thought is accompanied by feeling. Desire is a part of feeling and is accompanied by volition. Volition, will, pushes us to act in the outer world. When we act in the outer world we are actually making our thought visible. Each action sets off a further chain of events. We can create a schematic diagram of this whole process:

THE WHEEL OF THE MIND

DESIRE AND FEAR

Experience is stored inside as an impression, as *memory*. A strong positive memory will create the desire to repeat the experience, while a strong negative memory will create a tendency to avoid that experience. How often have we said to ourselves, "I like/hate this restaurant, I will/will not come here again"?

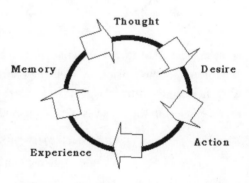

According to the yogic texts, memories are stored inside the subtle body in a vast catacomb called the *sushumna*. The sushumna is similar to the record or CD library of a large radio station. There is an inner disc jockey that selects the records or, in this case, the memories. Instead of the Beatles' and Rolling Stones' greatest hits, he plays your personal greatest hits: memories, hopes, fears, ideas, plans and so on. In any given moment a thought bubbles up into your mind, triggered by an association, or a physical sensation like hunger, or a sunset, or a song, or a person.

We spend our lives going around and around this cycle. Some yogis have called it not the *Wheel of the Mind*, but the *Wheel of Karma*, because it creates our destiny. In the grip of this cycle we unconsciously move from thought, to desire, to action, to experience, to memory. This momentum creates more thoughts, desires, actions, experiences and memories.

There is another parallel cycle of the mind, a shadow of this one. Just as there is a movement *towards* some things in order to satisfy desire, there is also a movement *away* from other things based on fear. Substitute *fear* for *desire* in the diagram. The satisfaction we experience in this cycle is relief when we have successfully avoided something we fear or loathe.

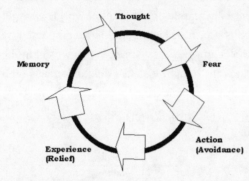

Let us look at the cycle of avoidance.

Much of our energy is tied up in these two cycles of avoidance and desire. All organisms move towards that which they want and away from that which they fear. Patanjali calls this *raga-dvesha*, attraction and repulsion. The desire cycle is the movement of attraction, while the fear cycle is the movement of repulsion. *Raga-dvesha* is the tension we feel when surrounded by people and situations we either want to attract or avoid. It is worth considering the amount of energy that we invest in these cycles of chasing and avoiding.

BREAKING THE DESIRE CYCLE

So far we have seen that ordinarily the desire cycle is broken only at the point of *experience*, that is, when a desire is satisfied. The forward careening mind separates us from the Self. However, meditation tells us that the cycle can be broken and the Self experienced at any point.

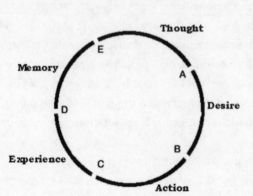

Let us rework the diagram:

Points A to E represent places where the cycle can be broken. We have been discussing point D where the mind becomes still when it enjoys an experience. Let us look at other places to break the cycle. Point B will be familiar to most of us. Here desire has arisen, but we do not act on it. Think of dieting, giving up smoking, or resisting a sexual temptation. While this does not usually give us immediate joy of the Self, it does strengthen us and often leads to joy in the long run.

In meditation the two main places to break the cycle are points E and A. At point E we try to prevent thoughts from arising. We strive to keep the mind blank. It is said that the famous 20th Century yogi Sri Aurobindo attained enlightenment in this way. His meditation teacher told him that he should simply keep all thoughts away from his mind. The teacher said that if he could do that he would attain Self-realization in three days. Aurobindo was a naïve subject; he had never meditated before. It never occurred to him that he could not do it. He also had exceptional powers of will and intellect. He followed his teacher's instruction and did indeed arrive at the goal. Of course, Aurobindo had a unique spiritual gift. This method takes enormous vigilance and mental strength, attributes most of us would have to build by years of practice. Let us try it right now.

Contemplation 8: Blanking your mind (2 minutes)
1. Close your eyes and turn within.
2. Try to stop your mind.
3. Do not let any thoughts arise.
4. Do this any way you choose.

Was that difficult? Did you notice a feeling of pressure—maybe in your brow, your third eye? Did you notice how strong the tendency to create thoughts is? The unformed thoughts silently scream, "Think me, think me!" This is a personal example of the universal creative power, the power of manifestation. The same urge on the cosmic level creates the universe, on a personal scale it leads to creating businesses, symphonies or offspring.

It is difficult to silence the mind directly. To do it we need to develop skilful means. In my meditation classes I have noticed that when I do this exercise—usually early in the course—students spontaneously invent all the classical methods of meditation. Some use a mantra like "stop thinking" or "blank, blank". Others focus on the breath. Others visualize a blank space. One man created a wall to keep thoughts out. In other words meditation techniques are simply sophisticated versions of common sense approaches to quietening the mind.

In fact, we can discover a skilful, intuitive meditator within ourselves. All we need to do is practise.

Point E, as we have seen, represents the attempt to stop thoughts from arising. Since this is so difficult, a more practical type of meditation is found at point A. Here, we allow thoughts to come up, but we do not allow them to build up strength and become full-blown desires. The technique of mantra is a point A technique. We allow thoughts to arise, but we let them go while repeating the mantra. This pulls the rug out from under the careening mental cycle, and serves to eventually quiet the mind.

Each of the other possible break points has been used by different schools of yogis as mental or physical disciplines designed to experience the Self. At point C we find the classical path of *karma yoga*, the yoga of service and action. This is suitable for active people who express their inner search through service to God or humanity. The karma yogi performs his work without worrying about the outcome. He does his duty; he does his best. He frees himself from worry about success or failure, he "surrenders the fruits of his actions". In terms of the diagram he performs *action* but gives up trying to control *experience*. He lets the "chips fall where they may". In fact, this is a good way for us to perform all our work in the world; it is a freeing attitude.

Many years ago all my hopes and aspirations were tied up in attaining my PhD. I studied for a solid year to prepare myself for my PhD qualifying exam, an exhaustive written examination. I went to sleep the night before keyed-up, but reasonably confident. But my underlying anxiety woke me after two hours of sleep and I had the panicky thought, "O my God, now I won't be able to get back to sleep and I won't be rested and I'll do poorly on the exam!" Needless to say, I didn't get back to sleep.

Success on the examination mattered too much to me, and my mind tortured me all night long. The exam was the next evening and I had all day to brood about my misfortune (a nap was not possible in my state). I decided I would not take the exam. Fortunately, a good friend of mine convinced me to give it a try. After all, I would have to wait another year for the next one, and I had worked so hard.

When I sat for the exam I noticed that something unusual had happened to my psychology. I believe that New Yorkers habitually think of the "worst case scenario" before they undertake anything. In other words, they imagine the worst that can happen and see if they will be able to handle it. Now, in my mind the worst outcome had already happened—there was no possibility of passing.

Therefore I had no reason to worry, and I felt clear and relaxed. And, I did well in the examination.

When we are intensely caught up in the desire for success and the fear of failure we sabotage our performance. When we let go of fear of failure we perform with more spontaneity and skill.

Point **D** is the path of *tantric* yoga, the yoga of experience. Though this yoga is a legitimate and highly intelligent way to achieve inner peace, it has been misunderstood in the West. We have come to associate it exclusively with sex. Most people think that tantra is having extended sexual encounters without orgasm. A witty fellow I know says that tantra is saying *Om* during intercourse. In actuality, the tantric approach involves allowing any experience (not just sexual experience) to happen, but shifting our understanding.

In our example, while some orthodox yogis would suppress the desire for pizza, and others would deny even the thought of pizza, the tantric yogi allows the thought, desire and experience of pizza all to occur. Normally, as we bite into the pizza we say, "This pizza is great!" The tantric yogi says instead, "Ah, this pizza gives me an experience of the Self!" He bases this on the understanding that all outer things which give us pleasure—pizza, music, sex, sport—are really triggers of the potential joy we already have within us. This is a useful path of meditation in the world for people whose understanding is stronger than their renunciation and self-discipline. If you find it far-fetched you should stay away from the tantric path and simply repeat the mantra!

While there are many approaches, my emphasis in this book is on point **A**. When we use the method of mantra or witness-consciousness we will not try to blank the mind. We will not get caught in warfare with the mind. We will allow thoughts to come and go.

KEY IDEAS OF CHAPTER THIRTEEN:
THE CYCLE OF THE MIND

- When a thought arises in the mind it sets off a subtle chain reaction.
- The mind is a fertile thought-producing factory.
- Thoughts create desire, desire creates action, action creates experience and experience creates memory.
- There is a second cycle of the mind based on fear and avoidance.
- All memories are stored in the sushumna.
- Much of our energy is tied up in avoidance and desire.
- We can break the cycle and experience the Self.

Chapter fourteen:
INTROJECTION - WORKING WITHIN THE MIND

maitri-karuna-muditopekshanam sukhaduhkha-
punyapunya-vishayanam bhavanatash chitta-prasadanam

The mind gives grace when it turns away from
misery and towards friendliness, compassion,
gladness, happiness and detachment.

Yoga Sutras of Patanjali I.33

THE MIND IS our best friend and our worst enemy. It is impossible to lead a happy and enlightened life without understanding and taking control of the mind. We are born with a mind that is unique and individual. One person has a mind which tries to make the best of every situation. It looks for the silver lining in every cloud. Such a person is fortunate: his mind is like a peaceful resort, a garden spot. Another person's mind is full of turbulence. Hurricanes and storms are always breaking out. Another's mind is as dry as a desert. Another person takes good things and looks for a bad way to view them. Such a person is unfortunate, and has difficulty finding satisfaction or happiness.

Why do our minds vary so much? A Freudian might say that some of us had deep traumas when we were young. A Hindu might say that we carry impressions from previous lives. A socialist might say we carry the scars of society's injustices. A psychologist might say that we reflect the patterns of our parents' minds. All of these theories probably have some truth in them. But the fact is that *we have the mind we have*. When we sit to meditate, we encounter what is given. That is our starting point.

Just as we have different bodies, so we have different minds. If I wanted to be a sprinter I could go to a coach, eat the right food, work with weights, learn proper technique and train intensely. But with the physical equipment I have I could never run faster than a certain time. Another fellow could beat me without any knowledge, any training, after having been out all night. Our minds, like our bodies vary.

Some of us are gifted with qualities like contentment, dispassion and a positive mind—others are not. The good news is that the inner Self blazes equally within each of us. The inner Self is democratic. Not only that, each of us can find skilful means to quieten the mind and access the Self.

THE GARDEN OF THE MIND

The mind is the mystery of human life. It is the garden of joy and the secret formula for despair and depression.

Swami Muktananda

If you had cultivated a perfect rose garden but then went to the top of the mountain and, like Rip Van Winkle, slept for 20 years, what would you find when you returned? You would be naïve to expect your roses still to be growing in orderly rows. Instead you would find your garden choked with weeds. There would be little sign of the original garden. These days it is likely that a condo would be growing on the spot.

The mind can be compared to an extremely fertile garden. Sprouts of thoughts and shoots of feelings grow in it at an amazing rate. It is not surprising then, that it is overgrown with weeds. We have done little to cultivate it. We have let negative patterns and bad tendencies grow. Often we have strengthened them by indulging them. It is easy to see that in proper mind culture we need to weed, prune and plant new seeds.

When you sit to meditate many unwanted thoughts spring into your mind. The mind is both voluntary and involuntary. You can use the voluntary aspect of mind to free you from old, bad habits. You can develop new and healthier habits. I call this process introjection.

INTROJECTION

Introjection is the act of placing new thoughts into the mind, based on our commitment to uplift the mind. It is a mental action of great value and is the essence of healthy mind culture. When we introject a thought we are saying, "My habitual attitude or pattern of mind does not serve my well-being. I choose to change it."

If we interpret an event as unpleasant we say: "That is bad." We experience a "downward shift" towards feeling bad. If we interpret an event as positive and say, "That is good" we will experience an "upward shift".

Unhappiness is the result of the negative thoughts we hold about our life. Unhappiness has nowhere to live when we feel happy. In this sense we create the experience of our lives with our thoughts. If we find ourselves in depression or without inspiration, it is essential to act creatively and not be at the effect of negative mental habits. We can practise introjection.

A yogi, a meditator, does not simply get lost in the *contents* of his thoughts— he is also aware of the *effect* his thoughts have on himself. Do they elevate or depress? When their effect is bad instead of following their negative direction he disciplines his mind and moves it toward healthier states.

I mentioned earlier how closely thought and feeling are related. When we use the technique of introjection we work with *thoughts* in order to change *feeling*. This is because feeling usually cannot be changed directly. When we are *within* a negative feeling we become identified with the images and pictures that arise in connection with that feeling. This feeds the feeling and makes it difficult to change. When we feel depressed we can hardly imagine feeling good ever again, and depression becomes our whole world. It colors the way we perceive our life and the future. Such "emotion-colored" thinking is dangerously unreliable and misleading. It is essential to become clear, to return to peaceful inner states. The most effective way to do this is to work with thought.

When we use introjection we discover that we have the power of choice. Sometimes we cannot change outer circumstances, but with a little effort we can *always* uplift our perspective. This is spiritual freedom.

We can develop the strength to say to ourselves: "My automatic, conditioned response leads me towards rage, enmity, fear and jealousy. These responses are not worthy of me; I have divinity within me! I choose to look at this in a different way, a way that will uplift and dignify my life."

TYPES OF INTROJECTION

Introjection is a powerful, pro-active way to deal with the mind. It empowers us. No longer at the effect of mental tendencies, we learn skilful means to uplift the mind by choice. The types of introjection I have already discussed or will discuss are: mantra, *mahavakya*, affirmation, inquiry, prayer, substitution and invocation.

1. Mantra

I have already discussed this powerful form of introjection at length in Chapter 7.

2. *Mahavakya*: Great Statements

The Vedas contain four great statements called *mahavakyas*. The most famous ones are *Aham Brahmasmi*, "I am the Absolute" and *Tat Twam Asi*, "You are that" (the Absolute). They direct us not to our body or mind, but to our real identity, to the divine Self within. I discuss this more fully in Part II, Chapter Five.

3. Affirmation

This is a popular form of introjection. A desired quality is *affirmed* - for example, "I am strong", "I am rich," by mental repetition. (Affirmations are discussed more fully in the Question/Answer section on page 120.)

4. **Inquiry**

Inquiry involves asking empowering questions of the Self.

Disempowering: "Why do bad things always happen to me?"

Empowering: "What can I do to improve this situation?"

The former question evokes an answer like, "Because you are a loser", while the latter elicits practical solutions.

The method of Self-inquiry based on the question "Who am I?", has been a means of Self-realization for centuries. Even on a mundane level asking precise questions inwardly is rewarding. I will discuss Self-inquiry fully in Part II of this book.

I discuss the other three types of introjection in the following chapters. They are:

5. **Prayer**

6. **Substitution**

7. **Invocation**

Thought is a powerful and creative force. One writer says:

> All thoughts and feelings are powerful agents of creative energy,
> regardless of whether thoughts are true and wise or false and limited.
> Likewise, whether the feelings are loving or hateful, angry or benign,
> fearful or peaceful, their energy must create according to their nature.
>
> Eva Pierrakos: - The Pathwork of Self-transformation

Thought is not, therefore, "mere thought" - it is intensely creative. Our whole life reflects the creation going on all of the time inside our minds. We are constantly creating outcomes. In the course of living we all have bad moments and bad days. From the point of view of the inner world, I mean times when we are overwhelmed by negative emotions like fear or depression or anger. The ancient texts call these negative states the "six enemies" or "toxic mind states", or "states of ignorance".

The most effective way of coping with bad days is introjection. The temptation is to act and speak from negative states. When we feel angry we dump our anger all around us. When we feel depressed we make negative decisions. Wisdom says, "Stop!"

- No decision, communication or action sourced by a negative state can have a positive outcome.

It is important to work on your inner state immediately. Only when you have shifted to a positive state can you make positive decisions, communications and actions. This is a hard, but extremely valuable lesson to learn.

The formula is:

- When in a toxic state, before you speak, act or make a decision, introject first.

This principle will save you a lot of pain.

If you find yourself angry or afraid, say the mantra intensely or use one of the methods of introjection. Sometimes you may be unable to shift the toxic state right away. In such cases simply being aware of the toxic state will help.

Look at these examples:

Example A

Negative Emotion:

"What's the use, I feel so hopeless, I will drop out of college."

Awareness of Toxic State:

"I am feeling depressed today so I am not making any decisions."

Introjection - focus on a desired quality:

"I contemplate strength, creativity and optimism."

Example B

Negative Emotion:

"You idiot, you know I like my coffee hot!"

Awareness of Toxic State:

"Dear, I am angry for some reason today, and I have to be careful what I say."

Introjection (mantra):

"Om Namah Shivaya, Om Namah Shivaya!"

KEY IDEAS OF CHAPTER FOURTEEN:
INTROJECTION

- The mind is our best friend and worst enemy.
- We have the mind we have.
- The mind is an extremely fertile garden.
- Introjection is the act of placing new thoughts into the mind, based on our commitment to uplift the mind.
- Unhappiness is the result of negative thoughts.
- A yogi disciplines his mind.
- No decision, communication or action sourced by a negative state can have a positive outcome.

Chapter fifteen:
PRAYER

Beggar, burn up the delusion of the mind in the fire of yoga.
Without realisation of Brahman it is not possible to know
the pristine state; the true bliss is not.
The sense of honour and respect do not go.
Preserve the bliss.
Bundle up desire in its abode, the mind.
Desire is sapless.
Give it up within yourself.

Bhagawan Nityananda

PRAYER IS A wonderfully effective form of introjection for many people. Some of us, however, are prayer negative whether because of inclination, prejudice or upbringing. Since there are many other effective methods available this is of little concern. But if prayer makes sense to you, you should make good use of it.

Notice the difference between the following two statements. "I am scared I might have a fatal disease", and "God, please let me be well". The former statement produces anxiety. The second one is much more empowering. When we pour our fear into a higher principle through prayer there is surrender and relief.

The most primitive form of prayer (and the most familiar) is praying for what you want or do not want. There are more subtle forms of prayer that connect us to the Self. In its highest form prayer is simply a bridge between the ego self and the awakened Self.

I am not at all against praying for what you want. In fact, it is a very good idea: it means you are being honest in your inner world. If it is a virtue to be honest with other people, how much more important is it to be honest with the Self or God?

A friend of mine used to say that all desires were disguised desires for the Divine. Thus if you want money, underneath that desire is a deeper desire for a sense of security or freedom from fear or for empowerment. Ultimately both of these can only come from God. He thought that if you wanted a person to love you, underneath it is the desire for divine love and open-heartedness. That also comes not from personal love, but from God.

There is undoubtedly a lot of truth in this view, however there is a danger. It can lead us to a denial of what we consider our "base desires" in an attempt to "be more spiritual". This can set up a state of inner warfare and self-hatred as well as denial. Refusing to look at our desires and fears is not the same as not having them. It is far better to be simple and humble. Begin where you are and ask, like Janis Joplin, "O Lord, won't you give me a Mercedes Benz," or "Send me money" or "Send me someone to love".

When you pray for what you want you have made your desire known to the highest court, the Divine. It is then appropriate to let what you want go and surrender to divine will. You may be given what you want or you may not. There are times when what we want is not appropriate—and there are mysterious reasons why. It could be the law of *karma*, cause and effect at work. Sometimes we look at others and want what they have. The mind creates new desires and cravings that are not necessarily the true desires of the heart. By prayer you fulfil your part by discovering and communicating your heart's true desires. The rest must be left to God.

You can also cultivate "higher" prayer. Give a little time to consciously pray for divine *qualities* (not things). For example:

- God (Self), please give me greater understanding.
- God (Self), please bless me with strength and quieten my mind.
- God (Self), please open my heart to divine love.
- God (Self), please help me let go of past hurts.
- God (Self), please let me feel connected to you!

And prayer for others is extremely helpful for *you* first of all.

We are aware how important it is to express what we want and need to say to others. We should also be explicit in the inner world. Prayer is an effective means of speaking to the Self. Every so often have an inner dialogue with God. Speak your hopes and fears. Ask for what you want materially and spiritually. Articulate your yearning on all levels.

By the way, it is never too late to speak to the departed in the *inner world*. In my private work many people speak of despair over loved ones who have passed away. Too often there are unspoken communications lingering. I reassure them that even though their dear one has left the outer world, he or she is still on "imail" (inner world mail).

PRAYER POINT

When you have thought about a situation to the limit of your ability, you will come to an inner place where further thought will not be productive. Your mind will worry and go over and over the same ground in a state of fear or doubt. I call the limit of useful thinking *prayer point*. At this point you should stop thinking and pray. Turn the issue over to the higher power. When you notice that you are starting to worry, prayer is helpful.

DEDICATING THE MANTRA

You can also use mantra at prayer point. When a block occurs or an issue will not go away in some area of your life, *dedicate* a certain amount of mantra repetition to the issue.

Let us say, for example, you have a problem at work. Say inwardly: "I dedicate 20 minutes of mantra to solve it. Let the higher power figure it out!" Then repeat the mantra dedicating it to that issue.

I knew a woman whose father was Indian and whose mother was American. She had lived her early life in India. She told me that her Indian grandmother handled stress in a fascinating way. Instead of torturing herself with choices and alternatives and the concomitant experience of anxiety, her grandmother would simply drop the issue and instead do mantra.

When you find yourself struggling without reward, say the mantra. Let the struggle go. The mantra raises the mind to a higher place, and in that place the true answer or solution is more likely to be received. Tension and anxiety block receptivity and clear thinking.

KEY IDEAS OF CHAPTER FIFTEEN: PRAYER

- Prayer is a bridge between the ego self and the awakened Self.
- You can pray for what you want.
- Higher prayer is to pray for divine qualities not for material things.
- Prayer point is when we turn an issue over to the higher power rather than getting caught in worry.
- Pray for divine qualities.
- Pray for others.
- When you reach *prayer point* give up worry and pray.
- You can use mantra at prayer point.
- You can dedicate a certain number of mantra repetitions to overcome blocks.

Chapter sixteen:
SUBSTITUTION

Seat yourself in the carriage and go to Kashi.
Reach the city of Shivananda.
Go to the city of Shanti.
Terminate at the city of Brahmananda.

Rub the sticks and light the fire;
cook day by day.
Make not distinction.
Pour into the fit vessel.
Give to him of happy thoughts.

Bhagawan Nityananda

SUBSTITUTION IS THE most direct form of introjection. Here we pull out the weeds of negative thoughts and take the *positive action* of planting the crop we want to grow. The classical formulation of substitution is in Patanjali. He says:

vitarka badhane partipaksha bhavanam

When the mind is disturbed by (negative) thoughts
repel them by contemplating the opposite.

Yoga Sutras of Patanjali II.33

In other words:

• When undesirable thoughts arise, substitute.

I have always found this an enchanting aphorism, since it demonstrates the common sense approach of yoga. The greatest wisdom is often the most simple. When we hear something profound we usually feel, "Of course! I knew that already." Since there is a place of perfect wisdom inside of us, that is true in its way. Plato said that we do not learn anything new, we only remember. The Eastern sages say that we *recognize* what we already know.

The idea of substituting a positive for a negative is natural. There is a song from a musical that goes, "Whenever I feel afraid, I whistle a happy tune". This is substitution. Patanjali says that if we feel angry we should contemplate love or forgiveness. If we are sad we can contemplate joy. If we feel afraid we can contemplate fearlessness. If we feel weak we should contemplate an image of strength like an elephant. Some portion of the feeling of the object of meditation comes to us when we contemplate it.

Once Baba told me to "sit like a mountain" in meditation. He meant that I should imagine that I was a mountain and I would draw the mountain-like characteristics of strength, solidity, immovability and imperturbability to me. The following chart gives some examples of substitution. As you practise you will discover the contemplations that work for you. Try some of the following to see which ones uplift and expand your feeling. Remember, we are learning to *follow the upward shift* not cling to the negative.

NEGATIVE THOUGHT/ FEELING	SUBSTITUTE
SORROW	
Grief	Forgiveness and love
Hurt	Joy or detachment
Weakness	Strength and power
Disempowerment	Empowerment
ANGER	
Desire	Fulfilment and compassion
Restlessness	Contentment and patience
Impatience	Faith and surrender
FEAR	
Worry	Confidence and certainty
Powerlessness	Insight, courage, acceptance and Shakti
Confusion	Clarity and the light of wisdom
THE BODY	
Physical pain or illness	Healing power and prayer
Tiredness or apathy	Shakti, spiritual energy.

A strong mind automatically uses substitution whenever it is assaulted by negative thoughts just as a healthy immune system fights disease. At the beginning, however, we may have to work for a while to establish the habit of substitution. In time it will replace the old habit of wallowing in the negative.

One of the things that I do in my own meditation is to ask myself what taste, flavour or quality my mind presently has. Sometimes we say: "That left a bitter taste in my mouth." Upon inspection we discover that our thought process actually has a bitter quality. Discovering that, I might say to myself: "Think sweet thoughts." Of course this would mean I would entertain loving thoughts, but I might also take it literally and think about chocolate and ice-cream! In the same way when the mind is tight, uncomfortable and negative I might reflect on such ideas as the following to change the "flavour" of the mind: *soften, lighten, expand, love, uplift, harmonise, energise.*

KEY IDEAS OF CHAPTER SIXTEEN
SUBSTITUTION

- Substitution is the most direct form of introjection.
- When undesirable thoughts arise, substitute positive ones.
- Contemplate qualities you wish to draw towards you.

Chapter seventeen:

INVOCATION –
I CALL ON THE SELF

vita raga vishayam va cittam

Fix the mind on those who are free from attachment.

Yoga Sutras of Patanjali I.37

TO INVOKE SOMETHING is to call on the presence and qualities of that thing. We can invoke a person, a deity, an experience, or something we love. We use the image to uplift feeling, to draw the highest quality of the object to us.

The mind takes the form of whatever it thinks. Unlike physical objects, the mind is made of pure Consciousness and is malleable. In every thought the mind takes a new shape. If we had instruments sensitive enough, we could measure in physical terms how each thought affects our bodies differently.

The following are some powerful invocations. You can invent your own. Take a few minutes now to experiment with some. Call on the higher power by silently saying:

- I invoke the power of the inner Self.
- I invoke the joy of creativity.
- I invoke the presence of Jesus (or Krishna or Buddha or Moses).
- I invoke love (or peace or strength).

Invocation is a strong mental act. It is also natural. As a young boy playing baseball I invoked the presence of my hero, the centre fielder for the Brooklyn Dodgers, Duke Snider. When it was my turn to bat, I would pound the plate, take my stance like him and say mentally: "the Duke is at bat." I had no idea what I was doing, but I got something from the practice. The Duke was great, but these days I would be more likely to invoke my guru or Buddha, Jesus, Krishna or even God or Shakti, the divine Mother. In fact one of the main practices I did for many years was to invoke the spiritual power of my teacher - a practice he himself had used.

Invoking a great being is a form of substitution. We substitute their divine qualities for our lesser ones. Then we participate in their qualities.

The great yogi Aurobindo points out that stilling the mind is very difficult. Witnessing is easier, as is invocation. Writing of invocation he says:

*"[In meditation] one can look up...imagining the force as there
just above and calling it down quietly, expecting its help...
Instead of fighting with the mind one keeps only a silent will
and aspiration for the power or the silence. Gradually the mind
becomes quiet and silence begins to descend."*

Here is a similar contemplation to try:

Contemplation 9: I call on the Self

1. Sit down, turn within and say mentally, *I call on the Self.*
2. Now remain quiet and open.
3. Note carefully if there is a response from the Self.

Some forms of response that I experience or my students have reported
are:

- a feeling of upliftment;
- the manifestation of lights in the third eye;
- a surge or quickening of energy;
- a quietening of the mind;
- a feeling of peace or joy;
- a stilling of the breath;
- an opening of the heart;
- an image or vision; or
- a feeling of sinking into the Self.

I find this exercise unfailing in its effect. It will bring in the energy of the
Self and swiftly uplift your meditation. Of course, if you prefer, you can call on
God or a spiritual teacher or one of the ancient or modern Great Beings.

KEY IDEAS OF CHAPTER SEVENTEEN:
INVOCATION - I CALL ON THE SELF

- The mind takes the form of what it thinks.
- The process of invocation draws the energy of the object to us.
- In meditation, invoke the highest principle or person you know.

Chapter eighteen:
BEYOND THE MIND – WITNESS CONSCIOUSNESS

sukhaduhkhayor bahirmananam

The meditator considers pain and pleasure as something external.

Shiva Sutras III.33

THE FIRST MOVIE I saw as a young child was the John Wayne film *The Wake of the Red Witch*. In it John Wayne plays a deep-sea diver who drowns. This upset me very much. My mother explained that only the character had died and that John Wayne was alive and well, thank you! I can remember the wonder and scepticism with which I absorbed her words.

Of course, I had become too involved in the story. I thought it was real. As I got older and more sophisticated I learned to step back from a film and view it in the double way (both involved and detached) that we view fiction. If we take this technique a step further and apply it to our own thoughts we can understand witness-consciousness.

It is important for every meditator to work *within* the world of the mind, to make the mind strong and pure. When working within the mind, we notice whether thoughts and feelings are negative or positive. We consciously work to expand and uplift the mind. Witness-consciousness is an even deeper level of meditation where work is *beyond* the mind.

The inner Self is pure awareness. That awareness is the eternal witness. Thought manifests from that awareness and dissolves into that awareness. When we move beyond the mind, thought—negative or positive—is simply thought, and feelings—negative or positive—simply are. *Witness-consciousness* involves detaching from the thoughts and feelings arising in the mind.

When we watch television the content makes a big difference. A situation comedy is different from a soap opera and an afternoon talk show is different from a golf show. We have preferences. The TV screen however, does not make distinctions. To it, there is only *on* and *off*. The contents do not matter to the screen and on and off do not matter to it either.

When we practise witness-consciousness, we watch our inner world from a distance. Thoughts arise and subside. Emotions come and go. The mind wanders in the past and the future, in positive and negative memories. Plans and fantasies arise, hold our attention, and then disappear. There is constant change and flow yet we do not move from the space of watching. The witness simply watches it all as the play of the inner Consciousness. My teacher once told a student:

> *What is your idea of yourself? Do you think that you are just a constant flowing stream of thoughts? Do not identify with your thoughts but with their source. Identify with the one who is beyond the mind, beyond all the thoughts. You are the Self, the constant witness of all these thoughts. Identify with the Self, your true reality.*

As you have grown from a child to an adult your life has changed. It is likely you have been in and out of love with one person and in love with another. It is possible you once held passionate political or philosophical ideas you no longer hold. Perhaps you used to be intensely involved in a job or an activity you are no longer doing. When you were engrossed in those people, activities and ideas, it may have seemed your entire life was identified with them.

Time has shown, however, that you have a life and an identity quite independent of them: your life has changed, perhaps profoundly, but you are, and have always been, *You*.

When we take the stance of the witness in meditation we feel the relief of detachment. Our vision becomes as broad and all embracing as possible. We do not judge or entertain preferences. Whatever thought forms and feelings appear, we understand that they are the play of our own awareness.

When I was a child I loved 'animal crackers', biscuits in the shape of animals. I would eat a lion, a giraffe, or a monkey. My mind differentiated them, but my palate discovered they all tasted the same. No wonder: they were cut from the same dough. In the same way, all thought is cut from the dough of Consciousness.

When we watch, we do not get drawn into the drama our thoughts suggest. We watch them come and go. The ancient sages taught that there is no bondage except the craving to acquire what we want and the anxiety to avoid what we fear. When we meditate as the witness we cultivate the vision of perfection: whatever arises is perfect, there is nothing to acquire or reject.

Everything that occurs in your inner world is a movement of consciousness. You are wide, broad, strong and spacious. All possible thoughts and feelings may occur. Some are uplifting and some are not. Those that are not uplifting can temporarily shake you. As the witness you include them in your awareness, and so much more. You remain as the background and watch them all. Just as the earth equally accepts everyone who walks on it, so you accept everything the mind creates. You are the empty blackboard on which the writing of Consciousness expresses itself. You are the *knower*, the underlying Consciousness that holds all potential meanings.

Contemplation 10: Witness-consciousness

1. If you like you can turn on your CD player and use the tamboura to accompany this meditation.
2. Sit for meditation and turn within.
3. Notice the movement of your inner world.
4. Slowly pull back and watch with detachment from a distance, as if you are watching a movie.
5. Let the thoughts and feelings come and go. Do not get drawn into the content or meaning of them. Let your awareness expand to hold them.
6. Accept everything. Reject nothing. Say to yourself: "This is the play of Consciousness", or "This is the play of my own thought and feeling", or "My awareness holds everything."
7. While you adopt the attitude just described, lightly watch the breath come in and out. *Watch the breath, and sit as the witness.*
8. When your mind gets drawn into the contents or dramas of various thoughts, gently go back to the witness position.

A variation on witnessing that works well for me is to imagine myself a few feet behind myself. I watch myself having thoughts and feelings from there.

The attitude of a witness is essential for a meditator. Even if we find ourselves identified with the people and objects in our lives, we can cultivate detachment in meditation. The practice of witness-consciousness will positively affect your meditation.

HAMSA MEDITATION

You have probably noticed a relationship between your breathing rhythm and your state of mind. When you are agitated, your breathing is also agitated. When you fall asleep breathing becomes slow and regular. The mind is calm in sleep. The breath is a powerful technique for entering deep meditation.

In my early days in India I studied with Hari Dass Baba, a great Hatha Yogi who taught me at least eight exercises using breath rhythms. In one I would breathe in, hold my breath, breathe out and then hold my breath outside - each part for a certain number of seconds. Another exercise involved a bellows-like breath, similar to hyperventilation. These techniques had a definite quietening effect on the mind and were conducive to meditation. They can be dangerous, however, and should only be practised under the supervision of an expert.

Some Buddhist traditions count the in-breaths: one, two, three, and four, up to nine as a method for witnessing. I used to wonder, "Why only count to nine and then start again?" I then realized it was so that you would not get too interested: "I am up to 3,700. I am first in the West. I am going for my personal best! Now, I am going for the world record!"

While the techniques I have just described all involve a manipulation of the breathing rhythm and are therefore somewhat artificial, the breath technique I will show you is both natural and safe. It is called the *hamsa* mantra. It is pronounced "*hum sah*." The breathing rhythm is left as it is. We simply watch the breath come in and listen for the sound "*hum*" and watch the breath go out and listen for the sound "*sah*."

Ham means "I am" and refers to the inner world. When you breathe in with the sound "*ham*" you bring the life force from outside into your inner world. You affirm your "I am-ness." "*Sa*" means "That" and refers to the outer world. When we breathe out we hear the breath as "*sa*" and we affirm our connection to the objective universe. The breath confirms our intimate relationship with the outer world and forms an ongoing and immediate connection. I consider this to be the king of methods of breath control.

As concentration increases you may find that the point between the breaths expands into a vast quiet space. This is the source from which all thoughts and feelings arise. This is the space of the inner Self. Breath meditation is closely allied to witness-consciousness. It creates spaciousness and detachment.

Contemplation 11: Breath meditation: Hamsa
- Close your eyes, turn within and become aware of your breathing.
- Focus on the sound of your breath as you inhale and exhale.
- As you breathe in listen for the sound *ham* and as you breathe out listen for the sound *sa*. (In the beginning you can quietly repeat *ham* on the in-breath and *sa* on the out-breath.)
- Let yourself move into a gentle rhythm. If your mind wanders bring it back to the breath.
- Remain in the witness attitude.

Give a bit of attention to each of the meditations and contemplations I suggest, since they are all valuable. You will discover which ones work for you. Respect your own intuition and interest. Go with the suggestions that appeal to you. You can review earlier contemplations and exercises later. You will see that different aspects stand out at different times. Let the teachings filter into your subconscious mind and expand the weapons you have in your meditation practice.

If you have been regular in your practice I have no doubt that you will have reaped benefits. If you have been a bit slack, I have a suggestion: *start again!* Re-read the early chapters and embrace the practice. I encourage you to work through the book slowly. This is preferable to racing through the practices.

KEY IDEAS OF CHAPTER EIGHTEEN:
BEYOND THE MIND - WITNESS CONSCIOUSNESS

- The attitude of the witness is essential for a meditator.
- From the perspective of the witness, thought, positive or negative, is merely consciousness in a specific form.
- The witness watches it all without attachment or aversion. As the witness, you are broad and open.
- Thoughts come and go and you are always the Self.
- Watch the breath and sit as the witness.
- "Ham" (I AM) refers to the inner world. "Sah" (THAT) refers to the outer world.
- Respect your own intuition and interest.

Chapter nineteen:
THE PRACTICE
OF SELF-ACCEPTANCE

Kneel to your own Self.
Meditate on your own Self.
Worship your own inner being.
Chant the mantra that is silently going on within you.
God dwells within you as you.

Swami Muktananda

IN ANCIENT INDIA the path of Vedanta held sway. It was a path for the few: only male Brahmin youths of intelligence and high moral character could practise it. It required purity and dedication and was entirely a path of the intellect. With most of the population left out, it was inevitable for other approaches to appear. The new ways were more democratic: women and the lower castes were permitted. Based on a realistic picture of human weaknesses, they were less forbidding and held that everyone could make progress through meditation, not just the gifted few. These new ways, one of which was Kashmir Shaivism, were less vertical and less hierarchic. They did not deny or loathe the body and were free from the duality of pure versus impure.

This vision sees human beings and life as divine. It acknowledges both the human and divine aspects alive within each of us. That is, God in the form of the Divine Mother, or Shakti and God in the form of Shiva, the absolute, the eternal aspect of the inner Self. The vision sees these two energies lying at the core of every person, object and event—if we could but discover them.

Sometimes this cultural evolution is recapitulated in the lives of individuals. My teacher practised Vedanta and yoga, an intense and disciplined spirituality. His concept was to control his lower nature by purifying his intellect through abstinence and hard practice. In *Play of Consciousness* he recounts how his lower nature turned the tables on him, making a mockery of his spiritual pride. He fully believed he had conquered his sexual desire until one day while meditating he was obsessed with lust. No matter what he did he could not control it. He felt humiliated and desperate—he was sure he had to leave the spiritual path. He left the hut where he was practising and wandered off with a heavy heart.

Eventually he arrived at the place of a great sage who, while not his guru, acted as a "spiritual uncle" to him. Baba told him of his problem and his despair. The sage comforted him and taught him the path of self-acceptance. He told Baba that it was arrogant to think he could control his mind and lower nature by force. They would rebel and prove themselves too strong. It was better, he explained, to accept whatever arose in meditation as the play of Consciousness. He taught Baba not to expect perfect purity, but to acknowledge both the light and dark of his psyche.

Next to meeting his guru, Nityananda, this was the most significant turning point in my teacher's inner life. He immediately relaxed. He opened. He accepted himself and worshipped all the parts of his nature as divine. He moved from the Vedantic power model of control to the Shaivite model of love and acceptance. If you look at his photographs before this event you see a man of great purpose and strength but also a man under a strain. If you look at his later photographs you see a man of radiant love, entirely at peace and comfortable with himself.

Buddhist tradition says that at a key moment in the Buddha's search he overheard two musicians talking. The older one was instructing the younger how to tune the *veena*, a stringed instrument. As they were tightening the strings the older musician said: "Tune it not too tight, not too loose."

Those words struck the Buddha with the force of realization. In that moment he saw what later became his famous doctrine of the middle path. His earlier life had been "too loose", too empty of higher purpose, too given over to pleasure and success. Later he had been "too tight", too obsessed by self-denial and self-mortification even to the point of starvation. He saw that the path of wisdom was the middle way between indulgence and asceticism.

When there is no self-acceptance there is inner warfare. One part of us struggles to repress or destroy another part of us. The result is not purity but tension. While it is true that sometimes a battle against an unwanted tendency is necessary, often a more loving approach is needed. Self-acceptance begins with establishing an accepting relationship with our mind.

The Bal Shem Tov once upbraided a disciple for his excessive austerity. He told him: "Abandon such practices which reflect a disordered mind. By tormenting your body you will not reach God, you will only offend Him. Instead of penance and agonizing over sin again and again, pray to God with a loving heart."

In his later years my teacher often told of an encounter he had had with a Brahmin priest in Benares. The priest wanted to perform a ritual for him and asked him to say: "I am a sinner, I am a sinner." When Baba heard that he drove the priest off saying: "I am not a sinner, I am a pure devotee of the Self. You are a sinner for asking people to repeat that."

TALKING TO YOUR MIND

Invoking the Self is talking to the Self. Patanjali's statement, "Yoga is to still the thought waves of the mind", as brilliant as it is, has probably created the wrong impression for many meditators. As I said earlier, Patanjali meant that in fact, yoga is *any* effort to still the mind. It is important to eliminate emotional agitation, mental confusion and delusion. Then, stillness spontaneously emerges.

Zen Master Daikaku, who brought Zen from China to Japan in the 13th Century, said:

> No mind means that there is no deluded, foolish mind, it does not
> mean there is no mind to discern false from true.

It is easy to see the mind as the enemy. However to fight it or suppress it by force is not conducive to meditation. If you have children or pets you know that force and repression is a temporary solution. In the long run, to educate and teach with a gentle and loving approach is the one which works. This is as true for your mind as well as your children and animals. They all will respond more enthusiastically to sweet and loving words. You can coax, cajole, flatter, or negotiate with all of them.

Experiment with the following and see how responsive the mind is.

Contemplation 12: Talking to the mind

In this contemplation speak softly and sweetly to your mind in whatever way your intuition suggests. The following statements are meant to be suggestive and show the range of ideas you can use.

1. Oh my mind, please become still.
2. Oh my mind, please be positive.
3. Oh my mind, let me merge with the Self.
4. Oh my mind, let me meditate now, you can be active later.
5. Oh my mind, please renounce anger and entertain thoughts of forgiveness and love.

Cultivate an affectionate relationship with your mind. Remember how much service it does for you. Think of it as a person, a beloved relative who is sympathetic to your needs and will listen to your requests. Have recourse to this approach whenever the mind is agitated or resistant in meditation.

KEY IDEAS OF CHAPTER NINETEEN:
THE PRACTICE OF SELF-ACCEPTANCE

- Self-acceptance is essential for inner peace.
- The path of wisdom is the "middle way", not too tight, not too loose.
- Cultivate an affectionate relationship with your mind.
- Speak sweetly and softly to your mind.
- Tell your mind what you want from it.
- The mind is a beloved relative or friend.

Chapter twenty:
BEGIN WITH
THE LOVE YOU HAVE

Love turns man into an ocean of happiness,
an image of peace, a temple of wisdom.
Love is man's very Self, his true beauty,
and the glory of his human existence.

Swami Muktananda

The heart is to be set on reality
and this is to be done by whatever means a yogi has.

Abhinavagupta

LOVE IS THE MOST powerful energy in the inner world. *Bhakti*, the path of love, is one of the classical ways of yoga. A meditator on the path of love cultivates and expands his or her love. The main spiritual practice is to express love in speech and actions and to increase love, moment to moment, day by day. When successful, the inner secret of life shines within and an ocean of happiness and joy is revealed. Life is lived from the principle of love. Love is met by love everywhere. The loving heart is reflected back in the faces and hearts of others, even total strangers.

To expand love we begin with the love we already have. The mind takes a keen interest in what we love. In fact, love and interest are intimately connected. If we can tap the natural flow of love, we simultaneously tap our interest.

Without love, life lacks *rasa*, the nectar of the inner Self. We may have knowledge, fame, fortune, power and control in our field, but if we lack love, passion and enthusiasm, life will feel dry. The same is true of our meditation. A great meditator is not one who can sit in a posture like a statue for long periods, but one who runs to his meditation with joy as though he were going to meet his lover.

Once a rancher came to a sage to learn to meditate. The sage gave him a mantra and sent him home. The next week he returned to say: "I can't make my mind concentrate; do you have another technique?"

The sage gave him a guided meditation on CD. But the next week he was back: "It doesn't work for me, what else do you have?"

This went on for many weeks. None of the techniques worked. Finally the sage asked him: "Look, is there someone you love?"

"No," said the man, "No one I can think of."

"Is there anything you love?" insisted the sage.

"Well," he shyly responded, "I love my prize bull."

"Terrific," responded the sage, "meditate on your bull, love your bull, merge in your bull. Do it every day."

The next week the rancher did not come back. Several weeks passed and the sage began to wonder about him. One afternoon he decided to visit the rancher at his house. He knocked on the door. No one came but he could hear a bellowing as though a bull were inside. He knocked again. He heard the rancher's voice: "I can't come out. My horns won't fit through the door!" His meditation had been so effective he had merged in the object of meditation.

Not long ago a concerned mother came to talk to me about her high school age son. He could not concentrate on his school texts and she was worried about his forthcoming exams, college entry and his future. She thought he might have a learning disability. Our discussion soon revealed that he read avidly about football with perfect comprehension and excellent retention. So, strictly speaking, it was not a "learning disability". The missing ingredient was interest.

Love and interest go together. Where our love is, there our interest is also. Where there is love and interest there is focus. Some people, as in the case of the rancher, find it hard to focus on this or that object of meditation—but easy to concentrate on someone or some activity they love. Interest may be the strongest force in our lives. Where our interest goes, there our mind goes. Where our mind goes, there we go. Tell me what a person does every day and I will tell you what he loves, and what are his interests.

In the first section of Yoga Sutras, Patanjali gives a number of meditative techniques and concludes with:

yathabhimata-dhyanad va

Meditate as desired.

Yoga Sutras of Patanjali I.39

It reminds me of a bit of New York street wisdom I learned in my youth, "whatever works". The point is made even more clearly in the ancient Shaivite text *Vijnana Bhairava*, another compendium of meditation techniques. The 51st technique reads:

yatra yatra manas tustir manas
tatraiva dharayet
tatra tatra paranandasvarupam sampravartate

Wherever the mind of the individual finds satisfaction
let it concentrate on that. In every such case the
true nature of the highest bliss will manifest.
Vijnana Bhairava: Dharana 51

Each meditator is responsible for finding the keys to unlock his or her inner doors. If our approach is too mechanical, too theoretical, or too "by the book", we leave our personhood out of the equation and our practice becomes dry. Through self-acceptance we customise meditation to make use of the love and interest each of us already possesses. Interest, like love, is not something we can impose or legislate. Rather, we discover it within ourselves. Of course, as understanding deepens, interest increases too.

Vijnana Bhairava, by the way, makes interesting use of this approach. Here are a few examples where natural interest, pleasure and love are used to enliven meditation practice.

jagdhipanakrtollasarasanandavijrmbhanat
bhavayed bharitavastham mahanandas tato bhavet

When one experiences the expansion of joy, of the savour arising
from the pleasure of eating and drinking, one should meditate on the
perfect condition of this joy, then there will be supreme delight.
Vijnana Bhairava: Dharana 49

gitadivisayasvadasamasaukhyaikatatmanah
yoginas tanmayatvena manorudhes tadatmata

When the yogi mentally becomes one with the incomparable
joy of song and other objects, then of such a yogi,
there is complete union with that joy.
Vijnana Bhairava: Dharana 50

lehanamanthanakotaih strisukhasya bharat smrteh
saktyabhave'pi devesi bhaved anandasamplavah

O Goddess, even without the physical presence of a woman, there
is a flood of delight, simply by the intensity of the memory of sexual
pleasure in the form of kissing, embracing, pressing, etc.
Vijnana Bhairva: Dharana 47

It is not difficult to see that these interesting practices can go too far and take us into the realm of indulgence. But a sincere seeker can find ways to use his personhood, the quirks of his personality, as a vehicle to transcend the personal. The experience of pleasure is a taste of the Absolute, human love is a small sample of divine love.

Contemplation 13: Meditate on love

1. Think of someone or something you love in an uncomplicated and peaceful way. Alternatively, you can think of an activity or place you love.
2. Visualize that person (place, or thing) in your mind.
3. Let the feeling of love arise.
4. Drop the image and go deep into the feeling of love itself.

KEY IDEAS OF CHAPTER TWENTY:
BEGIN WITH THE LOVE YOU HAVE

*   Love is the most powerful force in the inner world.
*   The path of love is a classic path of yoga.
*   A meditator on the path of love cultivates and expands love.
*   We begin with the love we already have.
*   A sincere seeker can find ways to use his personhood, his personality, to transcend the personal and experience the Divine.
*   The experience of pleasure is a taste of the Absolute; human love is a small sample of divine love.

Chapter twenty-one:
QUESTIONS & ANSWERS

asanasthaha sukham hrade nimajjati
Established in meditation on the Self,
the yogi plunges into the ocean of bliss.
Shiva Sutras III.16

THE QUESTIONS IN this chapter were asked of me in my meditation courses or other public talks.

WHO IS SHIVA?

QUESTION: When you say Shiva, are you referring to the Hindu God Shiva?

SWAMIJI: There are marvelous depictions of Lord Shiva as the cosmic dancer or as the great meditator. He has cobras around his neck and the river Ganges flowing from his head. I admire them aesthetically, and respond to them symbolically, but I use the term Shiva in a different way.

The philosophy of Kashmir Shaivism describes Shiva as universal Consciousness. Shiva in this case refers to the inner Self, Awareness. It is the stillness underneath all thoughts and feelings. When the mind is calm, the Self emerges. We sense it. We feel it. We know it.

MANTRA AND MEDITATION

QUESTION: Can you explain how to use the mantra for meditation?

SWAMIJI: Om Namah Shivaya points us to the Self. We use it to focus the mind. When you say, "Om Namah Shivaya, Om Namah Shivaya, Om Namah Shivaya", to yourself, your mind might jump around. Your job is to keep saying: "Om Namah Shivaya, Om Namah Shivaya."

When your mind protests: "I am bored", your response is: "Om Namah Shivaya."

When your mind complains: "My knee hurts", your response is: "'Om Namah Shivaya, Om Namah Shivaya."

When your mind attacks you by saying: "I cannot do this", you sweetly say: "Om Namah Shivaya."

When your mind worries: "What am I doing tomorrow?", you calm it by saying: "Om Namah Shivaya."

It is not the end of the world if your mind wanders off. Accept it. Bring it back to the mantra. Do not bring it back violently. Calmly and lovingly return to the mantra. Do not attack yourself for what you think are your meditation failures. There is nothing worse than self-attack thoughts. Love your mind. Keep saying the mantra. When the mind wanders, keep going back to the mantra. Remember that you can always have the meditation you are having. That is the best meditation. Accept yourself and try to be content.

Remember that the mantra is a bridge to higher Consciousness. Even better: it is higher Consciousness itself in verbal form.

QUESTION: At what speed should I repeat the mantra?

SWAMIJI: Repeat it at a speed that feels comfortable to you. When my mind is active I speed up the mantra. I say the mantra forcefully. When the mind is quiet I say it calmly.

QUESTION: Are you actually saying it out loud or is it in your head?

SWAMIJI: The most effective is silently. If it helps, you can visualize the words. It is important to hold the mantra lightly in your mind. When you concentrate, do not strain.

BELIEFS AND MEDITATION

QUESTION: Do you have to believe in God in order to meditate?

SWAMIJI: Meditation is not about beliefs. Meditation transcends the world of belief. It goes beyond the world of the mind. Meditation is about *what is*. This reminds me of a story.

Once Mulla Nasruddin was ill and thought he was dying. He began to call out: "Oh God! O Satan! Oh God! Oh Satan!"

After a while a friend who was attending him asked: "Nasruddin, I could understand if you called out 'Oh God! Oh God!' I could even understand if you called out 'Oh Satan! Oh Satan!' But I cannot understand why you are calling out to both!"

"My friend," whispered Nasruddin, "I am covering all of the possibilities."

So "God" or "no God" exist in the realm of duality, the realm of the mind. The realm of deep meditation is beyond that. All contradictions are resolved there. If you are asking me personally, I have a constant experience of God as my inner Self. That same One lives within you also. He craves your *attention*, not your belief.

Sleep works no matter what you believe about it, and so does meditation. However, it is hard to believe that you would continue to meditate if you did not have faith that the universe is meaningful, that there is a higher purpose and a higher power.

WHEN YOU HAVE AN AGITATED MIND

QUESTION: Sometimes I cannot seem to control my mind. When it is like that, I feel like stopping my meditation and doing it another day. I feel like this saves me needless heartache. Am I wrong?

SWAMIJI: That is like quitting a round of golf because your ball has landed in a sand trap. On the contrary, playing from a sand trap is an integral part of golf.

In the same way, meditating with an agitated mind is an essential part of the practice of meditation. You will discover that your mind shows up in a different condition every time you sit to meditate. Your task is to work with what is. Even though it is much more satisfying to have a clear, one-pointed mind that easily goes deep within, it takes regular practice and perseverance to achieve such a state regularly.

An agitated mind is an opportunity to study the nature of agitation. Try to welcome the mind, in whatever condition it shows up, with detachment and a little humor: "Ah, anger, hello." "Aha, sorrow, welcome." Take the opportunity to study the condition that arises spontaneously rather than resisting it. Ask yourself, what chakra is affected? What is the nature of the underlying emotion? Can you discover any cause for the agitation? Think about recent interactions, even what you ate the day before. Many things affect the mind, it is important to discover them.

In this book I suggest a range of contemplations and methods to use in meditation. These are skilful means. Contemplate whether any of those skilful means appeal to you in your present agitated state. A method that you choose during any particular meditation should appeal to the mind. Force yourself to sit there, but ask your intuition what way might be interesting to tackle the agitated mind. By the way, I prefer the word "discipline" to the word "force". As I have said, force does not work. However, we desperately need discipline in every aspect of life. Understand this distinction: discipline is not cruel but is a manifestation of kindness and self-esteem.

Remember that if in the course of a meditation you succeed in quietening an agitated mind, or improving its condition slightly, you have achieved a formidable spiritual triumph. It will greatly strengthen your inner resources.

TANDRA: MEDITATIVE SLEEP

QUESTION: I was repeating the mantra in meditation and the next thing I knew, the timer went off. I had fallen asleep or gone blank. This happened a few times. What can I do about this? It also happens with the Chakra Meditation. I sometimes cannot get through the whole CD without blanking out.

SWAMIJI: This is the state of *tandra* or meditative sleep. It is a nice state to get into and will refresh you enormously. You may have visions in that state.

Meditation is like conscious sleep. It is at the crossroads where waking and sleep meet. That crossroads can be approached either through the land of sleep or the land of waking. Waking meditation will gradually become more peaceful, while tandra meditation will become more conscious. I think you will notice the state you describe is actually distinguishable from sleep in that there is more awareness.

I had a number of discussions with Baba about this issue, and he reassured me. Gradually I learned from my own practice that the state of tandra is beneficial. Your mind is becoming still and you are going deeper. It is good.

When I was in my teacher's ashram in India my parents came to visit. Eager to learn, they would rise early and meditate. One day my mother said to me: "An odd thing happens to me when I try to meditate. I go into a state where I am not awake and I am not asleep."

I said: "Mom, that is meditation."

"Don't be silly," she said, "I can't meditate!"

But of course, she was meditating and continued it for the rest of her life.

CONTENTMENT IN ADVERSITY

QUESTION: I have health issues which distress me. There is also some adversity in my life situation. I find it hard to practise contentment. Do you have any advice?

SWAMIJI: I do not want to minimize what a burden illness and other adversity can be. But, fundamentally, the state of contentment is an already existing inner state that can be accessed—at least in theory—under any condition. It is important at such times to make an effort to get in touch with the place of contentment within.

Sometimes we have to enlist our highest wisdom to accept or understand particular situations. When you do get in touch with the peace of the Self, it has a positive effect on the way you handle your difficulties.

Just as a good night's sleep makes it easier for us to deal with life, so a good meditation helps in a similar way. You may not be able to achieve complete equanimity at this stage of your development, but a little effort will help a lot.

THE MANTRA IN DAILY LIFE

QUESTION: I use the mantra in meditation with good results. I find my mind repeating it at other times too, but I worry that this might affect my ability to work and go about my daily business.

SWAMIJI: The mantra will not diminish your ability to handle things. On the contrary, it will help you by eradicating subtle anxiety. When you need full concentration on some task, let the mantra go. As I have said, the use of mantra outside of meditation (*japa*) is a time-honoured method of stabilizing the mind.

THINKING IN MEDITATION

QUESTION: I have always relied on my ability to think rationally and analyze ideas. I like my mind, but it seems to be too busy. Meditating quietly is almost impossible. I feel torn between stopping my mind and encouraging it.

SWAMIJI: I am a great believer in fitting your method to reality, rather than forcing reality to conform to your preconceptions. As I have said, the mind shows up in different ways each day, and each of us has different characteristics of mind. For this reason I have given a variety of techniques in the hope that you will find one or more that particularly make sense to you.

If you have a strong and active mind, you can sometimes use the period of meditation to work out problems and issues in your life. Many inspirations and understandings take place in meditation, and you can think more clearly.

It is important to use what you have learned from the Shiva Process Chakra Meditation. If you are exploring some life issue in meditation, always pay attention to the feeling. What does each idea or alternative feel like? Feeling will be your guide.

When you find the right solution there will be peace or energy. The Self will be pleased. Sometimes solutions are well hidden. Be patient. Do not force a decision. True understanding reveals itself little by little, in the fullness of time.

When the explorer Balboa first saw the Pacific Ocean, it became visible to him only when he got to the last hill. No matter how he strained before then, he could not see it. Yet, without knowing it, he was getting closer and closer. Maybe the animals, the climate or the smell of the air told him he was close to his goal.

Meditate patiently and let wisdom chase you.

Having said this let me add that your meditation should not always be in the realm of the mind. It is good to withdraw from your life issues and transcend.

Use the mantra or witness-consciousness to take you beyond the grooves your mind usually works in. But sometimes a crucial issue in your life will force itself on you in meditation and insist that you contemplate it. When that happens use the method I have outlined here.

AFFIRMATIONS

QUESTION: During meditation the other morning I was working with affirmations. When I repeated the statements "I am strong", "I am perfect", it did not have a good effect. They seemed to make me sad. What do you recommend?

SWAMIJI: Affirmations sometimes have this paradoxical effect. Sometimes when you affirm, "I am strong" another voice declares "No you're not!"

It is possible that your mind has a hidden negative streak. For now my advice is simple: if affirmations work for you and produce good feeling and a sense of empowerment, use them. If they seem to have a negative effect as you describe, stay with the mantra.

The problem arises when we try to forcibly overcome our negativity by doggedly being positive. You cannot put a filling in a tooth before the decay is taken out. You cannot paste a smile over sadness or anger.

As you become more experienced in meditation you will learn how to go to the source of the problem and root out the negativity. For now the mantra will be effective.

SENSITIVITY TO THE WORKPLACE

QUESTION: Since beginning to meditate, I feel better about myself and I have experiences of peace and self-acceptance. However my work environment seems more and more negative to me. I have worked hard to get where I am, but my work seems an agitated and unhealthy place. I feel like I will have to leave, but I do not want to.

SWAMIJI: It often happens that a meditator goes through a phase of extreme sensitivity. Sometimes other people's vibrations or emotions overwhelm him; sometimes job situations seem intolerable. These are actually good signs: they show that your intuition is opening up and you are seeing some of the subtle aspects of the life around you. They were all there before you meditated, but now you are becoming aware of them.

In my earliest days of practice I saw so much ego around me (others' and my own) that I felt I was in a nightmare. I wanted desperately to go to a cave and be by myself. Rightly, Baba discouraged this and showed me how to wage my inner battle while living with people.

Understand that whatever job you took you would eventually see the same things. When people are not meditators their unconscious anger and anxiety spill into the environment.

Let me tell you a secret: even if you lived in a pure environment, filled with avid meditators who are working on themselves, the same thing would happen.

Try to use your new insight to your advantage. Do not take on the anxiety of others; rather try to help others remain calm. Be sympathetic to others, while remaining clear that their emotions are their own.

After a meditator learns the art of attaining peace in meditation, the next task is to be able to bring that peace into daily life. If you feel overwhelmed by others' feelings you can take refuge in the mantra or practice witness-consciousness. Try seeing the world as the play of Consciousness.

In summary, before you think about looking for another job, see if you can improve the situation by inner and outer means at your present job. When you learn how to remember the Self at work you will be an island of calm, an inspiration and a beacon of light for your co-workers. They will gravitate to you and look to you for advice and solace. A few may ask you your secret. You can give them a wink, a knowing look and whisper—"I meditate!"

THE WORLD AND I ARE ONE

QUESTION: I often feel I live in my own world, separate from others. In the moment this seems impossible to overcome, but in the same moment I know that it is not. Please give me a method of dealing with this.

SWAMIJI: What you say is true to the extent that no one else can enter your inner world. It is the world only *you* move in. Other people are always outside; other people are objects in your inner world.

A sage I met used to say: "I like myself, so wherever I go, I like where I am." Our inner world colors wherever we go and whatever we do. If we make our inner world a garden of delight, and this is possible only through yoga, meditation and contemplation, then we become joyful!

The paradox is that the more you explore your own inner world the more connected you feel with everyone, the more you can see the Self in every other person. Behind the facade, behind the personality, behind the differences we are the same One. You can meet others more fully by turning inward. Go deeper and you will find that Oneness and that feeling of relationship.

SELF-ACCEPTANCE

QUESTION: I judge myself. I especially judge my angry and sad feelings when I think they are inappropriate. Please help me find a way to discriminate and uplift myself.

SWAMIJI: It is important to accept your feelings when they arise. It is also important to be responsible with negative emotion like anger and sadness. It is irresponsible to dump emotion, to throw it at those around you. However, it is repression to deny it.

In Self-inquiry when anger arises we simply say: "I am angry", or "I feel anger arising within." We try not to blame others or to throw anger at them. Neither do we deny it. We investigate negative emotion with the understanding that under *all* negative states like anger, fear or sadness, there is joy and peace. If you inquire deeply enough you reach the inner Self. Have faith that inquiry into negative emotion will lead you to peace. Peel the onion of every moment and you will come to the joy of the Self.

Anger is a distortion of peace. Fear is a distortion of peace. Whenever there is an unhealthy state that arises within you there is some distortion of understanding lying behind it. Yoga teaches us not to indulge bad tendencies and negative habits.

After I had been with my teacher two or three years I understood that the main issue in my spiritual practice was self-acceptance. I had to recognize and accept the different movements and quirks of my own nature. I saw that the greatness *and* the horror of humanity were within me in seed form.

It is important to learn acceptance; it is a form of humility. Do not expect yourself to be 100 percent perfect. When a person demands too much from himself or herself, they either berate themselves when they fall short of the ideal, or they cultivate a persona, a false image. A persona is designed to convince yourself and others that you are okay, but the effect can be different. I am not sure whether a false image or self-hatred is harder to undo.

Get rid of negative tendencies and bad traits but do not attack yourself. Cultivate self-acceptance and it will help you to be more objective. You will learn what is true and what is false about yourself.

FOLLOWING THE INNER ENERGY

QUESTION: I feel there is no moral right or wrong in the spiritual quest, one only has to be receptive to the inner energy, to be true to it, to honor it and follow where it leads. Could you talk about this?

SWAMIJI: In yoga we call this inner energy "Shakti". When you become attuned to the inner energy, then your awareness becomes sensitive to whether the inner energy expands or contracts moment to moment. You then move towards joy and peace and away from fear and anger.

It is not a question of right or wrong. It is not about morality. A person who is attuned to the Shakti will act appropriately and compassionately. Lovers of the Shakti are always looking to unblock energy and to expand love and wisdom.

OVERCOMING FEAR AND ANGER

QUESTION: I have great trouble controlling my anger. Do you have any suggestions?

SWAMIJI: Anger is frustrated desire. Examine it. Discover what it is about. Gradually, you will learn to control it.

If you feel overcome by waves of anger, use the mantra, *Om Namah Shivaya*. Try to stay detached. As you meditate you will gain control of it.

Some people are afflicted by anger and some by fear. Each of us is afflicted by one or the other and sometimes both. When we practise Self-inquiry, we discover that some people have a contraction in the navel, others a pain in the heart and others tension in the throat or in the third eye. Each of us has our own configuration. If we have a problem with anger, anger will seem insurmountable, but if we have a problem with fear then that will seem like the big one.

Through understanding, meditation and mantra repetition you will gain the tools, the skilful means to overcome your difficulty. Your mind will get stronger.

When you meditate you can ask questions like:

- What is the foundation of my anger?
- What am I angry about?
- Do I need to change my understanding?
- Do I need to do something?
- What is my greatest spiritual obstacle?
- Am I not hearing something I need to hear?

- What would be the best approach for overcoming or diminishing this anger (fear)?

Instead of seeking outside, turn within. Become still. Let an answer arise. Then ask:

- Does it feel good?
- Does it feel uplifting and true?
- Does this bring me peace?

You will get answers to some, if not all, of these questions. In the stillness of the Self there is wisdom, insight, understanding and compassion.

The inner world is not an alien realm. It is intimate and, at its core, friendly. Once you learn to navigate that world every entry into it will promise peace and relief from stress. You will look forward to your meditations and enter them with anticipation and excitement.

Do not waste the opportunity to develop yourself. The purpose of human life is to grow in wisdom and joy and to help others. Meditate for your own upliftment. Meditate for your loved ones. Meditate for the world. Meditate! Meditate! Meditate.

KEY IDEAS OF CHAPTER TWENTY-ONE: QUESTIONS AND ANSWERS

- Every time you meditate, your mind shows up in a different condition.
- Meditating when your mind is agitated is an essential part of the practice of meditation.
- Welcome the mind; study its condition.
- Inquire: Where do I feel this? What is the emotion? What is the cause?
- Techniques of meditation that uplift the mind are called "skilful means".
- Tandra is the crossroads where waking and sleep meet. It is beneficial.
- When some issue haunts you in meditation you can inquire into it.
- Pay particular attention to feeling.
- After a meditator learns how to attain peace in meditation, his next job is to take that peace into his life.
- Be sympathetic to others, but do not take on their emotions.
- Help others process their emotions.
- Be a beacon of light for your friends and co-workers.

Part 2

SHIVA VYAPTI
MEDITATION IN THE WORLD

Chapter one:

THE HIGHER POWER – EVERYTHING IS CONSCIOUSNESS

na shivam vidyate kvachit

There is nothing that is not Shiva.

Svacchanda Tantra

ONCE, TEN MEN went on a difficult and arduous pilgrimage to a holy city. At one point they had to make their way across a dangerous raging river. When they got to the other side they counted everyone to make sure they had all crossed safely. The leader counted first and discovered that only nine men had made it across. He then asked each of the other pilgrims to count. Sure enough each one counted only nine. They were plunged into grief at the thought of the one who had been lost.

A wise stranger came upon the scene and discreetly asked what had happened to elicit such an outpouring of grief. "We are pilgrims," said the leader. "There were 10 of us when we began our journey. One of our brothers has been lost in the river."

The stranger quickly noticed that by his count there were ten pilgrims. He asked: "Sir, would you please count everyone again just to make sure?"

"Yes," replied the leader who began counting aloud, "one, two, three...eight, and nine! Oh alas, one is gone!"

"But sir," said the stranger, "you have forgotten to count yourself!" And so, the tenth man was found.

Yoga philosophy says that we are in the same predicament. In our analysis of the world we look externally and leave out the key figure—ourselves. When we notice the Self and begin to explore it we become aware of the most powerful thing in the universe: Consciousness. We discover that in the most fundamental way, we are our own awareness.

In the process of my second education I made a study of every system of thought that inspired me. Particularly in the ancient philosophy of Kashmir Shaivism, I encountered ideas so powerful that they transformed my understanding. The essence can be given in a single sentence—"Everything is Consciousness."

The elaboration: Western science takes the view that everything is matter. Darwinian evolution shows a history of material change. Science, however, has a problem in accounting for Consciousness. It is an embarrassment. How did Consciousness suddenly spring into being? No material solution satisfies. Would Darwin say that Consciousness was a mutation that proved useful? This seems far-fetched to me. Consciousness is not a detail like the opposable thumb. The presence of Consciousness utterly transforms reality. Reality is *unthinkable* without Consciousness. Let us look at the viewpoint of Kashmir Shaivism.

Kashmir Shaivism says that, far from being a by-product of a material process, Consciousness, or *Chiti*, is the primary stuff of the universe. Consciousness, characterized by *iccha*, will and emotion, *jnana*, knowledge and *kriya*, the power to act, pervades everywhere at all times. There is no place, no time or person where Consciousness is not. A religious person would call that Consciousness "God," but according to Kashmir Shaivism, it is God without form that becomes all the forms in the universe. The name for God in this system is "Shiva". However, here Shiva refers to Universal Consciousness. A Kashmir Shaivite would regard the specific depictions of Shiva to be symbols of Universal Consciousness.

How does Kashmir Shaivism account for matter? Quite elegantly: Shiva, Universal Consciousness, in exploring his own possibilities, creates the universe out of his own being. He does not go outside of himself for building materials. Therefore, Consciousness itself is the substratum of matter. Matter is simply a grosser vibration of Consciousness. Kashmir Shaivism defines 36 levels of creation, from pure Universal Consciousness at the top, down to the dullest, least conscious object in the universe: the stone.

Love, peace, wisdom, complete fulfillment, freedom, mastery and perfect relationship characterize Consciousness. It *is* everything in the universe. A stone is cold, isolated, dull, but even a stone has divine properties too—it is strong, content in itself, reliable and long lasting, to name a few. It is perhaps superior to human beings in these last named qualities. A Shaivite would argue that these attributes reflect the divine *essence* of a stone. A Shaivite author wrote, "The Self is the sweet core of everything." Since a stone is the most inert object, every person, animal and object has Consciousness as its essence.

THERE IS NOTHING THAT IS NOT SHIVA

In this part of the book I will be describing a technique of Self-inquiry. We will investigate the blocks within our subtle body and try to understand how they came about. We will then release them by using tools I will describe.

Blocks appear because there are aspects of ourselves we have not examined or thought about with our conscious mind. We are *in denial* about them. Jung would say that we push them into our unconscious.

Such a state of affairs is intolerable for a meditator. He is determined to make the unconscious conscious, to bring everything into the light. Nonetheless, even for an experienced meditator, such an undertaking is fraught with danger. After all, who but us has created the situation? Inevitably there is an emotional reaction to changing it.

When window washers work dangerously high up on the outside of a building, they wear safety belts. People who perform the trapeze act in the circus have a safety net under them. Our net, our safety belt, will be the contemplation and understanding drawn from Kashmir Shaivism - "Everything is Consciousness."

I learned to meditate with this awareness. My teacher's instructions are filled with the spirit of this attitude. One example:

> Sit quietly and follow a natural breathing rhythm. Witness the different thoughts as they arise and subside in your mind. Let your mind spin as much as it wants. Do not try to subdue it. When thoughts or images arise, maintain an awareness of equality—the understanding that all objects are nothing but different forms of the Self. Even the worst thought is God.

> Your goal is not to battle with the mind, but to witness it. Know that you, as the Self, are the witness, and let the mind go wherever it likes. Eventually, if you meditate with the awareness that "Whatever is, is God", your mind will become calm and peaceful.

The *Svacchanda Tantra* says, *na shivam vidyate kvachit*, "nothing that is not Shiva exists anywhere". When we look at the world from a material point of view we see it wrongly.

Once a man was walking along a road. Suddenly he screamed out in terror at the sight of what he thought was a large snake coiled on the side of the road. He had a powerful fear reaction. His breath came in gasps, his blood pressure went up, and his heart palpitated. When he looked again he saw that it was not a snake at all, but a coiled piece of rope. Nonetheless his reaction, based on his mistaken belief, had been the same as if it were a snake.

All of us see a snake in a rope when we think that the universe is far from

God or Consciousness. We react in fear. We fear the future. We fear other people and situations. We feel alone. We feel a lack. We despair. We have the snake-in-a-rope reaction when we think the Universe is material, limited and indifferent. But is our reaction appropriate?

When the man looked again he realized his mistake. His fear left him. He laughed. His blood pressure and heart rate decreased. Exactly thus, when true understanding of our real situation dawns, we feel intense relief. We understand that there is nothing to fear and that the Universe is the play of Consciousness.

Kashmir Shaivism says that everything is linked to everything else by supreme intelligence. Nothing is separate or alone because the same Consciousness underlies everything. There are links and correspondences everywhere. The well-known saying "as above, so below" indicates these correspondences. Kashmir Shaivism similarly says, "as here, so elsewhere". When we evolve spiritually, we move towards oneness. This can show up as uncanny coincidences that affirm that a higher power is running things.

Many years ago, I experienced a particularly dramatic coincidence. Before going to India in 1970, I taught English literature. Later, my literary tastes changed and I became an avid admirer of the poet-saints, especially the 16th Century poet-saint Tukaram. I was thrilled by his extraordinary expressions of love for God. I was teaching at the Ann Arbor, Michigan ashram at the time and I planned to teach a course on his life and writings. We set a date and announced it. I looked forward to it with anticipation. The ashram community was also excited.

On the day I was to start the course I received an envelope in the mail, postmarked Dehu, India, Tukaram's hometown. Dehu is an obscure and dusty little hamlet in the state of Maharashtra. Inside the envelope was *prasad*, blessed offerings from Tukaram's temple. I was stunned. To appreciate this you must understand that, in my whole life, I had never before, nor since, received a letter from Dehu. Moreover, it arrived on the day I was to start the course! I felt that Tukaram was speaking to me across the centuries. That experience was, for me, a powerful confirmation of a higher intelligence that unites us all.

Of course, there was also a mundane explanation for what had happened. An acquaintance of mine was on pilgrimage to holy sites in Maharashtra. When he arrived in Dehu, he thought of my expressed admiration for Tukaram. He put some prasad into an envelope and sent it off. He had no idea I was teaching a course. It did not diminish the "Chiti-ness" of the experience for me. Chiti had surely orchestrated the timing.

When we meditate on supreme Chiti, we honor the playful, interconnected, harmonious and benevolent power that underlies everything, including our minds. When we perceive the mind as Chiti, it merges in the Self.

The sage Vasugupta said that in the inner world, "There is no word, no thought, no image, no idea, no state which is not Shiva." That is the core understanding of our Self-inquiry. With this understanding as our "safety-belt", we can easily inquire into our blocks.

Do this contemplation a few times until you get a feel for it. Then incorporate this attitude into your daily meditation.

Contemplation 14 : "All is Chiti, all is Consciousness"

1. Sit comfortably. Turn inside. Allow all thoughts feelings, sensations, memories, images, and so on, to arise without judgment or preference.

2. Contemplate: *All is Chiti. All is Chiti. All is Chiti. All is Consciousness.* Witness, accept and enjoy.

KEY IDEAS OF CHAPTER ONE:
EVERYTHING IS CONSCIOUSNESS

- Everything is Consciousness.

Chapter two:
THE CONTRACTION OF SHIVA

jnanam bandhaha

Limited knowledge expressed in thought or speech is bondage.

Shiva Sutras I.2

I F WE COULD truly understand "Everything is Consciousness" there would be no problem. But, like the man who saw a snake in a rope, we do experience a problem. How does this problem—the problem of suffering—come about? Shaivism says that Shiva, Universal Consciousness, undergoes a contraction.

The power of contraction is also part of the divine nature of Shiva. The force of *maya*, the cosmic illusion (somewhat similar to original sin in Christianity) has come into being. Maya confuses even Shiva, and he forgets his true nature. Where he once felt at one with the universe, he now feels weak and separate.

Shiva's powers now seem limited: his perfect will becomes our contracted will; Shiva's perfect wisdom becomes our diminished wisdom; and Shiva's perfect ability to do or create becomes our limited ability to do or create.

CONTRACTION OF WILL

If Shiva were to speak he might say:

- I am perfect.
- I am content.
- I am complete and whole.
- I have everything I want.

When Shiva or supreme Consciousness becomes the individual we say:

- I am imperfect; I am weak.
- I want; I need.
- Something is missing.
- I lack something.

CONTRACTION OF KNOWLEDGE

Where Shiva said:

- I know everything.
- My mind is one with Universal Consciousness.

Now we say:

- I know only a few things.
- My mind is separate from other minds.
- My mind is weak and small.
- I am confused.

CONTRACTION OF ACTION

Where Shiva said:

- I can do or create anything.

Now we say:

- I can do only a few insignificant things.

We could substitute the phrase the *Awakened Self* instead of Shiva, since it contains no cultural implications. Then our term for contracted Shiva can be the *un-awakened self*. When you unlock your Awakened Self in every situation you feel empowered and expanded. Science has shown that powerful energy lies hidden within matter and can be released by nuclear fission. It is also true that powerful inner world energy lies hidden within us and can be released by appropriate spiritual means.

SELF-TALK

Notice that I have represented all these contractions in the form of statements. In fact, *language creates and reflects the contraction.* Human beings hold limiting ideas at an unconscious level and are deeply affected by them. The above statements: "I am lacking something, I am imperfect" are held subtly. You could say that they are held on a cellular level. Only a profound spiritual process can uncover them. All of the great mystics underwent such a spiritual process to discover divinity beneath the contracting statements and limiting ideas they held deep in their minds.

Self-talk goes on in our minds all the time. The mind ceaselessly thinks and comments about everything that happens in the waking state. Even when we go to sleep, mental activity continues and takes the form of dreams. Self-talk can be positive or negative. It can expand us and make us feel joy, or it can contract us and make us feel as though we are living in hell. The essence of yoga, spirituality and Self-inquiry is to become the master of our self-talk. We have to discipline self-talk, not let it control us. The methods by which we can understand and transform our self-talk are meditation and Self-inquiry.

KEY IDEAS OF CHAPTER TWO:
SHIVA'S CONTRACTION

- The power of contraction is also a part of Shiva's nature.
- When Shiva becomes the individual he or she says: "I lack something."
- Language creates the contractions.
- Another name for Shiva is the Awakened Self.
- Contracted Shiva is the un-awakened self.
- Self-talk can be positive or negative.
- The essence of yoga, spirituality and Self-inquiry is to become the master of our self-talk.
- The methods by which we can understand and transform our self-talk are meditation and Self-inquiry.

Chapter three:

SELF-INQUIRY -
THE SHIVA PROCESS METHOD

Inquiry is the highest branch of yoga since it distinguishes
between what is to be rejected and what is to be chosen.
Therefore, the wise person should practise inquiry.
Abhinavagupta: Tantraloka, Chapter 4 Verse 15

WHEN I WENT to India in 1970 it was with the purpose of understanding my inner world. I wanted to be able to shift at will from negative states to positive states. Meditation taught me how to do that. In the mid-seventies my teacher instructed me to teach meditation and to create an ashram in Ann Arbor, Michigan in the United States. The ashram grew as seekers came. But as time went by I noticed that my students wanted to apply their spirituality to their outer lives. I began to wonder if there could be a more specific application of meditation to daily life. I asked myself the following questions:

- Can meditative awareness be maintained at work, in relationships and for health issues?
- Why do meditators sometimes have great success in achieving peace through meditation, but have a lot of trouble maintaining that peace in their outer life?
- Is it possible to combine Western psychological insights with Eastern meditative insights to create a harmonious way of living in both the outer and inner spheres?

By late 1974 I had some ideas I wanted to try out and I discussed some of these matters with my teacher. I approached our talk rather apprehensively. Some of his aides had told me that I should stick to conventional techniques since he would never approve of such a radical line of investigation. Instead, he seemed to have an immediate intuitive understanding of what I was talking about and emphatically told me, "Do it!" Then he said: "Whatever you do, I am behind you."

I felt inspired by his support, and over the years I contemplated my project and experimented.

It wasn't until the mid-eighties that I discovered the answer I was looking for lay in a contemporary version of a kind of contemplation called Self-inquiry.

Self-inquiry is a powerful method of meditation, which has been honed by ancient and modern sages as an instrument of Self-realization. Not only that, it is also a method which brings wisdom into the mundane arena of our daily lives. Proper use of Self-inquiry will revolutionize and enliven every aspect of life: career, relationships, health and spirituality. It is the secret technique of the yogi who lives in the world, and it gives him an enormous edge.

QUESTIONS: A POWERFUL FOCUSING DEVICE

Let us look at the term Self-inquiry for a moment. An "inquiry" is an investigation. Science, for example, is an inquiry into the laws of the outer world. Philosophy is an inquiry into a broad conceptual understanding of life and the universe. Biology is an inquiry into the laws of organisms, and so on. Thus, Self-inquiry is an investigation of the Self.

The word "inquiry" suggests that questions are at the heart of the method. We are familiar with the method of science which asks questions like, "What is going on here? How does this work? If I did this to it, what would the reaction be? What is this made of?" Philosophy might ask, "What does this mean? What is its significance or value?" A question uses awareness to inquire into a specific issue. Good investigators in any field know a lot depends on the art of asking the right questions.

Self-inquiry is a classical means of contemplation which uses questions to invoke the profound wisdom of the inner Self. Self-inquiry directs precise questions toward the Self, fully expecting valuable answers. We practise Self-inquiry informally when we ask ourselves questions like, "Should I go or not? Should I marry him or not?" When we become adept at Self-inquiry, we are less dependent on others to tell us what to do. We discover the valuable answers which lie within.

Questions are the most powerful of all investigative tools. A good question is like a laser. It illumines the subject at hand and creates a focus with a strong intelligent power. It starts a fire of understanding.

A distinction to understand is that there are good and bad questions. A good question advances understanding; a bad question is a diversion or a negative thought. For example: A golfer needs a par four to win the Masters. His second shot lands in a sand trap. A good question to ask is: "How can I get close to the hole from here?" Another good question is: "What kind of shot should I play now?" Or, "How does the green slope?"

Each of the above questions will evoke a useful answer. Bad questions are:

"Why does this always happen to me?" (The answer would be: "You are a loser."); "How could I be such a jerk?" (Answer: "I am an idiot, that's why!")

Bad questions get bad answers. They create negative thoughts and lead us away from being present to the problem at hand. They prevent us from being productive in the moment.

The Buddha used Self-inquiry when he sat down under the Bodhi tree and watched the images, thoughts and feelings that arose within him. He discovered that even though they appeared real they were in fact void or empty. Shankaracharya, and later the great modern sage Ramana Maharshi (1879-1950), inquired into the Self by asking powerful questions.

Ramana's Self-inquiry (*atma vichara*) is probably the best-known method. When he was just 16 years old he was overcome by a feeling that he was about to die. He lay down on the floor and contemplated a series of questions like: "If the body dies, will I die?" Within a half-hour his questions were answered by a permanent realization of the Self. His inquiry resolved into one question that became the core of his lifelong teaching: "Who Am I?"

When Ramana recommended the inquiry "Who Am I?", he wanted the meditator to eliminate all merely mental answers to that question. He knew from experience that the answer would dawn concretely in the form of an experience of the Self. Asking "Who Am I?" works something like the windshield wipers on a car. It wipes away mental formations to get to the clear expressions of the Self beneath them.

Western philosophers have done significant work on Self-inquiry also. In the 17th Century this inquiry led Descartes to the conclusion, "I think, therefore I am." Sadly, it did not go beyond the mind and fell short of the Self. But Descartes' achievement was enormous considering he was a solitary explorer in the inner world with no supporting tradition around him.

The contemporary sage Da Avabhasa developed his own method of Self-inquiry, using the question, "(Am I) avoiding relationship?" This is based on the following understanding: since the Self is everywhere and in perfect unity, a Self-realized person will experience a sense of perfect harmonious relationship with all beings and objects in the universe. Wherever relationship is not perfect, there is a contraction, a discomfort that flows from the sense of separation. Thus, in pursuing Da Avabhasa's method, the meditator examines contractions within and asks the question, "Am I avoiding relationship?" Since these contractions must be a turning away from the pure relationship to the inner Self, such an inquiry will restore the sense of easy relatedness.

In general we can say:

- Self-inquiry discards all mental formations and instead investigates what is present in awareness.
- Self-inquiry seeks to let go of tensions and disharmonies, not by replacing them with "higher" concepts, but by dissolving them.

I call the form of Self-inquiry I have developed *The Shiva Process*. It is a discipline which opens ordinary living to an inner spiritual dimension.

It could be said that in ordinary consciousness we have both eyes open, in meditation we have both eyes closed, while in the Shiva Process we keep one eye open and one eye closed. The goal of the Shiva Process is to allow us to be simultaneously aware of the inner world and the outer world. When you use the Shiva Process Chakra Meditation compact disc, you are practising Self-inquiry.

During my years of meditative training in India, I developed the ability to meditate myself into a serene and joyous state. Many of my fellow ashramites also developed this skill. This was satisfying, but I noticed something else. After we came out of meditation, people and events could still disturb us. Some of my fellow students seemed to use meditation as a tool to escape from the problems of life. Maybe they were thinking of meditation in the 1960s mode, "Meditation is a natural high." More and more I began to see that this was a limited understanding.

Events taking place in the outer world create a reaction in our inner world. Self-inquiry is a method by which we become extremely aware of the nature of our reactions. Often these show up as stress held inwardly either consciously or unconsciously. By inquiry we seek to discover the blockages and release them, creating inner harmony.

- Stress creates inner blockages that cause emotional suffering, mental confusion and physical disease.
- Our reactions are entirely subjective.

The same event can happen to 10 different people and there will be 10 different reactions. We have different expectations, different emotional types, different upbringing, different concepts, different values and different nervous systems. All of these influence the way we react to specific events and people. We are extremely sensitive reactive organisms.

- Some of our reactions are appropriate and helpful to us, while others are inappropriate in the sense that they create stress and unhappiness.

The great spiritual teachers of all traditions point out that it is our reaction that creates our suffering, not the events themselves.

The goal of meditation and spiritual work is to be able to live life with ease and openness. There should be a free flow of energy within. This expanded energy gives a feeling of blissful peace and radiance.

Events are simply events. It is always our reactions to them—our thoughts and feelings—that cause contractions. Some of these reactions are subtle. They are *unconscious*. We carry tension within our body without consciously being aware of it. Nonetheless, it will affect our sense of well-being. We may be irritable and cranky, frightened or depressed and not know why. Effective Self-inquiry can reveal the reasons.

- Blocked thoughts and feelings create blocked or inappropriate actions and communications.

Self-inquiry is designed to bring our reactions into focus and to shift them when necessary. It is, however, more than an awareness technique; it is also an action technique. Our thoughts and feelings are related to actions and communications in the outer world. The Shiva Process is particularly effective in discovering appropriate actions and communications to unblock stuck areas of your life.

KEY IDEAS OF CHAPTER THREE: SELF-INQUIRY—THE SHIVA PROCESS METHOD

- An inquiry is an investigation.
- Self-inquiry is a classical means to investigate the inner world.
- Questions are the most powerful investigative tool.
- There are good and bad questions.
- Self-inquiry discards mental formations and investigates *what is*.
- Self-inquiry dissolves tensions and disharmonies.
- The Shiva Process is a discipline which opens ordinary living to an inner spiritual dimension.
- The goal of the Shiva Process method is to be simultaneously aware of the inner world and the outer world.
- Our reactions are entirely subjective.
- Self-inquiry is an action technique as well as a focusing technique.

Chapter four:
WHAT ARE BLOCKS?

chitireva chetana padadavarudha
chetya sankochini chittam

Universal Consciousness becomes the mind
through the process of contraction.

Pratyabhijnahridayam Verse 5

LET US TAKE a few moments to consider blocks. If we have a blocked artery or a blocked colon, or a blocked drain pipe in our house, or even a blocked fuel line in our car, we know that some material blocks a channel from flowing. When we talk about the chakras, our subtle energy system, we are talking about the subtle realm, not the material realm.

A block is a contraction, a tension within the subtle body. It comes about because of our *reaction* to a person, event or possibility in our lives. In meditation we can focus on a block from inside.

A doctor can examine the body and identify the symptoms that indicate an illness may be present. In recent years medicine has developed instruments which can examine blocks from *inside*. A tiny camera can enter the intestine or the arteries and return an image that identifies the block. Meditation is like that.

If there is a problem in the plumbing in your house, the plumber will locate the block, analyse it and then make an intelligent effort to unblock it. Similarly, it is important to locate the subtle blocks within us, so that we can release them.

Let us pause to find a block. Do the following contemplation.

Contemplation 15: Chakra Check

Part I

1. Take a moment to survey your navel, heart, throat and third eye.
2. Find the chakra that is most blocked (or unpleasant, or uncomfortable).
3. Do it now. (1-3 minutes)

Welcome back. You have found your worst chakra. Did it surprise you? Were you aware of it before you contemplated? Is this particular chakra often contracted?

Part II

Ask yourself the following question and contemplate it for two minutes now.

1. "What is the block in my chakra made of?"

Welcome back. What did you discover? Was it fatty tissue, rust, leaves or sludge? No, of course not. Here is my answer: subtle blocks are contractions of feeling. Thus, blocks in chakras are contracted emotions. Underlying these blocked emotions are contracted thoughts. So the whole answer is, blocks in your chakras are made up of contracted thought and feeling. This is an important understanding and provides a key to our work.

The 11th Century Shaivite writer Utpaladeva said,

> *Although thought-constructs are mental representations of objects*
> *once seen or present, they are in fact, products of the power of*
> *Consciousness and not of the objects they represent.*

In other words, although we often confuse thoughts with what they represent, we can be certain that whatever arises in the inner world is *Consciousness* and not matter.

Part III

Now, go to your blocked chakra and contemplate, as follows, for the time allotted:

1. Say to yourself and consider: "This block is made of my own thought and feeling."(30 seconds)
2. Say to yourself and consider: "This is my own feeling caused by my own thought or attitude." (1 minute)
3. Say to yourself and consider: "This block is a reaction to something in my life. What could it be?" (2 minutes)
4. Ask yourself the following and let an answer come: "What do I need to do to release this block?" (2 minutes)

Note: The answer may involve an action in the outer world or the inner world. For example: "I need to quit my job", or "I need to forgive someone."

In general we can say that blocks come from two sources: the outer world or the inner world. Outer world blocks are based in the present or recent past and are the result of our reactions to people or events. Inner world blocks come from memory (conscious and unconscious) and are sometimes the result of early trauma and conditioning.

In this four-part contemplation you have been doing Self-inquiry. You may have received a useful answer to the last question. ("What do I need to do to release this block?") Even if you did not, it is always worthwhile to practise this exercise. As soon as we creatively focus on our inner world, new understandings flood in. It is as though a film of ignorance starts to melt.

After you have done this contemplation a number of times you can practise a shorter version:

Chakra check: Short version
1. Find your worst chakra.
2. Ask yourself, "What is this block about?"
3. Ask yourself, "What do I need to do to release the block?"
4. Ask yourself, "Do I need to do something in the inner world or in the outer world?"

Do this exercise any time you need to—that is whenever you feel blocked or "off".

Now, if our blocks are nothing but contracted thought and feeling, it stands to reason that by Self-inquiry we can get to the heart of the matter and untie those knots.

KEY IDEAS OF CHAPTER FOUR: WHAT ARE BLOCKS?

- A block is a contraction, a tension within the subtle body.
- Blocks are made up of contracted thought and feeling.
- They come about because of our reaction to a person, event or possibility in our lives.
- Or, they come from the inner world, from memory of the past.
- As soon as we creatively focus on our inner world, new insights flood in.
- By Self-inquiry we can get to the heart of the matter and untie knots.

Chapter five:

SELF-TALK

jnanadhishthanam matrika

Language is the source of limited knowledge.

Shiva Sutras I.4

matrikachakra sambodhaha

Enlightenment takes place through the power of inner language.

Shiva Sutras II.7

UNDERSTANDING CAN MOVE in two directions: towards the light and the Awakened Self or towards the limitation and bondage of the un-awakened self. At the heart of both lies the power of language. Kashmir Shaivism calls this power *matrika*, which comes from the same root as matrix and mother. It is the collection of all intelligible sounds, an ocean of all possible meanings. It is the creative power of the Divine. Shaivism agrees with the biblical assertion, "In the beginning was the word and the word was God...." God's linguistic act "Let there be light" underlies all manifestation. Shaivism also says that the manifest world comes from the power of language.

Matrika is active in everyone's inner world. It ceaselessly creates positive and negative ideas, images, impressions and memories and consequently different feelings and emotions. I call the matrika of each person *self-talk*.

Shiva is Shiva because of his perfect self-talk. A self-realized being has eliminated negative self-talk and disciplined his mind to speak to him positively. To move forward in the inner world we have to understand and transform our negative self-talk.

Blocks come from negative self-talk, hurtful mental and emotional habits and tendencies. We have acquired some of these tendencies from our parents and some from our culture. A mystic might say it also comes from negative tendencies developed in past lives. The origin of self-talk is not so important. It is more important to become familiar with self-talk in the present, especially self-talk which is harmful to us.

ACCURATE AND BENEFICIAL STATEMENTS

To begin our Self-inquiry we work with self-talk by using techniques I call **Accurate Statements (A Statements)** and **Beneficial Statements (B Statements)**.

- **A Statements** are *simple statements of present feeling*. They locate where you are now.
- **B Statements** are *possibly uplifting statements*. They serve to expand our self-talk and put us in touch with the higher Self.

You could say that **A Statements** reflect our individuality, while **B Statements** reflect our Shiva nature, the Self.

I am going to discuss **B Statements** in this chapter and **A Statements** in the next. In this I follow the lead of the Shaivite sages, who always gave the highest teachings first and did not work up to them by degrees. It is like being airlifted to the top of a mountain. If you can remain on the summit, great, if not, you will slide down to your comfort zone.

BENEFICIAL GREAT STATEMENTS

Beneficial Statements make us feel more harmonious and closer to the Self or God. Notice that I defined them by saying *possibly* uplifting statements. That is because **B Statements** do not work for everyone all the time. You can tell a true **B Statement** by its result—it causes an "upward shift," an upsurge of energy, a relaxation, and an insight. For example, consider the statement "I am worthy." This will act as a **B Statement** for some people, some of the time. However, sometimes it might have no effect or even a bad effect (a downward shift). When we search for **B Statements**, we search for those statements which uplift us in the moment.

The ancient Scriptures of yoga are nothing but collections of **B Statements**. They are arsenals of mental weapons to fight against the tendency of the mind to fall into, and wallow in, darkness and ignorance. The Upanishads give four *mahavakyas*, which summarize in a single sentence the essence of the highest teaching. *Maha* means great; *vakya* means statement, so it is not difficult to see the relationship with **B Statements** as I have defined them. One of the four great statements is *aham brahmasmi*, which means, "I am the Absolute". Here the individual soul, (*aham* = I am) affirms oneness with the higher Self (*brahmasmi* = the Absolute).

When I was initiated as a Swami of the Saraswati Order my teacher told me to contemplate the statement *aham brahmasmi*. I asked him if he meant that I should say it like a mantra. He said no, and demonstrated what he meant. He repeated the phrase and then mimed a wordless contemplation. He taught me that the proper way to contemplate was to silently utter the phrase once or twice and then let myself experience the space towards which the phrase points. Any statement we say or hear will call forth a feeling state within us. In contemplation we silently voice a **B Statement** to ourselves and then dwell on the feeling state that is evoked by it.

As I contemplated *aham brahmasmi* I became peaceful and still. I felt a subtle energy, a vibration of a gentle, yet unmistakable joy. As I continued my contemplation, I merged more and more into that experience. I found that as soon as I said the phrase, I contacted the experience. However, if my mind was agitated or obsessed I could not hold it for long. Every time my mind went away from the place of stillness, I would again repeat the statement and rediscover that space. Under normal conditions, with a little effort, I was able to quieten my mind.

I AM THE SELF

On a different occasion, Baba gave me another **B Statement** which is an English version of *aham brahmasmi*. At the time, I was in a struggle and felt blocked. I saw ego everywhere, in myself and in others. I went to Baba about it and he told me that I could make my ego work for me. This shocked me because I was under the impression that the ego had to be destroyed. He told me to contemplate "I am the Self" and not to think, "I am great" or "I am a sinner." He said that to contemplate "I am the Self" was a healthy channel for the ego.

I learned a lot from this interchange. I understood that both praising and criticizing the ego-self only strengthens it. Identifying with the Self, however, was appropriate and liberating. At first glance this might appear dangerously inflating. Nevertheless, when we affirm "I am the Self", we are not making a comparison with others. We are "not less than" or "greater than", but…"one with". Wisdom tells us that everyone is the Self. To contemplate in this way carries us beyond the ego-self.

The ego-self is a movement of the Self which has made a wrong identification. The ego-self forgets "I am the Self" and says, "I am this body". It identifies with career, status, wealth and the myriad manifestations involving us in life. In this identification, the Self becomes smaller. Shiva becomes the individual, and the divine condition of unlimited joy becomes human suffering. When we contemplate, "I am the Self" we return to our true and original condition.

A scientist might say that I had a "paradigm shift"—my spiritual model changed. I understood that the Self was not something I had to create, construct, or realize after long travail. The Self is the substratum of everything we do and think, every minute of our lives. *The Self is the ever-present reality that can be contacted whenever we give it our attention.*

My notion of my spiritual journey changed. I was no longer climbing the mountain to reach a distant summit. Now I was at the summit and hanging on while the gale winds of my mind tried to blow me off.

Contemplation 16: "I am the Self."

This contemplation works brilliantly to calm the mind.

1. Close your eyes and turn within.
2. Bring in the thought "I am the Self". Repeat it gently like a mantra and let your mind focus on it.
3. As you repeat it, let the words trail off. Watch where they take you.
4. Notice your inner feeling. Does it change? Is there a response? Where does the response come from? Is there a response from the navel, the heart, the throat or the mind?
5. If your mind wanders away from it repeat, "I am the Self" until concentration is restored.
6. Let the space of the inner Self expand. Rest in that space.

In the path of Zen the master often wakes up the student by cryptic instructions, or by manifesting odd behavior or even hitting him with a stick. This technique is used to "blow the mind", to get the mind out of habitual grooves so the Self can manifest. In our inner world too, such "lateral thinking" is sometimes useful. You never know what can cause an upward shift, an enlightening experience.

The teachers of the wisdom path often tell us "You are not what you think you are." The emphasis here is on *think*. We create our ego personality with our thinking about ourselves. If we think differently we *are* different. We need to adopt a divine rebelliousness when we say, "I am the Self," that is we can refuse the conventional view that our friends and we hold. I have used a Zen-like version of "I am the Self" with equal success. It is the contemplation "I am not who I think I am." Try it.

Experiment and see what works for you. Each of us will resonate with different contemplations. Work with the one that inspires you, or uplifts you the most. Remember that we are learning to follow upward shifts.

KEY IDEAS OF CHAPTER FIVE:
SELF-TALK

- Blocks come from negative self-talk.
- To move forward in the inner world we have to transform our negative self-talk.
- In Self-inquiry we work with two kinds of statements: **Accurate Statements (A Statements)** and **Beneficial Statements (B Statements)**.
- **A Statements** are statements of present feeling. **B Statements** are possibly uplifting statements.
- The great statement *aham brahmasmi* affirms oneness with the universe.
- Praising or criticizing the ego-self strengthens it.
- Contemplating "I am the Self" is liberating.
- The ego-self is wrong identification.
- The Self is the ever-present reality that can be contacted whenever we give it our attention.

Chapter six:
WHEN YOU'RE HAPPY
SAY YOU'RE HAPPY

Aham sukhi ca duhkhi ca raktashca ityadisamvidah
sukhadyavasthanusyute vartante'nyatra tah sphutam

Thoughts like "I am happy; I am miserable,
I am attached" and so on, are strung together and seem to arise from
each other, in fact, they arise from Consciousness.

Spanda Karikas I.4

A S YOU MEDITATE you will discover that meditation sometimes carries a special grace. At other times your meditation may feel "dry". You may be in one phase or the other. Honor whatever is happening to you; do not compare yourself with other people. Do not let your mind trick you by devaluing your own process. Eventually you will see that in the realm of inner growth everything happens at the right time and in the right way.

Meditation and inquiry are subjective processes so we have to avoid the disease of looking at others and imagining that they are "doing it right" or "doing it better". True, they look serene sitting in their meditation with that little half smile. Be assured everyone has a struggle. Besides, if your friend does become the next Buddha, there will be one more person to help you! Meditation is not a competition. Let your meditation practice expand and let your understanding grow. There is no doubt that you will reach the goal.

What kind of inner world do you want? It is your choice. In expanded states you are in contact with the Self. In contracted states you are far from the Self. Yet, even then the Self is close at hand. By skilful means, by meditation and Self-inquiry, you can prevent the mind from contracting and encourage it to expand. That is yoga; that is spirituality; that is happiness.

A STATEMENTS: WHEN YOU'RE HAPPY, SAY YOU'RE HAPPY

A number of years ago I had a vivid meditation experience which was a defining moment in the creation of the Shiva Process. In my meditation I felt as though I were sitting in the presence of my teacher. The thought came to me that this was an opportunity to ask him a fundamental question, the answer to which could transform my understanding. I thought carefully about how to phrase the question. Finally I asked, "Baba what is the secret of freedom?"

He looked at me deeply, eyes twinkling and said: "Do you really want to know the secret of freedom?"

"Yes Baba," I answered.

"When you're happy, say you're happy," he said, "when you're sad, say you're sad. When you're scared, know you are scared. When you're angry, say you're angry. When you feel proud, know you're proud. This is how to be free."

When I came out of meditation, I felt uplifted and slightly confused. Intuitively I knew I had heard something profound, but I needed to contemplate it. Over the years, those words have echoed in my mind. Gradually, I understood that Baba was teaching me the value of what I now call **A Statements** or **Accurate Statements**; simple statements of present feeling like: "I feel sad. I feel happy. I feel angry. I feel nervous. I feel proud." A shortcut to trace inner tension is to ask: "Am I mad, sad, bad, glad or scared?" Such simple statements prevent us from believing the mind's complex "stories", which do nothing but increase our confusion. When the mind, in its capacity to invent and complicate, takes us far away, becoming aware of how we feel in the moment brings us present.

A STATEMENTS (ACCURATE STATEMENTS) ARE NOT THE OPPOSITE OF B STATEMENTS (BENEFICIAL STATEMENTS)

A human being has a dual nature. The 18th Century poet Alexander Pope described it wittily in *An Essay On Man*:

> (Man) hangs between in doubt to act, or rest,
> In doubt to deem himself a god, or beast;
> In doubt his mind or body to prefer,
> Born but to die, and reasoning but to err;
> Alike in ignorance, his reason such,
> Whether he thinks too little, or too much;
> Chaos of thought and passion, all confused;
> Still by himself abused, or disabused;
> Created half to rise, and half to fall;
> Great lord of all things, yet a prey to all;
> Sole judge of truth, in endless error hurled;
> The glory, jest, and riddle of the world!

Indeed, we are caught between two possibilities, and **Beneficial Statements** help us choose and move toward our divine nature. Through insight, wisdom, discipline and the correct use of our wills, we can choose the higher over the lower, joy over suffering. An **A Statement** is not really the opposite of a **B Statement**. An **A Statement** is a "simple statement of present feeling". A statement like "I am angry" or "I am scared" already has a great deal of truth-value. Often we do not know or will not admit how we feel. Instead, we allow negativity to become the fuel that spins a web of deluded thoughts. When we make an **Accurate Statement** like, "I am angry," or "I am scared", it cuts through the illusion and brings us to the present. An **A Statement** *is a reality check.* Present feeling is always valid and puts us in touch with what is real, while thoughts can lead us away. **A Statements** and **B Statements** are both highly desirable.

The act of telling the truth has two parts to it. We have to first of all *know the truth* and second, *decide to speak it.* If we are not actually in touch with the truth then whatever we say will be distorted by the underlying feeling, however much we want to speak the truth. If we are angry then anger colors what we say. If we are depressed, the "truth" we speak will be a depressed truth. Hence, the **A Statement** helps us know the truth and also acknowledge the feeling in the moment.

If a **B Statement** uplifts us and brings us closer to the Self, to our divine nature, its opposite is a thought that increases our misery and leads us far from the Self. I call such thoughts "ego-based" thoughts. There are two kinds of ego-based thoughts: falsely expanding thoughts or *inflating thoughts* and contracting thoughts or *tearing thoughts.*

INFLATING THOUGHTS

Inflating thoughts are arrogant thoughts that can seem like **B Statements** but are based on ego. They imply building up the ego falsely by comparison with others. They result in an inevitable crash into tearing thoughts in the future.

Some typical examples of inflating thoughts are:

- I know it all.
- I can get away with anything.
- I am better (smarter) than everyone else.

Once there was a gathering in the court of a great king. All the nobility and high officials took their respective places according to protocol. Into this resplendent scene came a shabbily attired hobo. He boldly sat among the peerage.

A page quickly went up to him and politely said: "Sir, pardon me, but this section is reserved for the nobility."

"Oh," said the hobo, "I am higher than that, much higher."

The page startled by this reply, said with biting irony: "Sir, only the king is higher than the nobility. Are you perhaps the king?"

"I'm higher than that," said the hobo, "much higher."

"I see," said the page, "but sir, only the Pope is higher than the king. Are you the Pope?"

"Higher," replied the hobo, "I am much higher than that."

"Umm," retorted the page, "only Jesus is higher than the Pope—are you He?"

"I am higher," answered the hobo, "much higher."

"Really," scoffed the page, "as far as I know, only God is higher than Jesus. Are you God?"

"I am higher," said the hobo, " much higher."

By now truly exasperated, the page snapped: "Nothing is higher than God!"

"Yes!" exclaimed the hobo *"I am that nothing."*

All the scriptures warn us against the dangers of pride and the comforts of humility. True humility, in fact, helps us participate in the nature of the divine because we do not become hard and resistant. We more easily flow with the movement of life.

My first spiritual mentor, the American teacher Ram Dass, used to call the spiritual path "nobody training"—it was an antidote for all our training to become "somebody", which only strengthened our ego. He threatened to run for president with the slogan "Nobody for President" and the affirmation, "Nobody loves you".

Certain personality types will be very given to inflating thoughts, but I think the particular problem of our time is the other variety of ego-based thoughts which I will discuss in the next chapter: tearing thoughts.

KEY IDEAS OF CHAPTER SIX:
WHEN YOU'RE HAPPY SAY YOU'RE HAPPY

- A true **A Statement** leads to awareness of present feeling.
- When you're happy say you're happy.
- When you're sad, say you're sad.
- Ego-based thoughts are of two kinds: inflating thoughts and tearing thoughts.
- Inflating thoughts are arrogant thoughts that may seem like **B Statements**, but are based on ego.

Chapter seven:
TEARING THOUGHTS

*The world is heaven for one whose mind
is pure and noble, in spite of all hardships.
One who is master of his mind becomes great and glorious.
The master of the mind is the one whose mind is steady.*

Swami Muktananda

MY TEACHER USED to tell a fable about a man who was traveling through a bleak and dry landscape on a hot day. Without knowing it, he sat down to rest under a wish-fulfilling tree. He began to brood about his difficult journey and what would make it easier.

"My mouth is dry, I wish I had a cold drink," he thought. A cold drink suddenly appeared in his hand.

"Wow," he thought, "I am hungry, I wish I had a nice meal too!" Immediately a sumptuous meal appeared.

"This is terrific," he thought, "but I am too hot, I wish I had an air conditioned mansion." Bingo! He was transported into a cool room in a mansion.

"Fantastic," he laughed, "now if only I had a beautiful girl to share all this with." Instantly the girl of his dreams appeared.

"Wait a minute," he thought, "What is all this? Where is it coming from? It might be a ghost!"

A ghost suddenly appeared. "Oh no," he screamed, "It's going to eat me up!"

It ate him up.

This is a wonderful bit of fantasy which does not overstate its teaching point: it is the mind which gives abundance—it is the mind which eats us up. The Self is indeed the wishing-tree, and the hell or heaven of the life we lead reflects the hell or heaven we create within our minds.

I would call the thoughts that created the ghost "tearing thoughts". A tearing thought is the worst kind of self-talk. Tearing thoughts are like red-hot arrows tearing into our own hearts. They undermine our self-esteem and scare us. They are full of self-hatred. They make us feel hopeless and fill us with despair. They sap our confidence and zest for life. They bring about depression.

I think of tearing thoughts as a design flaw in human beings. If God is listening, I would like to ask Him to please correct this flaw when He creates the next universe! The mind is quite remarkable and so helpful. It helps us do our work. It helps us conduct our relationships. It helped Shakespeare write his plays. It assisted Einstein in his work and theories. Yet, sometimes it turns against us and savagely attacks us with tearing thoughts.

What would you do if your beloved dog periodically went berserk and viciously attacked you? You would have to get rid of him. Like that dog, our friendly, helpful and loveable mind suddenly begins to snarl and bite us with no advance warning. Unfortunately, we cannot rid ourselves of our mind. We have to learn to live with it. We worry about what our enemies are saying about us. Is it not ironic that there is a voice within our own head which attacks us? It speaks to us in ways every bit as bad as our enemies, and worse! I never cease to be amazed by this. Thus, it is important to learn everything we can about tearing thoughts with a view to defusing them.

Here are some typical tearing thoughts:

- I am worthless.
- I am unlovable.
- I am destined to fail.
- I am a loser.
- He (she) is better than I am.

It is not surprising that when such thoughts play in your mind, you will have a downward shift of feeling. Thought and feeling always go together—as a horse and carriage and love and marriage. Positive thoughts create happiness; tearing thoughts create depression. Sometimes the thoughts are unconscious, that is, outside our conscious awareness. However, if we are depressed we can safely assume, "tearing thoughts are in the neighbourhood". Knowing this, we can search for them and find ways to dissolve them. After all, thoughts are only energy.

A few years ago I watched a BBC television program called The Master Game. It showed chess matches between top grandmasters. The players shared their thoughts and calculations as play unfolded. One match was between the then World Champion, Anatoly Karpov, and a lesser grandmaster. The difference between their inner processes was fascinating.

Karpov was completely focused on the game. He simply calculated different variations: "If I go here, he goes here, then I go here and he goes there—that is good for me. If he goes there and I go here, then he goes there and I go here— that is good for him. I choose the first."

However, his opponent let worry and extraneous negative emotional elements influence him. "Oh, my God, I am playing the World Champion! He is such a strong player, what chance do I have? He will easily beat me. His plans are so subtle!" and so on. A significant portion of his energy was wasted in tearing thoughts and worry. He lost clarity and Karpov won easily.

When you feel depressed, assume the presence of tearing thoughts. Instead of going through the day with an underlying feeling of depression, it would be much better to sit down as soon as you can, resolve it and shift it. If you do not do that, the depression will color all the interactions and experiences of your day. It will create a negative momentum. The day will deteriorate, or at least the music of depression will cast its discordant tones over everything.

Let us assume that you are vulnerable to certain tearing thoughts which arise under stressful conditions. The first step in conquering tearing thoughts is to *identify* them and turn them into **A Statements**.

For example, the tearing thought *"I am a loser"* takes you down the primrose path to your "I am a loser" thinking groove. You remember: *"Yes! That is right. I remember that French exam I failed. I remember the time I took that girl on a date and she would not kiss me good night. I remember that business venture that went under. Everything I do turns to dust. Richard is so successful. Tom is so suave, so handsome and so competent."* By now you are thoroughly depressed and lost in a whole cluster of bad memories that confirm your assertion, *"I am a loser".*

Tearing thoughts lie. They are a powerful seduction. It is important not to get involved in their downward spiral. The simplest way out is to make an **Accurate Statement**. Instead of "I am a loser," say, "I feel sad," or, "I feel hopeless." The virtue of an **A Statement** is that it does not lead to waves of negative self-talk but points to the experience of *present feeling*. The mind is not encouraged to feed on its negativity.

If there were only **A Statements**, we would be constantly going up and down according to the vagaries of the mind. Fortunately, there is the other self-talk I call **B Statements**. **A Statements** are accurate statements of present feeling, **B Statements** are "possibly uplifting statements." They cause an upward shift—they make us feel better, more harmonious and closer to the Self or God. With attention and effort, tearing thoughts can be resisted and overcome. One who conquers his tearing thoughts becomes more God-like than human. Observe them, fight them, and overcome them.

HOMEWORK

Contemplation 17: Self-observation: tearing thoughts

Everyone has tearing thoughts yet few pay much attention to them. We assume they are true. Now, I would like you to observe your tearing thoughts as follows:

- What tearing thoughts arise?
- Under what conditions?
- How often?

If you feel depressed, a good statement is to say to yourself, "tearing thoughts in the neighbourhood." Search for the tearing thoughts underlying your feeling of depression. Merely identifying them in this way is the major step in overcoming them. You can amuse yourself when they arise by saying, "Ah, tearing thoughts!" to yourself. Tearing thoughts hate humor—they want to make you feel contracted, small, heavy and tragic. Try this while you are meditating and while you are going about your daily business. If you find yourself in a stressful situation and you become aware of tension, look for the tearing thoughts. They are there.

TEARING THOUGHTS INTO **A STATEMENTS**

Turn your tearing thoughts into **A Statements**. Instead of following them into anger, fear or depression, *make a simple statement of present feeling*. Use the following statements as a guide to discover your present feeling. Ask yourself:

Question	A Statement
Do I feel depressed?	"I feel depressed."
Do I feel angry?	"I feel angry."
Do I feel worried?	"I feel worried."

When you hit on the right one you will feel a sense of relief. Remember: mad, scared, sad, glad or bad. This simple exercise will be empowering.

KEY IDEAS OF CHAPTER SEVEN:
TEARING THOUGHTS

- When our mind turns against us and attacks us we are having "tearing thoughts".
- Tearing thoughts are our worst spiritual problem.
- If we are depressed we can assume there are tearing thoughts in the neighbourhood.
- The first step to conquering tearing thoughts is to identify them.
- Turn your tearing thoughts into **A Statements**.

Chapter eight:

THE QUICHE

*atah satatam udyuktah spanda-tattva-viviktaye
jagradeva nijam bhavam achirenadhigacchati*

*The person who is on the alert for Spanda, the upward shift of
energy, attains the Self in ordinary life in a short time.*

Spanda Karikas I.21

A NUMBER OF years ago during the third lesson in one of my meditation classes, a woman shared two stories. In one story she was triumphant but the other was a comic tragedy. She was delighted to tell us that the previous week she had accompanied her husband on a short trip. As the plane came in to land, there was considerable turbulence. She was always nervous about flying at the best of times, and the degree of turbulence now made even the experienced crew look worried. But now she took refuge in the mantra she had received in the course, and was completely calm and even blissful during the whole event. Her husband had a much worse time than she did, and was amazed at her calm. He softened towards her practice of meditation and began to ask her respectful questions.

The comic tragedy had happened to her in a bakery a few days after the plane trip. Although it was intensely disconcerting for her, it was good luck for me. I have told this story many times since it illustrates important points about meditation in the world, in a way that *everyone* can relate to.

Magda (an alias) wanted to buy a quiche. When she entered the bakeshop she noticed a quiche on display and no one in the shop. The proprietor must have been in the back of the store. She waited. After a little while another woman strode into the shop. Seeing that the proprietor was not visible, the new woman rang the bell. The owner came out. He asked: "Who is next?"

The other woman said: "I am." Magda said nothing.

The proprietor asked: "What do you want?" (Reader, can you guess the rest of the story now?)

The woman said: "A quiche." The proprietor wrapped it up. The other woman paid and left.

He turned to Magda and asked: "How can I help you?"

"I would like a quiche," said Magda.

"I am sorry, that was the last one," said the shop owner.

Magda went into a fury. She went home and snapped at her husband. She dumped anger on her children. By the time she got to meditation class, she had begun casting racial aspersions at the other woman. She was a living demonstration of the un-awakened self.

After some discussion, I asked the class what the Buddha would have done in Magda's place. One man gave a great answer: he said the Buddha would have said: "Madam, I was here first, but I can see you are in a great hurry. Therefore, you can go first, but *I reserve that quiche*!" We agreed this would have been a perfect blend of compassion and wisdom. By now Magda was able to laugh about the situation.

Most of have us have been in similar situations. It is not easy when someone violates polite behavior and jumps in ahead of us. We can have "un-awakened" responses of two kinds: we might not speak up, like Magda, or we can react emotionally and angrily, out of proportion to the situation.

In a later class one of my students said that he had once unwittingly been the other lady! He had been in a teashop in England and people were standing around in a desultory fashion. He walked boldly up to the counter and ordered his cup of tea. Only later did he realize that those people were waiting in a queue, English style. How many crazed and frustrated tea drinkers he left in his wake, he did not know. Perhaps several of them complained to their meditation teachers!

Let us spend a little time with the story, because it can give us some insights. It is useful to look at it step by step:

Waiting for the proprietor

Comment: An "empowered" person is *on purpose*. Magda was on a mission to buy a quiche. Coming from her Awakened Self, she would have rung the bell and summoned the proprietor. In this event I imagine her to be vague and preoccupied. Of course, she could have been in any of a number of internal states, but I would wager she was in her un-awakened self. That state is characterized by a lack of focused energy, decisiveness, dynamism and joy.

- A POSSIBLE **ACCURATE STATEMENT**:
  I am Magda - *I am daydreaming; I am confused.*
- A POSSIBLE **BENEFICIAL STATEMENT**:
  I am Magda - *I am here to buy a quiche, let me get on with it!*

Enter the other woman

Comment: This woman is on purpose: she radiates her intention. We always know when someone is trying to get ahead of us! Even if Magda were lost in reverie or fantasy, a part of her would have been present to the other woman's intentions. Magda might have felt hopeless and disempowered and thought: *"This is the story of my life, it's happening again!"* She might have felt frightened and thought, *"She's too powerful I cannot do anything about what is happening."*

- POSSIBLE **A** STATEMENT:
  I am Magda - *I feel scared. I feel shocked.*
- POSSIBLE **B** STATEMENT:
  I am Magda - *This woman has awakened me. I can act. I can speak.*

The woman claims to be first

Comment: This is the crucial moment. Why doesn't Magda speak up? A frog is in her throat. Why? She may be shy; she may feel on her back foot (unable to act effectively). I think she felt an upwelling of anger and feared to dump it or she was afraid she would burst into tears. She was disempowered by her own intense reaction.

- POSSIBLE **A** STATEMENT:
  I am Magda - *I am angry. I am scared.*
- POSSIBLE **B** STATEMENT:
  I am Magda - *I can speak the truth without anger. "Madam, I was here first."*

Out goes the quiche

Comment: As in a Greek tragedy, the inevitable happens. Magda is on a downward spiral. Once a downward spiral begins it is hard, but not impossible, to save the situation. Opportunities to save the situation by skilful means exist at every stage. The quiche is gone, but Magda's inner state can be salvaged. It is important to see that the latter is far more important than the former.

POSSIBLE **A** STATEMENTS:

I am Magda ...

- *I am furious.*
- *I am angry with the woman.*
- *I am angry with myself.*
- *I feel sorry for myself.*
- *The quiche has been taken.*

POSSIBLE **B STATEMENTS:**

I am Magda ...

- *I give up my attachment to quiche.* (Renunciation).
- *Well, wouldn't you just know it?* (Irony.)
- *I can get something else.* (Flexibility.)
- *I can go to another bakeshop.* (Strength of purpose.)
- *That was a good lesson to learn.* (Life is a great teacher).
- *That quiche was not destined for me.* (Humour, wisdom).
- *That quiche was probably no good or too fattening.* (Everything happens for the best).
- *That quiche was an illusion.* (Vedanta).
- *What quiche?* (Zen).

Any response that did not lose energy, and put Magda in touch with her Awakened Self would have been suitable. Remember: whatever works is appropriate.

I recently read of a computer virus that enters your computer through email. It immediately sends 50 contaminated messages to people on your address list. Imagine the ripple effect! In the same way, the quiche had its own ripple effect. When Magda went home she was impatient and cranky with her family. They would have had no idea what was underneath her anger. In turn they felt victimized and angry themselves. Many bad communications took place leading to hurt and resentment. If Magda could have made a simple **A Statement** (*I am angry*), and if she had resisted the temptation to dump her anger irresponsibly, the downward spiral would have stopped.

Once two Zen monks were crossing a river. An attractive young woman asked if one of them could lift her across. The younger one said: "Certainly not, my vows preclude my touching a woman."

The older monk simply picked her up and carried her across the river. The two monks walked on in silence for some time. Finally, the younger one spoke: "I cannot get over the fact that you carried that woman across the river. Have you no sense of propriety, no self-discipline?"

The older one asked: "What did I do when I reached the other side?"

The younger one answered: "You put her down."

"Exactly," said the older monk, "And *you* are still carrying her!"

Proper mind culture includes the ability to let situations go when they are over and when you cannot change them. That Magda was still carrying her upset days later is not an auspicious sign. It is likely that what happened was not a one-time incident, but rather reflected some deep-seated tendencies in Magda. However, by working with meditation and self-inquiry Magda could eventually gain victory over the tendencies of her un-awakened self.

DAILY REVIEW

The analysis we made of the quiche massacre is a useful model for a daily review. Take a few moments to replay portions of the day just before sleep. By paying attention to the tensions in the chakras and searching for appropriate **A** and **B Statements** you can discover many hidden things and solve dilemmas. You can also let go of any toxic residue of the day.

KEY IDEAS OF CHAPTER EIGHT:
THE QUICHE

- An empowered person is on purpose.
- The un-awakened self is characterized by a lack of decisiveness and dynamism.
- Un-awakened responses lead to confusion and anger.
- We tend to victimize others when we become involved in quiche-like situations.
- Opportunities to save the situation by skilful means exist at every stage.
- Proper mind culture includes the ability to let situations go when they are over.
- Do a daily review before sleep to release the tensions of the day.

Chapter nine:

HOW TO DO SELF-INQUIRY

hridaye chittasanghattad drishyasvapadarshanam

When the mind becomes one with the heart,
the true nature of the world is perceived.

Shiva Sutras I.15

I N ONE OF the *Pink Panther* movies, Peter Sellers' bumbling French detective, Inspector Clouseau, searches a room looking for clues. He trips over himself and knocks over furniture and lamps while muttering about the next clue. In the course of five very funny minutes the whole room is destroyed. Inevitably Clouseau also loses his pants. No one else is in the room, and it is as if a room full of inanimate objects has risen up to attack Clouseau. Of course, it is all his own doing.

That scene rises above slapstick to make a metaphysical statement about how we defeat ourselves. Like Clouseau, Magda created the quiche tragedy herself. Although she continued to blame others, her own tearing thoughts and disempowerment were the source of the event.

One of our most essential spiritual goals is to eliminate tearing thoughts. Have you been able to ferret out the tearing thoughts which lie hidden within a bad mood? When you become familiar with the pattern of your tearing thoughts, you will be convinced of how pervasive and malicious they are. It will inspire you to go to war against them.

My dear reader, do not let your tearing thoughts depress you to the extent that you want to give up your inner quest. Please remember the most powerful divinity lives within you. It is easily attainable through meditation and Self-inquiry. In the Bhagavad Gita, Shri Krishna tells Arjuna: "Be a yogi, Arjuna, and fight!" We, too, have a yogic battle to wage. There is no human endeavour nobler or more important!

If you could eliminate, or at least substantially defeat, your tearing thoughts, you would be utterly transformed. You would be a new person, full of confidence and peace. The spiritual masters in all the traditions are men and women who have overcome their tearing thoughts.

It may be that Self-inquiry sounds complicated when you read about it. While it reveals an enormous amount about the mind and the Self, its technique in practice is simple and straightforward.

Accordingly, I will devote this Chapter to a practical illustration of Self-inquiry in action, which should help you grasp it better.

PHILOSOPHICAL BACKGROUND OF THE SHIVA PROCESS METHOD

The form of Self-inquiry I will describe is the same as the one I use in the Shiva Process work. So far we can summarize the tenets of Self-inquiry in this way:

- Supreme Consciousness, or the inner Self, is concealed within each person, object and experience.
- That Self is unknown to us because of contraction due to wrong understanding.
- Our experience of the Self is diminished by the tendencies of ignorance, fear, desire, anger and grief.
- We can discover the Self within by inquiry and meditation.

Through Self-inquiry we discover that the contraction of the Awakened Self that we all experience is nothing but the result of the self-talk going on within us all the time.

The way we speak to ourselves in our inner world is crucial to our experience of our lives and ourselves.

Negative self-talk underlies all states of contraction; positive self-talk is the key to all states of expanded awareness and joy.

Contemplation 18: Doing Self-inquiry

1. Close your eyes and survey your chakras.
2. Notice the area of greatest contraction.
3. Inquire into that contraction.
4. Ask yourself, "What is the emotion?"
5. Then: " What might have caused it?"

You may feel a strong feeling, or the face of someone may pop into your mind, you may remember an event from yesterday or 10 years ago. If you stay with it a message will arise from your inner world.

---

6. Make an Accurate (A) Statement

Remember, an **Accurate (A) Statement** is a simple statement of present thought and feeling. Instead of focusing on the "story" - "He/she did this to me.

I hope that will happen. I am afraid that might happen. I don't like X. X doesn't like me" - look deeply into what the feeling may be. Ask inwardly: "Is this feeling anger? Is this feeling sadness? Is this feeling worry? Is this feeling fear?"

You will come up with your own statements which may ring truer than the ones I am giving here. That is as it should be. Work with your own statements and you will discover how much innate wisdom lives within you. Sometimes pictures accompany these statements and that helps you discover what is causing the block, tension or stress.

Look for the statements which seem true. You discover what is true by noticing if there is a sense of relief or peace after the statement has been made. Peace follows **Accurate Statements.** There is an automatic response from the inner Self. The statements that increase the tension or stress should be discarded for they are not the truth in this moment, even though they could be true in the next.

Now that you have made an **Accurate (A) Statement,** you have reached your bottom line: you have stated your experience as an individual in this moment.

Always remember that behind your contracted or blocked experience of the moment, you are unobstructed Consciousness and bliss, you are in essence the Awakened Self.

To move from awareness of the contraction to expanded joy you can:

---

7.   Make a Beneficial (B) Statement

Beneficial (B) Statements are "possibly uplifting statements". There is a great fund of **B Statements.** Some are scriptural like "I am the Self; Aham Brahmasmi, I am Brahman; I am Shiva. I am in touch with the Awakened Self." Some **B Statements** are psychological like "I am OK, you're OK."

Accurate Statements are related to our personal reality, **Beneficial Statements** are connected to our higher reality. They put us in touch with grace or divine Consciousness, which is marked by an uplifting and expanded feeling.

Some **B Statements** are noble, some philosophical, some practical and some of them quirky and humorous (laughter at least temporarily removes your contraction); it is important to find one or more that work. **B Statements which** work cause an upward shift, that is, they make you feel better, more expanded, closer to your Awakened Self. Energy moves through you, your spiritual circulation is improved. It can be boiled down to this: *say something to yourself that causes an upward shift.*

8. Be satisfied with a "Shift."

Self-inquiry is not meant to "fix" you, or psychoanalyze you. It assumes that your real nature is your divine nature, your Awakened Self. Therefore, once a shift has happened, let that be enough for the present session. In your relaxed and free condition, go about the business of your life, remembering that you are the Awakened Self. Be constantly vigilant for your reactions which make you lose that awareness.

Look at events in your life the way we looked at Magda's tragic farce in the bakeshop. Such events are mirrors, reflecting our inner condition. Are you losing energy and aliveness in characteristic ways? Can you find skilful means to empower yourself? This is yoga; this is Self-inquiry. It makes sense to strive to live in such a way that your joy, your awareness, and your energy are at a maximum.

Continue to observe your tearing thoughts and your reactions to events in your daily life. You might want to keep a record of significant observations and insights.

SUMMARY OF CHAPTER NINE: HOW TO DO SELF-INQUIRY

- Tearing thoughts are hidden in a bad mood.
- Supreme Consciousness, the Self, God, or Shiva is concealed within each person object and experience.
- Wrong understanding hides our true nature.
- The way we speak to ourselves in our inner world is crucial to our experience of our lives and ourselves.
- Negative self-talk underlies all contracted states.
- Make **Accurate Statements.**
- Make **Beneficial Statements.**
- Be content with a shift.
- Always remember: your real nature is the Awakened Self.

Chapter ten:

TELL THE TRUTH, DON'T GET ANGRY

katha japaha

Even the casual conversation of a yogi
becomes as powerful as a mantra.

Shiva Sutras III.27

I N THE GREAT epic the *Mahabharata*, the young princes studied archery with the famous archery guru, Dronacharya. In ancient India, instruction in a particular art or skill was not limited to the techniques of that art alone but involved discipleship. The student would be trained in self-discipline, surrender, meditation and self-knowledge. The teacher would develop him morally, ethically and spiritually, as well as in archery, music or whatever skill was involved. A young archery student, for example, might spend long periods when he never touched a bow, but listened to teachings and served his teacher.

One day Dronacharya told the class: "My lesson for the day is 'Tell the truth; do not get angry.' Contemplate this and come back when you have mastered it." The princes wrote the lesson down and went off to consider it.

The next day all the princes except Arjuna arrived on time for class. Arjuna, of course, is a main hero of the epic. Later he would gain everlasting fame as the disciple who questions Sri Krishna in the dialogue of the *Bhagavad Gita*. Chapter Six of the *Gita* is called the *Yoga of Meditation* and is one of the most inspiring texts in the whole field of meditation. (See Appendix 3.) Dronacharya asked them: "Can I take it that you have mastered my last lesson, 'Tell the truth and do not get angry?'" The princes agreed that they had. Their lessons continued.

Days passed, but still Arjuna had not returned to class. After a week Drona sent for him. When Arjuna appeared he asked him why he had missed so many sessions.

"My revered teacher," Arjuna said, "you told us to contemplate 'Tell the truth and don't get angry.'"

"That is correct," said Drona.

"But," Arjuna said, "you also said that we were not to return until we had mastered it. So far I have only mastered, 'Tell the truth....'"

Dronacharya smiled: "My son, it is indeed easier to learn to tell the truth than not to get angry, and your fellow princes have not even learned that much."

He turned to the other students: "Learn from Arjuna, this is not a lesson to be mastered in one day. You have not demonstrated your cleverness, only your dishonesty!"

Communication moves between the two poles indicated by "tell the truth" and "don't get angry".

The sage Patanjali lists *satya* or "truth" as one of the essential virtues to cultivate. He says that if a seeker cultivates satya, all his words will come true. Someone who tells the truth is comfortingly reliable. In the old story, the boy who cries "wolf" too many times when there is no wolf loses all credibility. He is not believed when there is in fact a wolf. By lying, his words have lost power.

In any event, lies are hard to sustain and usually get exposed. Once Fatima, Mulla Nasruddin's wife, bought two kilos of meat from the market. During the night Nasruddin became hungry. He cooked and ate all of the meat. The next day when Fatima set out to prepare dinner she found that the meat was missing.

"Nasruddin," she asked, "Where is the meat?"

"The cat ate it," he answered.

Fatima went and got the cat and put it on the scale. It weighed exactly two kilos. *"If this is the cat,"* she said, *"where's the meat? If this is the meat, where's the cat?"*

On the other hand, we have the phrase, "the harsh truth, the brutal truth". We have the notion that too much truth of a certain kind will be more than we can bear. It will shake us, hurt us, and leave us distraught. Hence Patanjali lists *ahimsa*, or non-violence, as one of his cardinal practices. Gandhi, and later Martin Luther King, made ahimsa famous in the political realm. In the highest sense truth must always be accompanied by kindness, or it is no longer truth. At least this is the ideal.

TRUTH AND KINDNESS

From the point of view of perfect communication there must be a blend of truth and kindness. Some of us err on the side of truth, we say too much, too harshly. We hurt others with our bluntness, though often we do not know why or how. Some of us err on the side of kindness. We say too little, and do not speak up for ourselves appropriately. We want to keep the peace and please others at any cost to ourselves.

The goal of Self-inquiry in the realm of human communication could be summed up as a balance between truth and kindness. It is noticeable that in those situations in which there is more "truth" than kindness, the atmosphere is charged with a subtle anger and a feeling of hurt and fear. In situations in which there is more "kindness" than truth the atmosphere is filled with a somnolent boredom, a sense that nothing real is being said, only polite chitchat. The former situation is alive and electric, but painful; the latter one is calm and non-threatening, but dead and boring. A clever student of mine pointed out that **Accurate Statements** represent truth and **Beneficial Statements** represent kindness.

Sometimes anger masquerades as truth ("I am just being honest..."); sometimes weakness and fear masquerade as kindness ("Yes, we'll do it your way..."). Only through a profound Self-inquiry can we come to the point of balance.

Magda had not reached that point of balance in the bakeshop. Her false "kindness" (based on fear) did not really keep the peace; it later boiled up as anger that was vented at innocent members of her family and herself. The Tao of truth and kindness is attained when we say what we need to say with a quiet strength and energy characterized by compassion. We do not need to express our words with anger to make ourselves heard, nor do we need to choke down what we have to say, for fear of upsetting someone.

JUDGMENT

The Bible tells us to "Judge not lest we be judged". Jesus told the crowd that wanted the prostitute's blood, "Let him who is free of blame cast the first stone." We intuitively recoil from a person who takes a "holier-than-thou" attitude and condemns someone from a moral high ground. Judgment is a problem because it is anger masquerading as truth. There is self-righteousness and superiority behind it. In many works of literature our sympathies go to the all-too-human "sinner" rather than the self-righteous judge. Hindu folklore tells us that when we point an accusing finger at someone, our other three fingers point at us.

While I was in my teacher's ashram, I was plagued for a period by my own judgment. Looking around me, what I saw in minute detail was that every ashramite was lacking in understanding, discipline or effort. I felt I was being "objective", but I was really practising character assassination. I was burning and suffering in my own anger. One day as I stood in the courtyard I contemplated the situation. The thought came that far from being sinners, these people were great souls who had given up their comfortable and prosperous lifestyles to rough it in India. They were searching for truth. Why did I judge them so harshly? In that moment I clearly saw that my vision was skewed. I prayed silently to see with new eyes.

Miraculously, *in that moment*, I felt a powerful force, more intense than a mood shift, rise up within me and transform my awareness. I was uplifted and ecstatic. I was lifted out of judgment mode, and what I saw before me was suddenly a divine scene. The bell rang for the next program and I did my job, which was to hand out the texts for the chanting session. I chuckled inwardly, because I knew that while things might appear normal to other eyes, I was handing out the books to gods and goddesses! The experience lasted several hours. I had been given an unmistakable demonstration of two things: how my attitude and judgment affect my own experience, and the extraordinary power of true prayer.

JUDGMENT TO VALUES

Although judgment in the sense I have described is cruel and hurtful, it can be used in a positive way. The novelist Ken Kesey used to say that it is important to look at the donut and not the hole: the positive not the negative. Judgment is a negative spin on your deepest held underlying values. In the story I have just told I said that I judged that my fellow ashramites lacked *understanding, discipline* and *effort*. This judgment is "truth" vitiated by anger. By softening it with kindness I discover that *understanding, discipline* and *effort* are my values:

- I value understanding: it is the noble goal of yoga.
- I value self-discipline: by its means happiness is attained.
- I value spiritual effort: it is necessary and rewarding.

Interpreting my judgment in this way, I arrive at a helpful conclusion.

Contemplation 19: Judgments to values

1. Sit down and turn within.
2. Think of a person about whom you hold judgments.
3. Contemplate the qualities you dislike.
4. Ask yourself: "What is the positive or opposite quality of my judgment?"
5. Then say, "I value _____."

While this is somewhat unpleasant, it is a good way to discover your values in a concrete way. Judgments expressed in a positive way are values. For example, if you judge a person as lazy you might say, "Industriousness is good" or "I value hard work." If you judge a person as self-centered and insensitive you might say, "It is important to be open and sensitive to others."

This process is an interesting form of Patanjali's teaching, "meditate on the opposite." It will help you *stand for* something rather than merely being against someone or something. It will bring kindness to your truth.

KEY IDEAS OF CHAPTER TEN:
TELL THE TRUTH AND DON'T GET ANGRY

- Harsh truth is not really truth.
- Weak kindness is not really kindness.
- The goal of good communication is to combine truth with kindness.
- Judgment is a negative spin on our deepest values.

Chapter eleven:

PROXYING

prabuddaha sarvada tisthej jnanenalokya gocaram
ekatraropayet sarvam tato anyena na pidyate

Seeing oneness everywhere and realizing the Self is in everything,
the awakened person lives without fear.

Spanda Karikas 3.12

MEDITATORS OFTEN TELL me that they have become much more sensitive to the subtle play of feelings in interpersonal relations. They sometimes discover that their work situation, for example, has become painful because of their new awareness and sensitivity. But even if new meditators go through a phase of intense sensitivity, it is surely not good for them to become less able to cope with life than before.

- Meditators should develop so much insight and skill that they become much better at handling things arising in their lives.

A meditator will be more aware than other people. He or she will sense underlying currents of anger and fear in situations in which others may feel anaesthetized. Learning the technique of proxying will allow him to function in such circumstances, and even to help others.

I discovered the technique of proxying a number of years ago when I received a phone call from a certain person. He called me often, but I always tried to keep the conversations short. I found them unpleasant. In fact, I noticed people generally avoided this man because he seemed to broadcast bad feeling. His words were positive and "spiritual" on the surface, but contained dark, unprocessed feeling and subtle currents underneath. This lack of self-awareness made people feel strangely manipulated by him.

On this occasion, when I hung up the phone, I discovered I was carrying a bad feeling. I was annoyed at him, and my first impulse was to want to send this feeling, which I was sure had been transmitted by him to me, back to where it belonged. Instead, I had an inspiration. I immediately sat down and did the Shiva Process with the feeling as though I myself were that man. I made **A Statements** from inside the feeling. I felt as though I was discovering his real thoughts. I suddenly saw that the reason people found him so unpleasant was that his words were broadcasting the tearing thoughts that he held. Some of them were: "I am unlovable. No one cares about me. Pay attention to me. Help me." His **B Statements** were: "Please give me your love. Please spend time with me." Within a minute of making these statements, the bad feeling left me through the crown of my head. Later he commented that he had been helped by our conversation.

Instead of sending his unpleasant feeling back to him, which would be to reject him, I had accepted him by accepting his feeling. I sent it on to higher Consciousness by processing it within me.

It is debatable that we actually (as people claim) "take on" the feelings of others. But remember that feeling is a vibration in the subtle body, and if we are open in general, or at least open to a particular person, we may vibrate in sympathy to his feeling, *whether we want to or not*. This often causes anger in a relationship, when one of the partners is in a bad mood. Next time you feel that you are "taking on" or being infected by the feeling of another, try proxying rather than escaping. You may find it a revelation.

Proxying can be done in a variety of situations. Certainly, it can be done as just indicated when you have been affected by the feeling of another. It can also be used when it might be valuable to enter another person's point of view. Be aware that to proxy properly you have to be *in sympathy* with the person that you are proxying.

Think of proxying as entering the other person's inner world. Statements like "I am Alex and I feel lonely and unlovable" are much more appropriate and sympathetic than statements like, "I am Alex and I have a lot of ego needs". The second statement does not sound much like something from Alex's inner world, but rather it sounds like judgment from someone else.

Contemplation 20: Proxying

1. Think of a recent situation where you were aware of another person's unpleasant feeling.
2. Say: "I am X (the other person)." Let the thoughts and feeling manifest.
3. Note where the feeling arises, in which chakra.
4. Ask yourself: "What is the emotion?"
5. Become aware of the kinds of thoughts accompanying the feeling.
6. View the feeling as though you were actually X and make **A Statements.**
7. Let the feeling flow up and out of you. **B Statements** can be made, but are often not necessary.

You can have surprising results by proxying institutions, animals, buildings and nations as though they were persons, as well as people. Shaivism says that the Self is the core of everything, so everything has its own self-talk.

KEY IDEAS OF CHAPTER ELEVEN:
PROXYING

- Proxying is a way to clear feelings received from others.
- Make A **Statements** as though you were the other person.
- Make B **Statements** as though you were the other person.
- Turn the feeling over to Universal Consciousness or God.
- To proxy well you must be in sympathy with the other person.

Chapter twelve:
FOUR WAYS TO DEAL WITH A DIFFICULT SITUATION

Siddha svatantrabhavaha

*A great meditator lives his life
with freedom and creativity.*

Shiva Sutras III.13

A DIFFICULT SITUATION is one which creates tension. This is subjectively defined. A difficult situation for you may not be one for me. For most of us buying a quiche would be a neutral or even a pleasant situation. For Magda, it was unpleasant to a most remarkable degree. A meeting, a party, an encounter will have a different impact on each of us. Nonetheless, it is certain that everyone experiences tension-producing situations.

We cannot avoid the unpleasant or difficult. Motivational trainers lecture that life can and should be an endless flow of enthusiasm, dollars and successes. But, in the face of serious or chronic disease, for example, it would be foolish and uncompassionate to suggest there is an easy solution. The Buddha left his kingdom when he saw that disease, old age and death were unavoidable. But remember that Jesus was spiritually triumphant during his terrible death by crucifixion. When we have such a "cross to bear" we must call on the Self and move closer to it. There will always be inner resources if we seek them.

In a situation that is more fluid we do have choice. There are four ways we can (and do) handle a bad situation.

1. Leave It

A certain type of person will naturally, and quickly, leave an unpleasant situation. While this is right sometimes, at other times it solves nothing. An old friend of mine used to leave town when things started to get uncomfortable. He would go to a new place, get a new job and find a new girlfriend. For a few months he would be in bliss. Then he would begin to feel tense and uncomfortable as his boss and girlfriend became aware of his less attractive traits. He would say: "I do not like it here, it would be a lot better in Berkeley or Santa Barbara."

In the new place the pattern would reproduce itself. Eventually, he began to see that it was more than likely that the problem was in him.

People who leave situations as soon as they become unpleasant tend to be decisive action-oriented people. This is certainly a good quality, but sometimes there is a lot to be gained by persevering in order to understand yourself more fully and to arrive at the right solution.

Indecisive people tend to stay in difficult situations too long. They do not act until circumstances force them. They would rather hurt themselves and endure pain than upset others.

It is important not to perpetuate hurtful situations by denial, neglect, a misguided sense of duty, clinging, inertia or greed.

We should not be like Mulla Nasruddin. Nasruddin once visited a foreign city. When he got there he felt hungry and went to the market to buy something to eat. He noticed a lot of people ordering a beautiful green fruit. "That must be delicious," he thought and purchased two dollars worth. He sat down next to the road to enjoy his meal.

A while later a friend walked by. He saw Nasruddin eating. Tears were running down his cheeks and he looked miserable. "Nasruddin, what are you doing?" the friend asked.

"Oh friend," replied Nasruddin, "I am eating your popular local fruit. But I must say that it has 10 times more fire than my wife. How do you people eat it?"

"Nasruddin," exclaimed the friend, "that is not fruit, that is a bag of chillies! You only use a tiny bit in curry to spice it up."

"Ah!" said Nasruddin, "Now I understand this mystery. I never knew that." And he went back to eating the chillies.

"Nasruddin, why are you still eating them?" his friend asked.

"I paid for them," retorted Nasruddin.

It is surprising how often, for one reason or another, we are like the Mulla. We eat chillies. We suffer and cry and yet we continue to eat them. Sometimes we just have to stop.

We can leave a difficult situation too late, too soon, or at the right time. On the other hand, some "bad" situations should not be left at all. An adjustment is necessary.

2. **Change the Outer**

For many of us this alternative will be the most natural. If something is wrong at work we talk to the boss, or reorganize the office. At home we try to change our spouse or children, bring in more discipline or communication. On the macro level we try to change society or the government. While this is sometimes effective often it is quite frustrating. Some situations and people will not be changed no matter how hard we work at it.

There are times when taking outer action is valuable and appropriate. Through effective communication and the use of other skills, just the right change is brought about that relieves us of tension. We should be aware, however, that sometimes our efforts are doomed to failure. It is a great waste of energy to try to move an immovable object, or to be upset that it is immovable.

I know two women who spent years trying to change the way their husbands related to them. During the whole time they were under a lot of stress. Both of them eventually had breakthroughs leading to significant relief. One of them employed number (1) above and left her husband. The second one employed number (3) below....

3. Change Yourself

The latter woman went through a period of deep soul searching and contemplation. She began to see that the problem was in the way she *thought* about her relationship with her husband. She saw that he was the way he was and would only ever be different in detail, not in essence. In meditation she realized that she needed to forgive him and accept him. Peace and joy returned to her life and her relationship.

This third alternative is extremely valuable, yet little used. We have much more control of our inner world than of the outer world. Now that we are meditating we can discover when our thoughts and emotions are out of alignment and make appropriate adjustments. We learn to relieve tension in our inner world. If tension is not relieved an explosion is inevitable. That explosion can take the form of violence or ultimately a physical or mental disease.

Let me emphasize that each of the first three solutions can be appropriate or inappropriate. It is a matter of using subtle discrimination to find out which. For example, some people who are afraid to leave a situation will stay in it thinking they are working on their attitude and trying to accept it. They think that if they just tried harder things would be okay. But there are situations which are too hurtful to accept. In such cases, speaking up or leaving is perfectly appropriate.

If your hand is in a fire, no amount of work on your attitude is going to help. You must take your hand out of the fire. But if it is just that your room is getting too hot you can turn down the heater, or ask someone else to.

4. Do Nothing

Many of us do nothing when faced with difficult situations. Let me correct that: we do one thing, and that is whine. Complaining is one of mankind's vices. In rare cases complaining can bring acceptance. However, most of the time it is disempowering. Our complaints are like a broken record that endlessly repeats itself. We leak energy and stop our life from moving forward.

It is common to hear someone complain about a person who is not present. We do it ourselves! "Behind the back" complaining is a result of a block in communication with the third person: we cannot be heard or we cannot express properly. If you find yourself habitually complaining to others about an important person in your life, read this chapter carefully.

The urge to complain is a sign that you have not been able to express yourself effectively. When communication is blocked we become toxic with fear and anger. This is how we become disempowered.

Since we do not want to be stuck in number (4) it is important to deal effectively with bad situations by finding the appropriate solution.

The tensions you discover while meditating come about because of bad situations of one type or another. As you meditate you will discover these areas of tension and you will become more and more clear about what causes them. Instead of running away from the stresses of life or hiding them with drugs or alcohol, investigate them. The fruit of your investigation will be a solution which relieves the stress and creatively handles problems.

THE PATH OF ENERGY

From an inner point of view my discussion of the four ways is about the path of energy. Among all the choices and possibilities in our lives, some have energy and some do not. The art of skilful living involves consistently seeking the choice with dynamic positive and expansive energy and avoiding choices where energy is blocked and negative.

The Shaivite text *Spanda Karikas* says:

ataha satatam udyuktaha spanda-tattva-viviktaye
jagradeva nijam bhavam achirenadhigacchati

The person who is on the alert for Spanda, the upward shift of
energy, attains the Self in daily life in a short time.

Spanda Karikas I.21

This can be tricky at times because our minds and expectations might go in one direction and the testimony of the energy might go in another. At such times we have to surrender our preconceptions and our preferences. We hone in on the energy.

The *Spanda Karikas* continues:

> *yam avastham samalambya*
> *yadayam mama vakshyati*
> *tadavashyam karisye'ham*
> *iti samkalpya tishthati*

> Taking hold of the energy, the awakened yogi firmly resolves,
> "I will surely do whatever it (the energy) tells me."

The way to walk the path of energy is through vigilance and by asking questions like:

- What choice has the most positive energy?
- Does this choice uplift me?
- Is some surrender or letting go necessary here?

To live with such vigilance, pay attention to your inner experience of life from moment to moment. Seek the *upward shift* of energy with the faith that such an upward shift is proof that your choices are correct. Examine your life in this spirit. Meditate in this spirit. A person who commits to the expansion of inner energy finds that the whole universe supports his life.

The following contemplation is valuable in life situations. It can be the key that opens the door of relationship or career. If you have a block or tension in one of these areas try the following:

Contemplation 21: Dealing with a difficult situation.

1. Turn within and contemplate the blocked or tense situation. Ask inwardly, "Is this a relationship issue? Is it work related? Is it a spiritual block? Is it a health issue?"

2. Notice the images, feelings and thoughts that arise when you ask the questions.

3. Ask: "Do I need to *say* something to someone? Who?"

4. Or: "Do I need to *do* something in this situation? What?"

5. Or: "Do I need to *drop* something or *get off* something. Anger? Fear? Jealousy? Pushing?"

6. If the answer is "yes" contemplate whether your communications are free of anger, blame or other negative emotional colorings.

7. Are you using subtle force to control or convince someone? Be scrupulously honest with yourself. If you find such "forcing energies", eliminate them: try to find a way to say what you need with genuine kindness.

---

8. Imagine the situation from the other person's point of view.

9. At the end you can try **B Statements** like, "I patiently await the outcome. I accept what is. I surrender to the Higher Power. I allow the energy of the universe to sort it out." You can discover your own uplifting statements.

10. Let your mind and heart speak to you about the situation. You can imagine writing to the person, or saying what you need to say to the person.

11. Find a way to communicate your ideas without blame, with a peaceful and gentle voice.

12. If you find after a deeply honest inquiry that there is no possibility of such an expression, you may have to leave the situation. But only after examining all the possibilities. It is beneficial to seek the counsel of an objective third party.

13. Do not neglect prayer as a means of communication to the Higher Power in such situations.

THINKING MEDITATION

You may wonder about my emphasis on contemplating life situations. Isn't meditation about stilling the mind and not about thinking? Meditators discover that it is very difficult to still the mind during periods when some aspect of their outer life is very turbulent. They sit to meditate and try as they may to focus on the Self, their problems keep coming up forcefully. The temptation is strong at such times not to meditate or, alternatively, to forcibly suppress the mind. I recommend neither of those solutions. Instead use the period of meditation for productive thinking. Think deeply about the situation, considering various alternatives and perspectives. Keep part of your awareness on your feeling. Look for upward shifts: they are clues your thinking is moving in the right direction. In the same way downward shifts show your thinking is moving in the wrong direction. Such "thinking meditation" is very much in the spirit of Self-inquiry and can be extremely productive when external concerns assault you during meditation.

KEY IDEAS OF CHAPTER TWELVE:
FOUR WAYS TO DEAL WITH A BAD SITUATION

- A bad situation is one in which we feel a tension, a disharmony.
- There are four ways to deal with a bad situation: change it, change yourself, leave it, or do nothing.
- The first three ways can be empowering or disempowering; the last one is disempowering.
- In times of turbulence use "thinking meditation". During meditation think about problem situations in your life and be guided to appropriate solutions by the upward and downward shifts in feeling.

Chapter thirteen:
ATTITUDE IS EVERYTHING

ya drishti sa shrishti

The world reflects your vision of it.

Yoga Vashishta

MEDITATION AFFECTS LIFE, and life affects meditation: if you have been agitated and angry all day, your meditation that night will be difficult.

Life itself is a form of meditation. The challenge is to become more and more aware of your inner world as you live your life. Notice how different events during the day affect you. What uplifts and expands your feeling and what makes you feel unhappy or contracted? This is important information in your quest for self-knowledge.

The next step is to apply skilful means in the heat of the battle of life. If, for example, you find yourself in negative self-talk in the midst of a conversation with another person, use the mantra. No one will know!

In making your entire life your meditation there is an essential thing I would like you to consider...

- Nothing is more important to the quality and enjoyment of your life than your own attitude.

ATTITUDE

Have you ever taken someone to a party, a movie, a concert or a sporting event that you were enthusiastic about and he or she was not? Have you ever been asked to go to a dinner or a party that you were not looking forward to? Both have probably happened to you, and both situations could have taught you something about attitude.

Your attitude is far more important than what happens to you—more important than your good or bad fortune. No matter how hard you work, no matter how much you give, or no matter how hard you struggle, you will not be able to arrange your life so that only good fortune comes to you. No one can do that—not even supremely fortunate or enlightened people.

A sage I met in India once told me a person who becomes interested in meditation and the inner world is undoubtedly someone who has a relatively even balance of the good and the bad in his life. (He called it good and bad *karma*). He explained that an abundance of good karma and an abundance of bad karma pull your attention to the outer world and away from inner matters.

A person born in poverty or with a severe physical disability will likely have to deal with that first of all, while a person with great wealth or worldly success will get completely caught up in that. Of course, the Hindu view is that our existence on earth is a long story of which the present life is only a chapter. Thus, the sage believed that everything evened out in the long haul (over a number of lifetimes). It is likely that you are, like me, someone who has known both good and bad in your life. It helps to remember:

- There is no outer condition however good that a terrible attitude cannot ruin.
- There is no outer condition however bad that a great attitude cannot improve.

These two interesting statements are about inner world empowerment. The more independent of outer events and strong we are inside ourselves, the more we are empowered.

We know people who *have everything* and are still not happy. The gossip magazines are full of them. We also hear inspiring tales of people whose spirit is so strong they overcome adversity. It is when people have faced and overcome failure, enmity, or the dark side of life, that they become truly interesting. We intuitively know that a soul is tempered by adversity and grows towards greatness and compassion. Think about this: while we all accept that we can get what we want and still be unhappy (sentence one above), the following truth is less obvious: *you can fail to get what you want and still be happy.*

What an extraordinary idea! In fact, happiness does not solely depend on getting or not getting what you want. No bad thing that happens to you *forces* you to have a collapse. Nothing you want is so important that life is not worth living without it. Happiness is a balanced inner condition of the Self, available to us every moment, under all circumstances and even right now! I concede the practical truth that we feel happy in the moment of fulfilling a desire, but that is because in that state we get a taste of the Self.

A contemporary spiritual teacher writes:

> *Consciousness can take both positive and negative directions. You have within you the purest wisdom, flowing toward ever-expanding bliss, an infinite variety of new life expressions. This is the universal spirit. You also harbor within you the distorted expression of your creative consciousness with which you will create negative and destructive results. One could also say that this is the eternal fight between God and the*

devil, between good and evil, between life and death. It does not matter what you call these powers; whatever you name them, they are your own powers. You are not a helpless pawn in anyone's hands.

Eva Pierrakos, *Pathwork of Self-transformation*

This states an ancient truth that can be expressed succinctly as - "The world is as you see it" or "You create your own reality". We endlessly interpret and react to events. The various contractions and unpleasant feelings we have discovered residing in our chakras are our reactions to outer events and inner thoughts. How we manage our reactions is our responsibility. At a certain level of self-awareness we become responsible for our reactions: they are not automatic, we develop the ability to choose.

Everything I have been saying in this book supports that point of view. Events have no emotional impact on us until our minds interpret them. Our feeling response to events is a response to how we *think* about them, not to the events themselves. In the last chapter I described the options available to us when we are caught in a bad situation. The inner option—we can change our attitude—is always available. If we do not like the feelings we have, we can try to change our thinking.

Our inner world moves in two directions only: towards happy states of mind or towards unhappy states of mind. When we succumb to tearing thoughts we invite despair and hopelessness. We make wrong choices.

One of my teachers told me that he used to think life was about getting what he wanted. Then one day he realized that although he had been reasonably successful in life, he was neither happy nor fulfilled. He then made his priority his feeling of peace and joy moment to moment. He took the hypothesis that when he felt bad his thinking must be wrong. At such times he would ask himself:

- "Is there another way to look at this situation?"
- "Is there an uplifting point of view?"

There always was. He evolved the unique idea to tailor his thinking to situations so that it yielded him contentment and happiness. He had the theory that in every life situation there is an optimum way to think, and a person with wisdom and detachment could find it. His ideas had a big impact on me. I recognized they involved a 180-degree shift of my inner world. Instead of thinking that my reactions were "natural" or "justified" I began to evaluate whether they were functional or dysfunctional—did they increase stress or did they lead me to peace? If I discovered they caused me stress I would try to change them.

It is in our highest self-interest to view life from an expanded, peaceful and joyous state. The more we do that, the happier our lives, the better our health. We need no other justification for adopting such a view: a positive vision is its own justification and its own reward. But, we should not take this idea of tailoring our thinking to situations as far as Mulla Nasruddin did.

One day the Mulla was getting dressed for a very important function in which he was to receive an award. He could not find his gold cufflinks which were his pride and joy. (Yes, his caftans had French cuffs.) He became more and more distressed as his search went on. Finally, he sat down at a table cradling his head in his hands in despair. He called out, "O God! If you find my cufflinks I will contribute 20 dinars to the mosque! Yes! Twenty dinars!"

His bosom heaved with the sincerity of his prayer. He gradually opened his eyes. There on the table, *which a moment before had been entirely empty,* were his gold cufflinks. With joy, Nasruddin turned his eyes toward heaven and called out, "Never mind God, I found them myself!"

Earlier I mentioned the Chinese conception of the Tao (pronounced "Dow"). The Tao is a mysterious essence that exists within every situation, every activity and every action. When we are in touch with the Tao we feel a wisdom, harmony and energy that fairly crackles. In touch with the Tao we will act naturally and spontaneously, we will meet all situations with creativity and calm. We will enhance and not deplete our energy, our life force.

The Chinese philosopher Lao-tsu wrote:

> *Empty yourself of everything. Let the mind rest in peace. The ten thousand things rise and fall while the Self watches their return. They grow and flourish and then return to the source. Returning to the source is stillness, which is the way of the Tao. The way of nature is unchanging.*

> *Knowing constancy, the mind is open. With an open mind, you will be openhearted. Being openhearted, you will act royally. Being royal, you will attain the divine. Being divine, you will be at one with the Tao. Being at one with the Tao is eternal. And though the body dies, the Tao will never pass away.*

Little by little you will become more and more aware, more attuned. You will be present to every moment of your life. You will be clear-sighted. You will notice the reaction you have to every thought, word and deed. As your awareness grows, you will develop the ability to choose energy over depletion, joy over depression, empowerment over disempowerment. Your intuition will open, you will know what to say and do in every situation. You will become an inspiration for others. I am not exaggerating. Everything I describe is within you. Right now it exists as potential. All that is needed is a bit of work and regularity in your practice to bring it out. You will begin to notice when you are blocked and ask yourself if your attitude is off. And right there, in the heat of battle, you will develop the ability to shift your attitude and relax into peace.

CONTENTMENT OF MIND

samtoshad anuttamah sukha-labhaha

Superlative happiness comes from contentment.

Yoga Sutras of Patanjali II.42

The mind is a rich and complex topic. Volumes could be written about it. When I look back to some bad years I had before I studied meditation, I see that the reason for them was that I had no understanding of my mind from the perspective of Second Education. Charlene Spretnak writes, "The failure to know the nature of mind condemns us to the misery of agitated mind states, a misery we rarely keep to ourselves but inflict on everyone whose life we affect." (States of Grace, p.46)

In my travels in India I met a number of great beings, yogis and sages before I met my teacher. One of these outstanding sages was Neem Karoli Baba (Maharaji) a renowned holy man, given to odd, child-like ways. Still, he was a great teacher. He would often mutter his mantra *Ram, Ram, Ram* to himself. One day he was repeating *"Thul thul, nan nan,"* over and over in his high-pitched voice. This was not a mantra. A devotee said that *thul* meant "too much," and *nan* meant "too little," in his native tongue.

The enigmatic saint continued repeating this unusual mantra. Finally, one of the devotees worked up the courage to ask him about it. "Maharaji, please tell us what is too much and too little?"

The sage said: "Everyone comes to me to complain they have *too much* suffering, *too much* trouble; they have *too little* money, *too little* joy. It is all in the mind! Their minds have this habit to think 'too much; too little' all the time. Why can't they learn to say 'Just right, everything is perfect, I am grateful to God?' Then they would be happy."

Indeed, contentment of mind is rare and can only be attained by meditation and inner work. *There is nothing more valuable to attain than contentment.*

Many years ago I was running a meditation ashram in the United States. It was doing well: lots of people were coming and the programs were dynamic. I felt expansive and I proposed to my teacher that we buy an adjoining property since many people wanted to live or visit there. He wrote back: "Be content with what you have."

The words stunned me, but they carried a power. I was certain that he was not against a natural expansion of my work. What was he getting at? That phrase began to echo within my consciousness. I saw that I had been worrying and felt a sense of lack. That feeling had been with me my whole life. And, I had been operating from it.

I saw that whenever we act out of a negative emotion, the outcome is not good. Only actions performed out of fullness, not lack, will be productive in the highest sense.

Contentment can be triggered by outer events, but it is a feeling space within the Self. There may be many goals you want to accomplish, but cultivate contentment now, *before* you pursue them. And, learn to be content *while* you are pursuing them.

One of the early golfing greats used to say that he always took time to "smell the roses". He did not let his competitive mind dominate him so much that he was not present. Every moment has the potential for the experience of contentment.

Contemplation 22: Be content with what you have.

1. Sit quietly and focus on the quality of contentment.
2. Contemplate the things in your life for which you are grateful.
3. Contemplate those aspects of your life and yourself with which you are satisfied. You can say to yourself, "I am grateful for..." Or, "I give thanks for...."
4. Search for the feeling of contentment within yourself. Find it now. Contemplate thus for 5-10 minutes.

Contentment exists in potential in every moment, in every situation. Some minds doggedly resist contentment and actively search for the negative. To realize that you have such a mind is self-knowledge. Do not despair—it is only a *tendency*. Fight against it, be aware of it, and take control.

KEY IDEAS OF CHAPTER THIRTEEN:
ATTITUDE IS EVERYTHING

- Meditation affects life. Life affects meditation.
- Examine your attitude.
- There is always good karma and bad karma in life.
- There is no outer condition however good that a terrible attitude cannot ruin.
- There is no outer condition, however bad, that a great attitude cannot improve.
- You can fail to get what you want and still be happy.
- The world is as you see it.
- There will always be an uplifting way to view any situation.
- Tailor your thinking to uplift yourself.
- A positive vision is its own justification and its own reward.
- Discover when your attitude is off and shift!
- To live in the Tao is to live with skill and attention so that our life crackles with energy.
- The mind is as vast as the universe.
- Contentment of mind is rare, but can be gained by inner work.

Chapter fourteen:

RELATIONSHIPS AND THE LANGUAGE OF LOVE

Nothing in the world is higher than love.
Love is the wealth of the heart.

Swami Muktananda

A LITTLE WHILE ago I spoke of the path of energy in which we look for upward shifts in all our experiences in the outer world as well as the inner world. This is a deceptively difficult path to walk: it seems obvious that we should always look for upward shifts, uplifting energy, yet in practice we are often drawn towards the negative influences which increase our suffering.

To walk the path of energy we have to ask questions like: "Does this increase my energy? Does the inner Self like this possibility? Am I moving towards peace and happiness?" Whatever choices we make, whatever interactions we have, even whatever thoughts we entertain, part of our awareness must watch our inner response. We operate under the assumption that for anything to be truly beneficial to us the inner Self must give assent.

The principles of the path of energy apply perfectly to relationships. A relationship is the creation of a new individual (the couple) from two separate individuals. The couple has its own "inner world" based on what is said, thought and felt together. Some relationships have a lot of love in their system, others a lot of anger. Just as the individual must learn to eliminate negative thoughts and feelings and move towards upward shifts, so the couple must unify its inner world and move in the direction of love and harmony.

THE LAWS OF LOVE

I am going to talk about relationships here in the light of the Shiva Process. The discussion will be, I think, easy to understand, but like the path of energy it is deceptively so. I do not have to tell you that relationships can be difficult. There is no greater hell than a relationship gone wrong. To keep your relationship moving towards heaven there is no substitute for good will and hard work.

Love is lawful. It is an inner movement of two people towards oneness. It transcends the egos of the lovers and moves towards joy and peace. A couple must learn to make their communications move in the right direction. Communications that move in the wrong direction can be said to "violate the laws of love". For example, affectionate remarks move in harmony with the laws of love. Critical remarks violate the laws of love—they cause contraction and withdrawal. Just as tearing thoughts are the worst elements in the inner world of an individual, so blame is the worst element in the inner world of a couple. Statements such as: "You did this; You did that; It's your fault," diminish and ultimately kill a relationship.

THE LANGUAGE OF LOVE

Two people in a relationship must keep part of their awareness on the feeling state of the relationship. They must ask themselves (and each other): "Is this conversation moving towards harmony or separation?" It is very easy for unconscious anger to enter the situation. Before you know it there is an argument and blame is everywhere. The couples should watch their inner experience and as soon as they perceive a downward shift, they should acknowledge it by saying something like: "We must have violated the laws of love."

When a lover sees that something he has said has caused a downward shift he should immediately acknowledge it. He might say: "I think I have violated the laws of love", and apologize.

As I said, blame is always in violation of the laws of love. But sometimes a person in a relationship does something thoughtless, hurtful, selfish or downright cruel. What to do then? Instead of blame, the partner should have recourse to **A Statements**.

Accurate Statements: "I feel hurt. I feel angry. I am devastated", do not violate the language of love. Blame makes the other person contract into defensiveness and decreases love. **A Statements** do not decrease love, but rather give the other partner a space in which compassion and openness can flow. The language of blame kills love but **A Statements** stop the bleeding.

To increase love the couple must use **Beneficial Statements**. The relational **B Statements** will be different from the personal **B Statements** but the effect will be similar: it will move the couple towards greater love and peace. Remember: whatever works, whatever moves the couple or the individual toward more expanded feeling is the movement towards love. Of course, conventional methods that people have used for ages will have merit, but each relationship has its own laws and the discovery of true **B Statements** will deepen the relationship.

In the widest sense every conversation or group is a temporary relationship. These relationships also follow the laws I have set out here.

In other words all day long we move in and out of relationships, some of which are close to the Self, and some of which are far from the Self. We should keep working with the relationship at hand.

DEDICATING THE MANTRA TO YOUR RELATIONSHIP

Earlier in the book I spoke about prayer point and about dedicating the mantra to overcome blocks when the mind cannot solve them. Here is an exercise you can try when your relationship is blocked:

Sit with your partner for an agreed upon time period (I suggest 15 minutes). Both of you say inwardly: "I dedicate these mantra repetitions to uplifting our relationship." Then do the mantra silently in each other's company. This is a mysterious but extraordinarily effective method.

KEY IDEAS OF CHAPTER FOURTEEN:
RELATIONSHIPS AND THE LANGUAGE OF LOVE

- A relationship is the creation of a new individual.
- Love is lawful.
- A relationship has its own inner world.
- The inner world of a relationship may be full of love or full of anger.
- Blame kills love.
- **Accurate Statements** help the relationship get back on track.
- **Beneficial Statements** expand the love in the relationship.
- Every conversation or gathering is subject to the laws of love.
- Sit with your partner and dedicate mantra repetition to your relationship.

Chapter Fifteen:
SELF-REALIZATION IN THE WORLD

Chitta sthitivaccharira karana bahyeshu

That same state the yogi achieves
in meditation can remain even when the mind
is turned outward towards the world.

Shiva Sutras III.39

THERE WAS ONCE an eager disciple who wanted to speed up his spiritual progress. He went to his teacher and asked: "Master how can I achieve self-realization?"

The master said: "Go to the graveyard at midnight tonight. Walk among graves and abuse the corpses. Come back tomorrow."

The disciple did as his master told him. He walked among the graves and swore at the corpses. "You fools, all you do is lie there, you're so ignorant!"

The next day he went to his teacher and told him what he had done. The teacher said: "Good, now go again tonight, and praise them."

That night the disciple obediently went back to the graveyard. He praised the corpses saying: "You are so talented, magnificent and beautiful."

The next day he reported to his teacher: "I have followed your instructions."

"Good," said the teacher, "what did the corpses do when you abused them?"

" Nothing," replied the disciple, "they just lay there."

"What did they do when you praised them?"

"Nothing," he answered.

"When you are similarly unaffected by praise and blame," the Guru said, "you will be enlightened!"

I love this story, but it is misleading if there is an implication that enlightenment is like a state of death. Perhaps some of the Eastern teachings make it sound that way too. I have a problem with that: the great beings I have met, both Eastern and Western have been anything but dead. They have been full of energy, humor and the unexpected. Enlightenment is a state of enhanced aliveness. It is a fire, in which all attachment is burned moment to moment.

The German psychoanalyst Karlfreid von Durkheim said:

There is a stillness of life and a stillness of death. The stillness of death is where nothing moves any more. The stillness of life is where nothing holds back the movement of change any more. This stillness is one of the fruits of the inner way.

One day after I had been six months or so with my teacher, a friend told me Baba liked to watch nature programs on television. Instead of thinking of this as a charming personal trait, it plunged me into my first crisis in faith. That he watched television at all is what troubled me. I assumed that enlightenment was an inner state of such richness that any outer pleasure would pale into insignificance. If a person had wave after wave of bliss coursing through them why would they want to entertain themselves with television or other things?

The concept of Self-realization or enlightenment is simply not in our culture. When Westerners start to walk the inner path they learn a new language. Many seekers from my generation misunderstood some of the concepts we encountered. However, as we became more at home with Second Education, our assumptions became more realistic.

In 1975 my teacher had a series of violent seizures which seemed life threatening. He recovered from the attacks and spoke about them in this way.

I don't know if I was just being tested or some of my past actions got in my way. I cannot say…To this day I can't figure out whether this is the grace of the guru or destiny testing the firmness of my inner state. Perhaps it is just a test. The reason I say this is because when you see me here at the retreat you will not see me as a sick man…They say the real test of the Self is in times of difficulty or danger…I was calm. There was a picture of my guru in front of me, and I kept looking at it and repeating the mantra "guru om, guru om, guru om." I didn't say: "Oh guruji, please save me!" I just kept speaking to my body: "Oh body of mine, this is your destiny. Work it out. This is the fruit of your karma. Go through it peacefully." I had no desire to cry, "Save me, save me." So, this is my inner state. This is what I have earned in my life…What really matters is that my inner state was not disturbed. My purity was not affected. I did not ask you to pray to Baba Nityananda for my sake.

I remember being surprised by this. I had thought that Self-realization meant there was no question of ever wavering from inner connectedness.

A chess grandmaster I knew once told me: "It's not enough to be a good chess player. You also have to make good moves!"

It could also be said that: "It is not enough to be Self-realized, you have to live it under all circumstances." Self-realization is not a gold card that grants immunity from disease, death, old age and loss. There is no guarantee that some future possibility or difficulty will not disturb Self-realization. Rather, it is a skilful way to meet the challenges which arise moment to moment.

Does this mean that Self-realization is fiction? Certainly not—as we meditate and pursue Second Education we grow in knowledge of the Self. In Gurdjieff's language, we live more and more in our essence rather than our personality. The deeper our process goes, the more established in the Self we become. But a Self-realized being is not a creature from another planet, rather he is a man (or woman) among other men and women.

The sage Aurobindo was once teaching a disciple and told him "this is how I did it!"

"What has that to do with us?" asked the disciple. "You are a spiritual superman. I can't be like you!"

A horrified Aurobindo told him: "When you speak like that you make me feel that my whole life is wasted. If I am different from you what is the point of my teaching you? You are just like me and what I did you can do also."

The Self-realized being teaches how to live life from the position of the Self. Enlightenment culminates in the experience of God in the world. It is a natural state and lives as potential within all of us.

In the middle eighties I visited Ojai, California, some miles north of Los Angeles, where the well-known spiritual teacher J. Krishnamurti had lived and taught for a long time. I was curious as to what my experience of his ashram would be.

As I walked through the grounds I came across a beautiful and peaceful oak grove. I was particularly drawn to a rock and sat down to listen to the quiet. I closed my eyes and was immediately plunged into a deep meditation. From within I heard a voice say: "Teach about independence." Intuitively I associated the voice with Krishnamurti. I later found out that he often held programs there and taught from that rock.

Independence is the essence of Self-realization. True independence is a state of love, wisdom and joy. False independence is tinged with fear or anger. The Self-realized soul relies on inner resources and is never at the effect of other people or externals.

Certain yogic texts distinguish different degrees of Self-realization. The interesting book *Tripura Rahasya* talks about three levels of Self-realized beings. The lowest struggles against ignorance and has spells of remembrance of the

Self, broken by intervals of forgetfulness. He sometimes gets caught in pleasure and pain and identifies with the body and the un-awakened self. Still, because his essential identification is with the Self, he makes progress against ignorance.

The middle level sage never forgets the Self. He has perfected the vision of the Self but is attached to meditative states. He wants to remain in samadhi, deep meditation, all the time. However, contact with the outer world shakes his inner state to some degree.

The highest class of sage has perfect vision inner and outer. He moves through the world with his realization utterly intact. He makes no distinction between meditation with his eyes closed and ordinary living. He is at perfect peace. His detachment and inner state are deep and unshakable.

TRANQUILITY AND EQUANIMITY

I have followed Kashmir Shaivism in calling the first section of this book, **Atma Vyapti, "Meditation on the Self"**, and the second part **Shiva Vyapti, "Meditation in the world"**. Some Buddhist schools recognize a similar distinction with the terms *tranquility*, inner peace and *equanimity*, outer peace.

In my years at my teacher's ashram in India, I knew many fine meditators. The emphasis then was on practising the inner attainment, but Baba had his eye on the complete picture. An American friend I lived with in the dormitory was an avid meditator. He got in as many hours a day as he could, and he practised the mantra when he was not meditating. Certainly, he had many meditation experiences, but he was sorely lacking in the aspect of equanimity. He would flare up at anyone who spoke or made a noise. This created an unpleasant atmosphere around him, and, inevitably, some of the others resented him and were not above purposely agitating him.

This went on for many months. He got angrier and he also got thinner. Then one day Baba told him to go back to New York, get a job and save money in order to be able to tour with Baba in the States the next year. My friend accepted this and made preparations, but he began to brood about it. After a few days he went up to Baba and said, "If I get a job what will happen to my meditation and my experience of God?"

Baba said, to the delight of those of us who happened to be there: "Don't worry about that, money is more important than God!"

This was not an expression of Baba's atheism or materialism. Rather, it was an example of his skilful and earthy style of teaching. Baba was humorously pushing my friend towards bringing his practice into the world, in order to develop equanimity. And he was blowing his concepts in a Zen-like manner to boot. Meditation takes a lot of energy, and one or one and one-half hours a day are enough as a regular practice for even the most passionate meditator.

The story is worth finishing, for it is a tale of tranquility and equanimity. My friend went back to New York, but his lust for meditation was such that he could not follow Baba's instructions. Instead, he meditated many hours a day until finally his health broke and he wound up in the hospital with a debilitating illness. That must have also broken the back of his delusion, because when I saw him in the U.S. a year later, he had gained weight, was working as a taxi driver in New York City, and was radiantly happy and relaxed. He told me that Baba had forced him to find God in the world. It was obvious that he had.

People who are successful generally have a lot of equanimity in their chosen area of life, even if they are not meditators. A great businessman will operate with a lot of power, intention and poise; he will be comfortable in the arena of business. He will not fall apart in adversity, but will react to bad situations with creativity and practicality. Such a one may, however, have difficulty in unwinding, in achieving tranquility without the requisite number of martinis.

As we have seen, some good meditators may have a talent for tranquility, but lose their equanimity as soon as they engage in the practical affairs of life. Little things might upset them or make them emotional. Enlightenment requires both tranquility and equanimity—the abilities to go inside and become quiet, and also to take that inner attainment into our outer life.

Equanimity is not a passive state. We must be able to transform the energy and feeling that comes at us. It is a focused and creative way to live, and can only be perfected by hard work, toughness and understanding. It is a goal worthy of our effort.

Only a great being can live with an open heart under all conditions. Normally, fear, anger, jealousy, or other reactions close the heart from time to time, or often. A child is naturally openhearted, but by puberty the heart has closed to some extent. Self-realization is a state in which we live life with open-heartedness.

I have a different version of the Zen story I told earlier. Once there was a Zen master, whose teaching was to do everything with total focus. "When you sit, you should just sit!" he would say, "when you walk, you just walk. When you eat, you should just eat.

One day a student happened to look through a window and see the master eating his breakfast and reading the morning paper. He became confused and upset. Later that day he announced to the master that he was leaving the monastery. "Why?" asked the master.

"Because you are a hypocrite!" the disciple cried out. "You teach us 'just eat when we eat, and just read when we read', but this morning I saw you reading the paper while eating your breakfast."

"Correct," responded the master, "when you eat you should just eat. When you read you should just read. And, when you eat and read, you should just eat and read!"

Why did my teacher watch television? Why not? After enlightenment we do what we have always done, we "chop wood and carry water". The inner state, however, has irrevocably changed.

shivatulyo jayate,

The yogi who has reached the supreme state of Shiva
becomes a divine being.

Shiva Sutras III:25

The words of a Self-realized being acquire the power of truth. He radiates love and spiritual energy. His gift to those who seek wisdom is knowledge of the Self and divine love.

Contemplation 23: Tranquility and equanimity

Tranquillity can be likened to a still lake, equanimity to a powerful, unmoving mountain. To call on these two attributes, I suggest the following:

1. For tranquillity visualize a still, quiet lake and let your mind become as still as the lake you imagine.

2. For equanimity imagine yourself to be as strong and immovable as a mountain. Visualize moving through your day with that strength and certainty.

KEY IDEAS OF CHAPTER FIFTEEN:
SELF-REALIZATION IN THE WORLD

- When Westerners start to walk the inner path they learn a new language.
- Self-realization is not a gold card that grants immunity from life.
- Independence is the essence of Self-realization.
- Enlightenment culminates with the experience of God in the world.
- Tranquility is the ability to quieten the mind and become peaceful.
- Equanimity is the capacity to take the peace and stillness we have achieved through the practice of tranquility, and move in our lives from this state.

Chapter sixteen:
THE PRACTICE
OF NATURAL HAPPINESS

Madhya vikasat chidananda labhaha

By meditative unfoldment the bliss of Consciousness is acquired.

Pratyabhijnahridayam 17

WE HAVE REACHED the end of this journey together. I hope that I have inspired you to meditate and I hope you continue to meditate once a day for the rest of your life. It is easy to let meditation slip to the bottom of your list of priorities. After all, it is a *non-doing*, and so many *doings* claim our time and attention. Fight against this tendency. From the widest viewpoint your spiritual development deserves first place in your life. Every part of your life is an aspect of your spiritual development. Thinking from that view will add meaning and energy to your life.

I love the path of yoga and all the techniques of self-development that ingenious yogis - of all traditions - have invented. Meditation and Self-inquiry are the twin jewels, the distillation of that. These practices give us a higher understanding and bring us to the knowledge of the Self. Paradoxically, that Self is always with us whether we meditate or not. My teacher, who was a poet of the Self, gave exquisite expression to this truth.

We who are the Supreme Self have become individual souls. How repulsive! This is our only hell. Get out of this hell this minute!

And there's only one way to do it. Right now, this very instant, start saying, "Shivo'ham"...I am Shiva...I am Brahman...I am Consciousness, I am Consciousness.

Jump and dance without caring about anything else. Dance with one idea—I am the Self...The Self is eternal and always revealed...It is always liberated....

Really speaking there is nothing to do to attain the Self. Even without doing the mantra or other spiritual practices the Self is with you.

Know that attainment. Be peaceful. See how beautiful it is from within. How pure! What inspiration! What delight! It is the Self that is man. It is the Self that is woman. It is the Self that is the universe.

Nonetheless, to grasp and sustain such wisdom and such ecstasy, most of us have to do some practice. It is also hard to do it alone, hence the sages always recommend seeking the company of fellow seekers and a good teacher. Such company nourishes and sustains our inner life, which often receives blows in the external world.

Find a good company of meditators in your area. There are a number of excellent teachers in my tradition and many in other sound and reputable traditions. Take your time with a teacher, be open, but do not accept him or her until you are sure that your growth is being fostered. You can write to me for recommendations if you like. For that matter, you can come and spend some time here at the Shiva Ashram, in Australia.

Before my guru sent me away to create an ashram and teach I had lived with him for years with great joy. During that time I experienced kundalini awakening and a powerful experience of the inner Self. I was convinced that my happiness depended on proximity to him, that my inner world would be bereft without his physical presence.

On the last day I was with him, he invited me on an early morning walk. We walked through the streets of Piedmont, California where he was teaching. I was fearful and confused about the task that lay ahead. Tears streamed down my face. He started making zany jokes to lighten me up. It worked and by the end of the walk I was laughing with him. As we neared the end of the walk he turned to me and said: "Do what I do, mimic me and the work will flow."

I took his words seriously and imitated him every way I could. Gradually this imitation became less physical and more internal. I discovered him as vigilance and attention within. I discovered him as knowledge within myself. Finally, I discovered he was with me as inner joy.

Remember the Self. The same Self dwells within you as in Jesus, the Buddha and the Masters of yoga. To discover it takes a bit of effort but nothing is more important than to know the Self. You can acquire riches and honors all your life but it is empty without Self-knowledge. That alone is real wealth and that alone will accompany you on your final journey.

Meditation is the practice of natural happiness. You do not need to go to India or Tibet, to a cave or a monastery. Your normal life is a perfect arena of spirituality. Divinize and energize your life. A life lived with attention to the inner world gradually triumphs over suffering.

May you always grow in awareness. May you always live every aspect of your life in the natural happiness which is the gift of meditation and Self-inquiry.

KEY IDEAS OF CHAPTER SIXTEEN:
THE PRACTICE OF NATURAL HAPPINESS

- Every part of your life is an aspect of your spiritual development.
- "Dance with one idea—"I am the Self."
- "The Self is eternal and always revealed...it is always liberated."
- Seek the company of fellow seekers and a good teacher.
- Remember the Self.
- Meditation is the practice of natural happiness.

Chapter seventeen:

QUESTIONS & ANSWERS

tat parijnane chittameva antar mukhi
bhavena chetana padadhyarohat chitihi

By turning within in meditation the individual mind
rises to the status of Universal Consciousness.

Pratyabhijnahridayam 13

THIS CHAPTER HAS more answers to questions I have received in courses and lectures. I hope that reading these will help clarify any obscure points.

DORMANT CHAKRAS

QUESTION: When I do the Chakra Meditation, I cannot feel anything in my navel chakra. Does this mean that I do not have a navel chakra?

SWAMIJI: It is normal to have one or two chakras in which there is less feeling and energy. Sometimes there may be no energy or feeling at all. There is no cause for alarm. There are several possibilities in such cases. One is that the main arena of your development at the moment is in other chakras, other areas of life. When you do not feel much in a chakra, it generally means that everything is all right. Continue to investigate the chakras which grab your attention. They will have a lot of feeling. They will feel contracted or expanded. You can ignore the other ones for the time being.

It is possible that the energy may shift later, and a "dormant" chakra may start to have intense feeling in it. The Kundalini energy works on what is necessary for your evolution. It does not mean that you are "missing a piece".

This situation is analogous to astrological charts in which some houses have a group of planets and others remain empty. Such a configuration does not mean the person does not experience the aspect of life governed by the empty houses—far from it! Nevertheless, the houses which hold a number of planets will certainly be interesting ones and call attention to themselves. For karmic reasons, beyond what we can ordinarily know, certain essential issues are emphasized in any single lifetime. Keep working with the obvious. Deeper and subtler layers of understanding will be revealed.

It is possible to make a typology of people who are navel centered, heart centered and third-eye centered. In fact, I have done so! People who are passionate and love to act in the outer world usually have issues in the navel chakra. People who have a lot of feeling in the heart chakra are concerned with their relationships with friends, family and co-workers. People with a lot of energy in the third eye are intellectual and usually focus on issues of understanding and control. Therefore, you can see that a tilt towards one chakra or another is normal.

TEARING THOUGHTS

QUESTION: I see unpleasant images in my chakras sometimes. I keep reading accounts of glorious meditation experiences that other people have, not just saints, and I want them too. Does this mean I am a low sort of person?

SWAMIJI: You are simply having a "tearing thought". You would be surprised how insecure people are about their meditations.

When we meditate, we go into a world in which there is no one else. Some of us have doubts about whether we are doing it well, or if what is happening is appropriate. When others boast of magnificent cosmic experiences we doubt our experiences. Understand that everything which happens in the realm of meditation is under the guidance of the inner Self, universal Consciousness. Some people will have out of the body experiences, some will have visions of Gods and Goddesses, and others will have nothing of the kind. They may feel peaceful or gain new insights into themselves or their lives.

Be content with the meditations you are getting. If you honor what happens in meditation, you please the inner Self. However, the best way to honor the inner Self is to be regular in your practice, no matter what is happening.

When my teacher first published his spiritual autobiography, *Play of Consciousness*, I also had the experience you indicate. I compared my meditations to the glorious ones he described. Finally, I had to shake free of the comparison and simply accept what was happening to me. That turned out to be more than adequate. By the way, read that book: it is full of Kundalini energy.

Everyone eventually confronts the dark images of their psyche. No one has only sweetness and light within. Look at the world—there is suffering, disease, old age and death. We would already be enlightened if we did not have blocks, knots and areas of ignorance.

Kashmir Shaivism agrees with the Jungians in saying that the dark is as much a manifestation of the Divine Mind as the light. As we progress along the path we assimilate the totality of experience. We begin to see how it all makes sense. It is indeed unutterably beautiful and poignant when viewed from a higher perspective.

When the unconscious emerges into the light of awareness we become free of unhappy impressions. See everything as the play of Consciousness, the play of light and dark. Do not be afraid; be the witness. Knowledge and understanding will reveal itself. This is sadhana, the process of enlightening yourself.

QUESTION: What is the difference between a tearing thought and reality?

SWAMIJI: A thought like, "I am worthless", is a tearing thought. A thought like, *I am not six feet tall*, is not a tearing thought if you are five foot eight. It is a simple statement of truth. However, if anger and self-hatred accompany a thought, then it is a tearing thought. The key distinction lies in feeling.

An angry thought directed outward, at another person, could be called an "attack thought". Direct a similar thought against yourself and you have a tearing thought. Angry, judgmental thoughts, whether they are directed inwards or outwards, hurt the heart and confuse the mind. They take us away from the natural enjoyment of the Awakened Self, towards the un-awakened self, the ego.

When your assessment of a situation moves you towards despair, you can be sure that tearing thoughts have entered the system. Remember that from the point of view of the Awakened Self, every situation has divinity at its core. Oppose your tearing thoughts. Search for a way to view the situation that gives you peace and puts you in touch with the Awakened Self.

SOLVING PRACTICAL PROBLEMS

QUESTION: Can I use Self-inquiry to deal with practical problems in my life or is it just for spiritual dilemmas?

SWAMIJI: You can use Self-inquiry to uncover the truth in any area of life: career and money, relationships (family, friends/enemies, romance, communication), health/body, spirituality (relationship to God, Self, Self-esteem, the mind and philosophical issues).

When you want inner guidance on a specific issue you can use your mind in your meditation. The first step is to concentrate on the area or issue in question. Become aware of where you feel the stress or tension, in which chakra. Let your true thoughts and feelings emerge. Identify the feeling. Witness your thoughts. Say **Accurate Statements** like, "I feel sad. I feel anxious or I feel frustrated" to yourself. Notice the statements that uplift you and release the tension. Work with **Beneficial Statements** like, "I am the Self. Everything is Consciousness. Peace is within me." Take note of those which uplift you. Follow the upward shift. It will lead you to the Awakened Self.

From the highest point of view, the distinction between "spiritual" and "worldly" is a false one. The spiritual dimension lies within mundane reality, hidden by a thin veil. All the spiritual masters tell us to pierce that veil and experience God in the world. Meditation and Self-inquiry allow us to penetrate beneath our habitual ways of responding to events in the world and to other people, and attain joy and wisdom.

Our minds and personalities have been conditioned to perpetuate the illusion of the world. We have a strong belief that happiness and fulfillment are impossible. We sometimes think other people are our enemies and rivals, and that there is not enough good stuff to go around. Spiritual reality, on the contrary, tells us there is infinite joy and peace.

Please pay close attention to the stories at the end of this chapter. Each of them illustrates the skilful use of Self-inquiry in unlocking doors in the mundane world.

THE NATURE OF THE MIND

QUESTION: Why is it that one day I am happy and the next depressed?

SWAMIJI: It is the nature of the mind to fluctuate. It is unstable. It takes the form of innumerable thoughts minute by minute. It is not surprising that it moves from mood to mood. Underlying these differing moods are unformed thoughts. These thoughts are so subtle we can call them unconscious. If you bring them to consciousness by means of Self-inquiry, your mind will become more stable. To make the mind steady it has to become established in the Awakened Self.

Do not recoil from less than ideal states of mind. You can regard negative states as an opportunity to study that particular state. For example, if you feel depressed say to yourself: "Ah, now I have an opportunity to study depression from inside. How intriguing!" The more intimately you know and understand the various mind states you experience, the more wisdom you will have, and the greater will be your capacity to shift out of them.

A AND B STATEMENTS

QUESTION: Do **Beneficial Statements** always follow **Accurate Statements**?

SWAMIJI: This is a good question, and the answer is both yes and not necessarily. The Scriptures and the teachings of the saints are filled with **B Statements** like "You are the Self." Such statements express the Awakened Self, and tie us to God. At the same time, the sages emphasize that we must also study ourselves and become familiar with our habitual patterns. **A Statements** reflect this process of self-study and self-observation.

Using B Statements exclusively without attention to the A Statement can be like building a beautiful house on a shaky foundation. I know of many so-called *jnanis* (people of wisdom), who have repeated "I am the Absolute" over and over but have neglected to purify the personality. They believe they are enlightened, but in fact they have strengthened their egos. There have been remarkable individuals throughout history who have been transformed and manifested various psychic powers. But because their Self-inquiry did not go deep enough, their egos created impurities. One such person might have been Rasputin, and I could name others.

To have an experience of the Self is not uncommon, but to become established in it usually takes a long, disciplined effort under the guidance of a Self-realized teacher. In fact, the relationship with the spiritual teacher is a safeguard against such "false enlightenments".

Thus making B Statements without A Statements risks the possibility of "delusory afflatus", thinking that our attainment is greater than it actually is. Of course, A Statements without B Statements has its own problems. Here we do not rise out of the personal and the neurotic, we imagine that there is no aspect of ourselves higher than our ego. Some forms of psychology that do not recognize the existence of the Awakened Self are in this category.

In practice, it is quite all right to use B Statements without A Statements in cases where A Statements are already understood. Also, when A Statements do not create an upward shift, or actually cause a greater contraction, it is appropriate to go to B Statements. I am aware that this is a fairly technical answer; so do not worry if you cannot follow it entirely. For our purposes, A Statements represent the personal or un-awakened self, B Statements represent the transpersonal or Awakened Self. Both are necessary.

QUESTION: What should I do when I feel too scared to turn inside and make an A Statement?

SWAMIJI: It sometimes happens that certain issues upset you so profoundly that you cannot sit calmly. It is for this reason I give the mantra to all my students. The mantra is a universal technique, which is particularly good when you feel panic. It will calm you down. When you encounter such obstacles, say the mantra intensely.

QUESTION: I felt like a mature adult until I started doing Self-inquiry and now I realize that there's so much in my inner world I do not know about. Is this normal?

SWAMIJI: We can become confused and overwhelmed by the depth and complexity of the inner world. In the early stages of any investigation, outer or inner, there are always more questions than answers, more unknowns than knowns. Keep at your inner work and you will go through a series of breakthroughs in understanding. Light will be shed on your inner world and you will start to understand the laws that operate there.

Your question reminds me of the teaching of the great and mysterious spiritual teacher G. I. Gurdjieff. He distinguished between *essence* and *personality*, saying people could have a well-developed personality, but an immature essence. You might encounter a highly educated, cultivated and sophisticated person, an acclaimed author or Nobel laureate, who still has tantrums like a three year old when he does not get his way. On the other hand, Gurdjieff said many simple and uneducated people—particularly in rural areas—might have strong essences. They would have the capacity to endure adversity without complaint or breakdown. This is not just nostalgia for pastoral life; Gurdjieff felt that *both* essence and personality had to be developed.

The reason that our essence lags behind our personality is that our education and culture focuses on personality. We develop our intellects, but we ignore our emotional development almost entirely. When we offer a PhD in peace of mind, then we will be moving towards development of essence. The inner work you are doing will strengthen your mind and emotions, your essence, and your inner sophistication will catch up to your outer sophistication.

QUESTION: I have been using **A Statements**, but they seem to be pushing me further into the problem. What can I do?

SWAMIJI: B Statements! **A Statements** go to the brink of tearing thoughts. The reason they are useful is that they give us a certain level of understanding. Often we do not know what we are feeling and why. It is important to know what disease you have before you are given medicine. Sometimes a good diagnosis begins the cure immediately. But once you know what the disease is, it is time to stop having more tests and move on to the cure. I would guess you already have a good knowledge of the tricks of your un-awakened self. Move strongly to **B Statements** and contact the Awakened Self.

CALL ON THE HIGHER POWER

QUESTION: Sometimes nothing works. I just feel bad and cannot shift it; no matter what technique I use. What can I do?

SWAMIJI: Let me suggest three possibilities. The first is prayer: pray to have the feeling shift, or to be shown the cause of the feeling. Prayer has great power because it is a direct communication with the Awakened Self. Since it works in relationship with other people to ask for what you want, and not to pretend you do not want it, so in relationship with the Self, it is good to be honest and direct. You can pray to Self, God, or guru—to the form of the higher power that is meaningful to you.

The second possibility is to say the mantra doggedly. I love mantra yoga, and I want you to understand that mantra repetition is always, in every inner case, a possible alternative. There will be occasions when the intellect will not work well at all. Mantra repetition is a great technique because you do not have to try to work anything out intellectually. You just do it. Mantra is a great B **Statement.**

Finally, there is the intelligent tactic of doing nothing. Here you do not try to shift out of the feeling or escape it in any way. You just be with it. This is one thing you can do in all situations: you can surrender to what is, and experience it. Often, this can shift the feeling. At least you will learn something as your observation of your condition goes to a deeper level. When you do not accept things as they are, you create a tension. You experience "the divided self"- a part of you is at war with another part. When you surrender and become one with even an unpleasant experience, you are likely to feel more integrated.

My faith is that there is always a skilful means which can work. Take your time to be with the situation and allow understanding to manifest. Sometimes our blocks prevent the messages from the Awakened Self from getting through. Relax, take your time, look and listen inwardly as calmly as you can. Understanding will dawn.

TRUSTING THE INNER SELF

QUESTION: How do I know when an answer that comes from my inner world is right?

SWAMIJI: You know it by the feeling. Baba frequently used to tell a story in which the key line was "peace follows renunciation". Since hearing it, that phrase has reverberated in my mind. When we inwardly let go of the struggle, or the wrong understanding, an unmistakable sense of harmony and peace comes in. Peace and harmony are characteristics of the Awakened Self, and show that the Self is "pleased".

According to yoga, peace and harmony are our natural condition. By holding wrong ideas and wrong desires and unnecessary fears, we ourselves destroy our own peace. When we let go of these we return to our natural and peaceful state.

KEY IDEAS OF CHAPTER SEVENTEEN:
QUESTIONS AND ANSWERS

- When you do not feel much in a chakra, it generally means that every thing is all right.
- Everything that happens in meditation is under the guidance of the inner Self.
- An angry thought directed at another person, could be called an "attack thought".
- When you want inner guidance on a specific issue you can use your mind in your meditation.
- From the highest point of view, the distinction between "spiritual" and "worldly" is a false one.
- It is the nature of the mind to fluctuate.
- Using **B Statements** exclusively without attention to **A Statements** can be like building a beautiful house on a shaky foundation.
- The mantra is a universal technique, which is particularly good when you feel panic.
- In the early stages of any investigation, outer or inner, there are always more questions than answers, more unknowns than knowns.
- Prayer has great power because it is a direct communication with the Awakened Self.
- Mantra is a great **B Statement.**
- Peace and harmony are characteristics of the Awakened Self, and show the Self is "pleased".

Chapter eighteen:

SELF-INQUIRY SHARING

drashtir drishyoparaktam cittam sarvartham
Having been purified by the Witness,
the mind understands everything.
Yoga Sutras of Patanjali IV.23

WHAT FOLLOWS IS *a small representative sample of sharing by students who regularly practise the Shiva Process method of Self-inquiry.*

One day I was feeling happy and decided to take the dog to the beach for a walk. As I walked I became aware that I felt sad. I was confused because a minute earlier I had been happy. I asked myself: "What is this? What is happening?" I stopped walking, closed my eyes and focused on my third eye. As I concentrated I could see the letters of the alphabet playing in my mind. They were spinning around, doing somersaults in my head. I could detect each one. They had not yet formed into words and sentences. I had the intuition that they were the cause of my sadness. I saw that they were unformed tearing thoughts contracting my good feeling. They were so powerful but I knew they were not real. I laughed at myself and felt happy again.

Comment: *This person is a highly developed meditator. She has been able to discover how tearing thoughts bubble up from the unconscious. There is always a reason that you feel sad even if you cannot find it. Look for it.*

I had only been meditating for about two weeks when my mother told me that she had given up twin boys for adoption before she was married to my father. During a private meditation session with Swamiji, I became aware of a longing and yearning in my heart. I realized that this pain had been there for as long as I could remember.

Swamiji suggested various **A Statements** but the feeling would not shift. The breakthrough came when he said: "This is my mother's feeling. This is my mother's grief." When I repeated the statements the intensity immediately shifted. Insight flooded my awareness. My perspective on this feeling changed. I was amazed to discover how much her sorrow had affected me. When I understood this I could let it go.

Comment: *When we love another person, when we are open to another person, we can take on or vibrate to their feelings. To proxy (See Part 2: Chapter eleven) is an act of compassion and service to those we love and to ourselves. We can always unblock the inner world no matter what the encounter.*

I was unhappy and struggling with a co-worker who was difficult. I had become increasingly despondent because my boss was not listening to me. I felt exhausted from the tension. I had spoken to him months before and nothing had changed. It became so unbearable that I thought I would have to quit.

One night during the meditation class Swamiji led the Chakra Meditation. When I got to my heart I discovered hurt and fear. When I got to my throat I discovered anger. When I asked what the anger was about the answer came immediately—my boss. The impulse to yell at him was lodged in my throat. I asked about the hurt and fear and again the answer came—I felt hurt that he did not listen to me and was afraid of exploding and acting inappropriately. I wanted to have a conversation with him, but my anger was in the way.

Swamiji suggested that I "tell the truth and not get angry." I went away and thought about how to do it. I kept repeating "tell the truth, don't get angry; tell the truth, don't get angry" over and over to myself. I scheduled a meeting with him, still not knowing what to say.

One night at home I sat down and experimented with some **A Statements**. I said: "I have angry words I need to say to my boss. I feel trapped. There are difficult things I need to say to my boss. I am scared my boss won't listen. I am scared I will get angry when I speak to him. I do not know how to handle this. I am afraid I will explode. I have to leave. I cannot cope."

I then made **B Statements**. I said: "I will speak to my boss. I need to have a meeting with my boss. I have a plan." I shifted off my anger. Creative ideas as to how to handle the situation came into my mind. I had shifted from unconscious anger to creative action.

In the meeting I told my boss, without anger, that I wanted to review how the office ran and that I had some ideas on how to change it for the better. He was impressed and followed my advice. I felt so relieved and empowered. Miraculously, a short time later, the difficult co-worker left.

Comment: *This is an ideal bit of Shiva Process. It demonstrates how mysteriously the outer and the inner go together, and how you can transform the outer by inquiring into the inner. Try this in your own life. You can review Part 2: Chapter nine, How To Do Self-inquiry.*

My boss' garage was a mess. He was convinced that his missing bicycle seat was hidden there. He asked me to look for it. I pulled everything out but could not find it. He sent me back several times to look again. He was acting normal even though tension was mounting. After three hours of searching I began to feel a bit weird. I had had enough.

When I got home I became aware that I was carrying a feeling and that I was trying to push it down. The feeling became so uncomfortable that I sat down and made statements inside myself. The **A Statements** were: "I feel traumatized. I am carrying a lot of emotion. I do not want to look for that bike seat again. That was a waste of time. I am angry with my boss. Do not make me do useless things."

I then asked myself if there was anything I could do about the situation. I said **B Statements**. The uplifting statements were: "Buy a new seat. Look in the Trading Post for a used one."

The next time I saw my boss he said: "About that bike seat!" Instead of reacting in anger I felt humorous and said to him. "Wait! Why don't you ring up the manufacturer and ask them if they can send you a new seat?" Within a week they sent him a new seat for free.

When I contemplated what happened I remembered that I thought it was strange that I should have such a big reaction over such a small issue. During the process I realized that there are every day events in life to which people have big reactions. At the time I was trying to talk myself out of my reaction. I was thinking, "This isn't the end of the world. I shouldn't worry about it. I shouldn't have these feelings about it. Some people are having marriage break-ups, what am I so worried about?" However, the experience was real, my reaction was happening. When I processed it I had a real shift. That experience transformed my understanding.

Comment: *A silly event, but a big emotional impact. Instead of denying it, this person went through it to a happy conclusion and learned something valuable. Every moment of life is potentially full of joy and wisdom.*

I was on my way to Cairns via Brisbane for a showing of my film. My feeling had been building for two days and now I was panicking about what it could be. By the time I got to Brisbane it had become steadily worse until I felt as though I had a dozen monsters living inside my chest. I could not figure out the issue.

By the time I got to Brisbane I was desperate, so with two hours to kill I decided to probe into the feeling until it was nailed. I was determined to be totally honest and look directly at whatever was bothering me.

I found a quiet corner of the airport, sat down and started meditating. I focused on the centre of the feeling inside. At first the heart and navel chakras felt so painful it was almost impossible to stay with it. But, this lifted as soon as I asked myself some questions.

"Is this about my work?" "Is this about my relationship?" When the feeling felt better after the second question, I knew I was moving in the right direction. When I felt stuck and blocked I would repeat the mantra for a while and pray for wisdom on this issue.

My tearing thoughts slowly fell away and my mood lifted. Eventually I realized the feeling had started over a small argument I had had with my girlfriend (what colored sheets to buy) but had a deeper core. I was afraid of surrendering some of the decision-making in our relationship. On a deeper level, it was about trust.

I traced the fear to a painful experience in the past and with that realization I forgave myself. The negative feeling immediately dissolved.

It took two hours of intense effort, but I had moved from a state of agony, to a state of bliss and joy.

Comment: *First we become aware of psychic discomfort and then instead of suppressing it or avoiding it or numbing it with alcohol or substances, we inquire into it. With inquiry comes insight and finally peace.*

I always become nervous when I have to speak in public. Recently I had to give a series of short talks to a group of people. I tried a number of different techniques to try to overcome the fear preventing me from speaking freely. Before each talk I meditated. Over the weeks I tried repeating the mantra intensely. I tried a breath meditation, breathing in calm and breathing out nervousness. I prayed to God. I made affirmations to myself. I contemplated strength. I tried squashing the feeling down and I tried to ignore it. I made copious A **Statements** like: "I am afraid what others will think of me", "I am afraid I will say something wrong." I tried to rationalize the situation with reassuring thoughts like: "It's not the end of the world; it's only a small talk." I was still nervous. I came to realize that out of all the emotions, fear was the one I disliked the most. I hated being afraid.

By the last week I was beginning to get angry with myself. I had been pushed to the limit and my resolve to shift it was intense. I sat to meditate and focused inside. I could vividly feel the fear inside me. It was so clear it was like a separate entity. I made the statement: "This is irrational fear." That seemed correct but the fear was just as intense. I concentrated even harder. Then a curious thing happened. The harder I focused the more it seemed like the fear was outside of myself. My consciousness seemed split in two. I was still aware of the fear, it was still there, but somehow I felt separate from it. It was like I was watching as an independent observer. The observer inside said: "I am not this feeling." I felt sudden joy. Another statement came: "I am not this feeling. I am the Self." The part of me that made those statements was fearless and independent. It was an immovable sense of Being. I realized how strong my attachment to the fear had been, and how powerful a person I would be if I always came from that witness perspective.

I stood up to give my talk. I was not nervous.

Comment: *Here intensive inquiry leads to spontaneous* **B Statements** *that come from deepest intuition. "I am not this feeling. I am the Self", reminds me of classical Vedanta. The ancient sages received such wisdom from the Self and when we pursue our own inquiry we find the same wisdom within ourselves.*

Appendix 1

SHIVA PROCESS CHAKRA MEDITATION WRITTEN FORM

THIS MEDITATION CAN be used in case the Shiva Process Chakra Meditation CD is not available. Set aside at least 20 minutes a day for it. I suggest that for the first few times read a bit and then do the practice. Then read a bit more and practise more. Later you will be able to do it all from memory.

I Self-inquiry

1. Bring your attention to the **navel chakra**. Feel the feeling in the navel area.
   - Is it pleasant or unpleasant?
   - Is it tense or relaxed?
   - Is it calm or energized?
   - Is there a feeling of wanting or pushing?
   - Is there a feeling of harmony or struggle?
   - Be aware of the feelings in the navel area.

2. Bring your attention to the **heart chakra**. Feel the feeling in the heart chakra.
   - Is it pleasant or unpleasant?
   - Is it sad or happy or some other feeling?
   - Is the heart open or closed?
   - Is it loving or withholding?
   - Feel the feelings in the heart chakra.

3. Bring your attention to the **throat chakra**. Feel the feeling in the throat.
   - Is it pleasant or unpleasant?
   - Is it blocked or open?
   - Are words or emotion caught there?
   - Feel the feeling in the throat chakra.

4. Now bring your attention to the **third eye**, the point between the eyebrows.
   - Is it pleasant or unpleasant?
   - Is it tense or relaxed?
   - Is there confusion or worry?

- Is it expanded or contracted?
- Is it light or dark?
- Do you see any colors?

Now review the four chakras you have just surveyed and determine which of them is the best or most comfortable one and which is the worst or least comfortable. Go on to the next section

II Healing Meditation

1. Get in touch with the feeling in the navel chakra. The navel has to do with issues of will. Sometimes it becomes tense when we are resisting divine will.
    - Relax the navel and say: "I let go. I relax. I surrender."
    - Imagine yourself floating on a calm lake.
    - Let the current gently take you and say: "Everything will be okay."
    - Bring in the thoughts: "I feel safe and relaxed."

2. Now feel the feeling in the heart chakra. The proper function of the heart chakra is to love. Contemplate love and forgiveness.
    - Bring in the thought: "I let my heart open" or, "I call on the power of love."
    - Practise forgiving and accepting yourself. Bring in the thoughts: "I forgive myself. I accept myself."
    - Let go of grievances against people who have hurt you. You can say: "I am willing to forgive those who have hurt me."
    - Ask for forgiveness from those whom you may have hurt consciously or unconsciously. You can say: "Please forgive me, I forgive you."
    - Let love expand and say inwardly: "I give my love."

3. Bring your attention to the throat chakra. The throat chakra has to do with communication of words and feelings. Say to yourself the following statements.
    - "I communicate my thoughts and feelings."
    - "I say what I need to say to the people that I need to."
    - "I speak with truth and kindness."
    - "I speak powerful and loving words."

4. Bring your awareness to the third eye. Become aware of the feeling in the third eye. The third eye is the centre of wisdom and insight. Say to yourself:
    - "I open my mind to higher wisdom."

- "I open to truth."
- "My mind is illumined."
- "Wisdom is within me."
- "I see the truth."

To conclude the meditation you can select the most positive chakra and contemplate it for the rest of your meditation period. You can play some gentle meditative music or sacred chanting as a background for your practice.

Appendix 2

SUMMARY OF CONTEMPLATIONS AND MEDITATION TECHNIQUES

dhivasat sattvasiddhihi

The essential nature of reality is attained
by mastery of the intellect.

Shiva Sutras III.12

MEDITATION TECHNIQUES

IF YOU DO not have the accompanying CD please refer to the Shiva Process Chakra Meditation Written Form on page 217.

1. **Self-inquiry with CD Track 1** (Chapter two, page 36)
   On this track you investigate the thoughts and feelings in four of the seven chakras: the navel, the heart, the throat and the brow. This gives you an awareness of any tension and blocks you may be carrying and also puts you in touch with expanded and uplifting feelings.

2. **Healing meditation with CD Track 2** (Chapter two, page 36)
   Relaxation and well-being is emphasized on this track. You return to the four chakras with a view towards acceptance, love and peace. Experiment with each idea and image. At the end you can find the best feeling and focus on it for the rest of the meditation.

3. **Mantra: Om Namah Shivaya** (Chapter seven, page 58)
   The mind is "many-pointed," like the spikes of a porcupine's coat. It jumps and moves in many directions. Your job is to focus the mind, to make it one-pointed and to eliminate obtrusive thoughts. When you repeat the mantra watch your reactions. There will be a never-ending flow of thoughts and feelings. Watch them and keep repeating the mantra. Meditation is the time when you can allow your thoughts to come and go. Sit as if you are watching a movie while lightly concentrating on repeating the mantra.

4. **Japa with CD Track 3** (Chapter seven, page 65)
   Japa is the practice of silent mantra repetition either during meditation or outside of meditation. The mantra is a wonderful means of cultivating

and strengthening the mind. There are many times in a day when your mind may tend to go towards negativity or worry. It is at such times that japa can be practised.

5. **Witness-consciousness** (Chapter eighteen, page 109)
    The inner Self is pure awareness. That awareness is the eternal witness. Thought manifests from that awareness and dissolves into that awareness. When we move beyond the mind, thought—negative or positive—is simply thought, and feelings—negative or positive—simply are feelings. Witness-consciousness involves detaching from the thoughts and feelings that arise in the mind.

CONTEMPLATIONS

These are valuable "thought experiments" designed to show you various aspects of the mind, or to put you in touch with the Self. You can incorporate any that really work for you into your regular practice. I suggest that every six months or so you read through them again and try the ones that appeal. Enjoy them. Use the summary below as a reference guide.

Part One

1: **I am asleep while sitting up.** (Chapter five, page 53)
    Let go as if you were going to sleep.

2: **What is the condition of my inner world?** (Chapter six, page 56)
    Become aware of your inner world and bring in thoughts to uplift the feeling.

3: **Having the meditation you are having.** (Chapter eight, page 68)
    Contemplate "acceptance" using statements such as: "This is the perfect meditation."

4: **Samyama** (Chapter nine, page 73)
    Part I: **Samyama on a desirable human quality.**
    Focus on a quality you would like to acquire or increase.
    Part II: **Samyama on the qualities of an object.**
    Focus on an object that embodies the qualities that you desire.
    Part III: **Samyama on the image of a great being.**
    Focus on a great soul with the idea of drawing his/her desirable qualities towards you.

5: **Breaking through – Buddha's Resolve** (Chapter ten, page 78)
    Make the inner statement, "I resolve not to move until understanding dawns."

6: **Inner weather** (Chapter eleven, page 80)
Become familiar with your inner weather.

7: **Being present** (Chapter twelve, page 86)
Part I: Listen to the sounds around you.
Part II: Become aware of your body, breath, thoughts and feelings in the present moment.

8: **Blanking your mind** (Chapter thirteen, page 91)
Try to stop all thoughts from arising.

9: **I call on the Self** (Chapter seventeen, page 106)
Invoke the power of the inner Self.

10: **Witness-consciousness** (Chapter eighteen, page 109)
Watch the breath and sit as the witness of your thoughts.

11: **Breath meditation: Hamsa** (Chapter eighteen, page 110)
As you breathe in listen for the sound *Ham* and as you breathe out listen for the sound *Sa*.

12: **Talking to the mind** (Chapter nineteen, page 114)
Speak sweetly to your mind with statements such as "Oh my mind, please become still."

13: **Meditate on love** (Chapter twenty, page 119)
Think of someone or something you love and let the feeling of love arise.

Part Two

14: **All is Chiti, all is Consciousness.** (Chapter one, page 135)
Allow all thoughts and feelings to arise without judgment.

15: **Chakra check.** (Chapter four, page 144-6)
Part I: Find the chakra that is most blocked.
Part II: Ask yourself, "What is the block in my chakra made of?"
Part III: Ask yourself, "What do I need to do to release this block?"
Part IV: Shortened version of the contemplation.

16: **I am the Self.** (Chapter five, page 150)
Let the space of the inner Self expand. Rest in that space.

17: **Self-observation: tearing thoughts.** (Chapter seven, page 159)
Observe your tearing thoughts.

18: **Doing Self-inquiry.** (Chapter nine, page 166)
Inquire into inner contractions.

19: **Judgments to values.** (Chapter ten, page 172)
Contemplate the positive or opposite quality of your judgment.

20: **Proxying.** (Chapter eleven, page 175)
Where you become aware of another person's unpleasant feeling, view the feeling as though you were actually the other person and make **A Statements.**

21: **Dealing with a difficult situation.** (Chapter twelve, page 181)
Contemplate a blocked or tense situation by asking inner questions.

22: **Be content with what you have.** (Chapter thirteen, page 189)
Search for the feeling of contentment within yourself.

23: **Tranquility and equanimity.** (Chapter fifteen, page 199)
Let your mind become as still as a quiet lake. Imagine yourself to be as strong and immovable as a mountain.

Appendix 3

THE YOGA OF MEDITATION BHAGAVAD GITA VI

Chapter VI of the Bhagavad Gita is one of the great traditional texts on meditation. Its wealth of ideas is valuable on many levels and its discussion of the practice of meditation still yields helpful hints to a meditator. Krishna, the guru, teaches the doubting and uncertain student Arjuna to establish his mind in the inner Self.

Lord Krishna said:

1. He who does his duty without depending on the fruits of his actions is a true yogi, not one who does nothing at all.

2. Oh Arjuna, a true yogi has the spirit of renunciation and has learned to discipline his mind and his intention.

3. One on the path must perform detached action with great enthusiasm. After the attainment of the goal all actions may be given up.

4. When one is no longer ruled by the senses and by addictions and performs actions with detachment and has also brought his mind to peace, he is said to have attained the goal of yoga.

5. Let one lift himself by his own Self alone, let him not degrade himself, for the Self alone is the friend of oneself and the self alone is the enemy of oneself.

6. To him who has subdued the lower self by the higher Self, the Self acts as a friend. But to him who has lost his higher Self by the dominance of the lower one, the self is like an enemy at war.

7. In one who has conquered his mind, the Self remains steady and unperturbed in the experience of the pairs of opposites like heat and cold, pleasure and pain, honor and dishonor.

8. A yogi whose soul has attained contentment through wisdom and knowledge, who is unperturbed, who has mastered his senses, who sees that a lump of earth and a bar of gold are both made of Consciousness, is said to have attained the goal of yoga.

9. He who is even minded in his outlook towards friends, companions, enemies, the indifferent, the neutral, the hateful, towards relatives, the virtuous and evil people is especially great.

10. Let the yogi meditate everyday, controlling his mind and keeping it free from desire and longing for possessions.

11. In a clean place one should create a seat made of suitable materials, neither too high nor too low.

12. Seated there, controlling the actions of the mind and senses, let him make his mind one pointed and practise yoga for the purification of the self.

13. Let him hold his body, head and neck erect and still, holding his attention within himself, without looking around.

14. Serene and fearless, firmly in control of his senses and his mind, he should sit in harmonious communion with Me, thinking of Me and Me alone.

15. Withdrawing the mind from outer things and keeping it calmly focused on the Self a yogi attains liberation.

16. Success in yoga is not for those who eat or sleep too much nor for those who eat or sleep too little.

17. Yoga becomes the destroyer of pain and sorrow for him who is moderate in eating, work and recreation and who sleeps neither too much nor too little.

18. When the disciplined mind rests in the Self alone and is free from craving, then it is said to have attained union.

19. As a lamp placed in a windless spot does not flicker—so also is a yogi's mind that is well controlled and united with the Self.

20. When the mind, restrained by the practice of yoga, becomes quiet, and when, seeing the Self by the Self he rejoices in the Self;

21. By means of his purified intellect the yogi grasps that infinite bliss which transcends the senses and becomes established there.

22. Having obtained That, he thinks there is nothing superior to it, established in the Self, he remains unshaken by even the worst afflictions.

23. That severance of connection with pain is yoga, it should be practised with determination and without despair.

24. Abandoning without reservation all desire born of the mind and completely restraining the senses by the mind on all sides;

25. Little by little he should attain tranquility by means of his firmly held intellect; he should establish the mind in the Self and abstain from every kind of thought.

26. Whatever causes the wavering and fickle mind to wander, it should be brought under control and made to rest in the Self.

27. The yogi who has attained a peaceful mind, calmed his desire and is free of negativity attains the divine state and experiences supreme bliss.

28. The yogi who is steadfast in his practice and who frees himself from bad tendencies easily enjoys infinite bliss in contact with the Divine.

29. The man of spiritual awareness sees oneness everywhere. He sees the Self in all beings and all beings in the Self.

30. He who sees Me in all beings, and all beings in Me—to him I am never lost, nor he to Me.

31. The yogi who is established in the vision of oneness worships Me in all beings, that yogi is one with Me whatever way of life he leads.

32. Oh Arjuna, I regard the yogi as the highest who sees equality everywhere because he sees the same self in all, whether they are in joy or suffering.

Arjuna said:

33. Oh Krishna, it is very difficult for me to be firmly established in this yoga of equanimity due to the fickleness of my mind.

34. Oh Krishna, truly the mind is restless, turbulent, strong and unyielding. I think it is as difficult to control as the wind.

Lord Krishna said:

35. Oh Arjuna, I agree the mind is restless and difficult to control but it can be brought under control by spiritual practice and dispassion.

36. My view is that yoga is difficult to attain by men of uncontrolled mind, but it is possible for those who control their minds to attain yoga by use of the proper means.

Arjuna said:

37. Oh Krishna, what happens to a man who has firm faith but is not steadfast in his practice because he is distracted and therefore fails to reach spiritual perfection?

38. Oh mighty armed Krishna, losing both the material and spiritual worlds does he not perish with no support, bewildered in the path of Brahman?

39. Krishna, only you can dispel this doubt of mine completely; there is no one but you to dispel this doubt.

Lord Krishna said:

40. Arjuna, he does not suffer doom in this world or the next. Truly, oh dear one, he who does good action never comes to grief.

41. One who has not completed the path of yoga reaches a higher world and lives there for unnumbered years. Later, he is reborn in the house of a pure and prosperous family.

42. Or he is reborn in a family of yogis, full of wisdom and spirituality. Such a birth is very difficult to obtain.

43. There, oh Arjuna, he will regain the wisdom he had attained in his previous birth and then he will strive harder than before for perfection.

44. His former practice drives him on irresistibly. One who seeks the knowledge of yoga quickly goes beyond mere ritualism.

45. But the yogi who strives diligently conquers his ignorance and gains spiritual perfection after several rebirths. Finally, he reaches the highest state.

46. A meditating yogi is superior to one who practises austerities; he is superior to a scriptural scholar; he is also superior to a ritualist. Therefore oh Arjuna, be a yogi.

47. He is the greatest of all the yogis who worships Me with abiding faith and becomes one with his innermost Self.

GLOSSARY

Affirmation: Positive statement.

Asana: Yoga pose and posture for meditation.

A *Statement (Accurate Statement):* A simple statement of present thought and feeling.

Ashram: A spiritual institution or community; where yoga and meditation are taught.

Ashtanga Yoga: Eight-fold path of meditation and yoga.

B *Statement (Beneficial Statement):* Possibly uplifting statement.

Chakra Meditation: A method of meditation that investigates thought and feeling in four chakras or energy centres within the body.

Chakras: Subtle energy centres in the body.

Chiti: Divine Consciousness; the essential creative energy that underlies the universe.

Devi dollar: Spiritual merit.

Dharana: Short contemplation of the Self.

Dhyana: Meditation.

Downward shift: A negative movement of thought and feeling.

Introjection: Mental act of substituting a positive thought for a negative thought

Invocation: Calling the presence and qualities of a higher power or respected person to us.

Japa: Repetition of the mantra.

Jnani: One who practises the path of wisdom or one who has attained the goal.

Karma yoga: The yoga of selfless service to humanity

Kashmir Shaivism: Non-dual philosophy, which sees the entire universe as the play of divine conscious energy.

Kundalini: The divine creative energy of the universe which, when awakened, moves upward through the chakras, purifying the entire being.

Maha yoga/Maha Kundalini yoga/Purna yoga: Different names of ancient yoga that comes from Shiva.

Mahavakya: Great statements from the Vedas **(Beneficial Statements)** which express the oneness of the Self with God.

Mala: String of beads used when repeating the mantra.

Mantra: Sacred phrase which protects and uplifts the mind.

Matrika: See *self-talk.*

Pranayama: Breathing exercise designed to quieten the mind.

Pratyahara: Turning the attention from the outer world to the inner world.

Purascharana: A set number of mantra repetitions to be achieved over the course of some days, weeks or months.

Raga-dvesha: Attraction and repulsion.

Sadhana: Inner work, spiritual practice.

Samadhi: Deepest state of meditation.

Samyama: One-pointed focus in meditation.

Self-inquiry: A method of meditation that turns the mind within to ask empowering questions.

Self-observation: The act of noticing your reactions to various events in your life.

Self-talk: Thoughts in the mind.

Self-realization/enlightenment: The goal of meditation; becoming anchored in peace and wisdom.

Shakti: Spiritual energy.

Shaktipat: Awakening of spiritual energy.

Shiva: The supreme, ever-present reality. One of the Hindu trinity of gods, symbolizing the destruction of spiritual ignorance or separation from the Self.

Shiva Yoga: An ancient tradition of yoga which features the awakening of the inner power, Kundalini.

Shiva Process: A form of Self-inquiry as taught by Swami Shankarananda.

Siddha: Self-realised being.

Spiritual materialism: Acquiring spiritual merit through intense effort.

Substitution: Replacing negative thoughts with positive thoughts.

Sushumna: Subtle spinal column where chakras are situated.

Sutra: A short aphoristic scriptural statement.

Tandra: A meditative state resembling sleep.

Tantric yoga: A path that attempts to see divinity in everyday life.

Tat twam asi: Literally "You are That" - a mahavakya.

Turiya: The Fourth State - the state of deep meditation.

Upward shift: A positive movement of thought and feeling.

Witness-consciousness: A meditative practice in which the mind is observed from a distance.

COURSES AND PROGRAMMES
Taught by Swami Shankarananda

ONE OF THE BEST ways to deepen your meditation is to be in the company of a master. Swamiji invites you to further your practice at his Shiva School of Meditation, established in 1991. Courses and programmes are offered at the residential ashram in Mt Eliza and also in the city of Melbourne.

Swamiji loves to meet new people and is readily available to help with any questions or problems you may have.

LEARN TO MEDITATE -LEVELS 1 & 2

Introductory courses on the essential techniques of meditation and the Shiva Process Chakra Meditation.

MEDITATION WORKSHOPS

Meditation workshops are held on various topics and designed to enhance and enliven your meditation practice.

SHIVA PROCESS GROUPS

Through mastering the techniques of the Chakra Meditation and conversation, you can uncover unconscious patterns and dissolve inner blocks.

SHIVA PROCESS INDIVIDUAL SESSIONS

One-on-one Shiva Process sessions are ideal for improving your meditation, deepening spiritual insight and solving problems in your daily life.

SATSANG WITH SWAMIJI

Take this opportunity to meet Swamiji in a programme which includes talks, chanting and meditation. (No charge.)

YOGA AND RELAXATION

Learn the *Golden Eleven* yoga postures designed to invigorate you physically, mentally and spiritually.

INTENSIVES

During these programmes Swamiji gives Shaktipat initiation; the mysterious and ancient tradition of awakening the Shakti of the inner Self.

RETREATS

Spend some time in retreat at the Mt Eliza ashram in this residential programme. Take part in daily activities and increase your spiritual awareness.

RECORDED MATERIAL

A range of Music for Meditation CDs and copies of the Chakra Meditation can be ordered. A lecture series by Swamiji on the teachings of G. I. Gurdjieff is also available.

WEBSITE

You can find us on the web at www.shivayoga.org. Email us at askus@shivayoga.org if you have any questions or require further information.

SHIVA SCHOOL OF MEDITATION
27 TOWER RD, MT ELIZA, VIC 3930 AUSTRALIA
TELEPHONE: 03 9775 2568   FAX: 03 9775 2591

SHIVA
SCHOOL OF MEDITATION

Swami Shankarananda

SWAMI SHANKARANANDA (SWAMIJI) is a meditation master in the ancient tradition of Shiva Yoga. He grew up in Brooklyn, New York, the son of an artist father and high school teacher mother. A brilliant student, he won many academic awards leading to a teaching position in English literature and Renaissance poetry at Indiana University. He was a member of the national championship chess team at Columbia University and became a US Chess Master.

His search for enlightenment led him to India in 1970 where he met many of India's saints and sages. He became a student of the great Swami Muktananda (Baba). After Swamiji attained self-realisation Baba told him to awaken seekers and teach meditation. Baba wrote at the time, 'He (Shankarananda) has the power to make people experience the divine presence.'

Swamiji is one of the few Westerners to be initiated into the ancient Saraswati order of swamis. He has headed ashrams in Ann Arbor, Michigan, New York, Los Angeles and Melbourne. Swamiji has written numerous articles on spiritual topics and his book *Muktananda Siddha Guru* has been translated into German, Spanish and French. He edited *Siddha Meditation*, a collection of Baba's writings on Kashmir Shaivism and was the founding editor of *Siddha Path* magazine.

Swamiji has taught thousands of people to meditate, touring the USA, India, Canada and Australia conducting meditation courses, workshops and Intensives. Politicians, police officers, doctors, lawyers, firefighters, homemakers and college and university students have successfully learned to meditate with Swamiji. He is the director of the Shiva School of Meditation, at the Shiva Ashram on the beautiful Mornington Peninsula near Melbourne, Australia. He teaches and lives with his students, guests and two chow chows, Bhakti and Ra Ra, and in his spare time explores the golf-rich area near his home.